Rekindling
our PASSION for
Jesus!

**FINDING AND EXPERIENCING
TRUE INTIMACY WITH CHRIST**

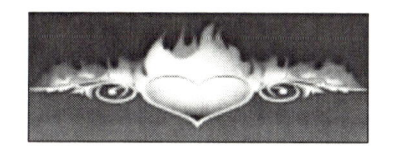

REGINA ELLIOTT

Xulon
PRESS

Copyright © 2012 by Regina Elliott

Rekindling Our Passion For Jesus!
"Finding & Experiencing True Intimacy With Christ!"
by Regina Elliott

Printed in the United States of America

ISBN 9781619966611

All rights reserved solely by the author. The author guarantees all contents are original and do not infringe upon the legal rights of any other person or work. No part of this book may be reproduced in any form without the permission of the author. The views expressed in this book are not necessarily those of the publisher.

Unless otherwise indicated, Bible quotations are taken from The HOLY BIBLE, THE NEW OPEN BIBLE, NEW KING JAMES VERSION (NKJV). Copyright © 1990, 1985, 1983 by Thomas Nelson.

Copyright Permission was granted for book quotes and lyric quotes by letter or email from ministries represented below. Reference page numbers are for placement location in this book.

The Wisdom Center –
Lyrics by Mike Murdock - I Love Sitting at Your Feet - page 26

Bill Gaither Music
Lyrics by Rusty Goodman - I Am - page 44
Lyrics by Lanny Wolfe - Jesus Be the Lord of All - page 51-52

Ken Davis - Jumper Fables - page 56-57

Dr. Joseph M Stowell - The Weight of Your Words - page 132-133

Lyrics by Phillips, Craig & Dean - *I Wanna Be Just Like You* - pages 79-80

Chariot Family Publishing - Stuart &Jill Briscoe *The Family Book of Christian Values* page 136

Zig Zigler Corporation - *See You At the Top* - page 139

Lyrics by Rosemond Herklots - *Forgive Us Our Sins* - page 197

Health Communications
Jack Canfield - *Chicken Soup for the Soul* - Story by Dr. Charles Garfield - page 228-230

Public Domain
St Francis of Assisi - *Eternal Life* - page 235

Helen H Lemmel – *Turn Your Eyes Upon Jesus* – Page 240

Charles H. Gabriel - *My Savior's Love* - page 253

Levina M Hall Jesus *Paid It All* - page 284

www.xulonpress.com

ACKNOWLEDGEMENTS

There isn't an undertaking quite like a person's very first published book. This one began through the Holy Spirit's working in my own heart as thoughts, words and truths pervaded my understanding. With new perception I began to understand what it means to have a *passionate, personal, even intimate relationship, with Jesus*. This revelation inspired my book. A manuscript in hand is nothing short of life-changing.

My soul sings praises to such an awesome God. He calls and equips. Thank You Lord for moving in me to write what You have stirred up in my spirit, written on my heart. Thank you for inspiration; creative thoughts; words; paragraphs; and chapters. Thank You for your precious, sweet anointing when I felt there wasn't another word to write. Thank You **Holy Spirit**, in advance, for moving in the hearts of readers also, as they open this book. Transform them with new *passion for Jesus!*

Special Thanks to my Aunt Joyce Ketner, from Manteca, California, who painstakingly proofed the book to make sure the flow of phrases, grammar and punctuation, was correct, and for any other errors she felt needed attention.

Special Thanks to my dear friend, Meredith Storer, from St. Joe, Indiana for her labor of love as well, for her keen eyes to also check for spelling errors, grammar and typo's, as yet a second look to hopefully catch anything we may have missed.

One more special friend I must mention, Lenare Yoder, another resident of St. Joe, Indiana, for your last minute read through when there was still apprehension on my part; a very big thank you.

Then last but not least, to Michael D, *preacher man,* from the bottom of my heart for your time perusing through the manuscript. For your expertise on things like *ice fishing,* that I know nothing about, and a few other pointers only you could have given. Thank you for the God I see in you every day. You are one in a million.

You are all appreciated and loved more than words can say. What a rich blessing to me and Seasons of Hope Ministries.

DEDICATION

This book is lovingly dedicated to my Mother, Ina Riddle, who taught me many things, but on the spiritual level: To love Jesus passionately, to pray, to read God's Word, to listen to His voice, and to walk obediently no matter how difficult the road became. We have God's promise that He is our faithful, forever friend, who will *never leave or forsake us*.

Mother's address changed to *The Father's House* on May 1, 2011. She will be missed greatly. Heaven is sweeter and a more meaningful destination for those of us who are yet to arrive. Yes, we will see her again. That's a guarantee. I now officially have more family in heaven, than on earth: My mother and father, both sets of grandparents, aunts, uncles, cousins, nephews, nieces and 5 brothers. What a reunion that's going to be with family; not to mention so many friends. Among one of our newest is Andy Crow, from St Joe, Indiana. I know he and my dad are having a grand time in heaven. They have the same vibrant charisma, the-never-met-a-stranger personalities, and almost identical passions: their love for God, family, America, sports, music, life, and people.

I miss you Mom, especially your *advice* and *instruction*. I miss hearing you whistle while you're sewing, the way you played the piano and sang in your deep *base* voice. I miss our sometimes heated, but always fun and enlightening, discussions about God's Word. I miss hearing your *anointed spirit-filled intercessory prayer*. Most of all I miss your laugh and the joy that was evident in your eyes every time you preached, or talked about the Lord.

I awoke just a few mornings ago and thought, *"I've just got to call Mother today, I haven't talked to her in so long."* Then of course it hit me that you aren't here anymore. Though we lived thousands of miles apart we were always as close as the phone or computer. Such is the reality of those we love who have gone to live with Jesus. Jesus, the one we are growing more passionate about every day.

Most of all, I trust you are somehow aware and proud of this accomplishment for the Kingdom for the Glory of God. So with joy I dedicate this book to you and to your memory. Thank you for your wise Godly counsel. Thank you for being my mother, for your love, and for your prayers and mentorship during our lifetime together.

INTRODUCTION
Invited to Experience Intimacy

A.W. Tozer once said *"the only book that should ever be written is one that flows from the heart, forced out by the inward pressure. These books will not only be to the writer imperative, but one day inevitable."*

And so it is. *"Rekindling our Passion for Jesus"* has not been written in any mechanical sense, but rather born out of an inward working by the Holy Spirit for a number of years nudging me to pursue the Lord Jesus with fervor and desire as a *"deer pants for water."*

This book is about getting answers for people like you and me – ordinary, everyday people. It's about learning to understand, embrace, cultivate, have and keep genuine passion for Jesus. To realize that church and God isn't just something we do; rather, it is about the greatest journey we will ever embark upon. It is about the most intimate relationship we can ever experience, which is what God purposed from the beginning. God never intended for us to treat Him as some *far off being* in the cosmos, to be addressed only during times of major catastrophe or need; rather, He has always longed for a personal, intimate relationship with mankind. God created us because He wanted a family. He desired companionship. He needed people with a passion to praise, worship and adore

Him, for who He is — followers who could never be content or fulfilled outside of Christ.

This passion will only be experienced and developed as we spend time in His presence; as we embrace the desire for intimacy. When we do this, we will experience a deepened relationship and closer companionship with Jesus. Everything will change; from once knowing *about Him,* to truly *knowing Him.* We will understand more fully *who He is.* Intimacy with Him is more powerful than anything the world could ever offer. *There's nothing like being in the presence Jesus.*

This writing is born out of my own struggles and joys in life; experiences during my growing-up years as the daughter of parents who were both ordained preachers. They were an amazing, positive influence in my life. Most importantly, they taught me how to know and love Jesus.

I attended Bible College, married, and sixteen years later faced a tragically devastating divorce. More life lessons were learned as I accepted *the call,* beginning then to cope with the challenges of entering full-time ministry myself. In the midst of it all God has been so faithful. There's been a constant awareness of His deep caring for me; yet somehow still not experiencing even greater closeness with Christ that I knew was obtainable.

It's seems that the church, (not referring to the building, of course) but those of us who comprise the body of Christ, are just *going through the motions.* We're posing as the *bride.* We've recited the vows, agreed to the covenant, yet have stood outside the bedchamber never fully embracing or experiencing the depth of intimacy that Jesus longs for us to have; genuine, unhindered, continual, life-changing, joy-filled, indescribable, passionate, intimacy. His presence transforms and heals. He is God. He has so much more to give us. Oh, it's true, He's given us gifts, even abilities and opportunities in life that can bring a certain amount of success or satisfaction, even euphoria, but *nothing compares* to what we can experience in Him.

I have been telling Jesus since the age of three how much I love him. Yes, even at that young age I knew I loved Him.

Introduction

I received Him as my Savior and followed Him in baptism at the age of five. But loving someone and knowing how to show it are two very different things. Somehow, as the years flew by and I reached adolescence and even into adulthood my sacrifice for Him—to be with Him—rarely portrayed that love. Oh, I didn't live in sin, or willfully walk in disobedience, but somehow I just didn't spend time with Him that demonstrated a desire to love Him more passionately or to simply sit at His feet, in His presence. There were always other things that vied for my focus and attention.

Why isn't there more discussion or teaching, or preaching for that matter on "how to" have more passion in our relationship with Christ? Rarely is the necessity of an ongoing *intimate love relationship* with Him ever discussed or guidance given to understand what it means to passionately pursue Jesus. It is not just a simple matter of accepting Christ; asking Him to forgive your sins, make you His child and come into your heart—end of story. Actually, that's just the beginning of our relationship with Jesus. Isn't it amazing, that's all most people are ever really told? Just receive the salvation experience. Yes, some learn about sanctification. Then there's the gift of the Holy Spirit, which is actually a two-fold experience; we receive Him through salvation, then there is a deeper infilling with an outward manifestation. We are taught to pray, read the word, and grow in our walk with Christ. **But passion for Jesus, what's that?** We seem to save our passion for sports, fun, family and community. It's a little ironic. We'll sit at a football game for 3 hours, no problem. But if our worship service goes longer than 1 hour, we're looking at our watches. Then we'll fellowship for thirty minutes after the benediction. Does that make any sense? Why do we place time limitations when we meet for worship, or with God? Isn't that supposed to be the most important thing we do in life?

My hope is for each reader to be enlightened as to what it *really* means to *fall in love* with Jesus. To give Him first place; to begin to involve Him in every aspect of your life. Not out of duty. Not even out of fear, or desperation. Nor to love Jesus

Rekindling Our Passion For Jesus!

because you're experiencing happiness—life is good and God's hand of blessing is obvious. No. Commitment should be simply out of love for Him. Realizing how empty and futile life is without Christ and how blessed and complete it is with Him. Crazy how out of all our passions in life, Jesus often scores last place, yet He should receive the highest priority. Why? *Who has ever done for us what He has, and continues to do?* I honestly feel that even if we weren't promised heaven, I would still want to serve and love Jesus. Life without Him is meaningless and futile.

We can walk in our divine destiny and experience the abundant life Christ promised as we understand how, choose to love Him more passionately and live for Him more fervently.

So we begin the *"Rekindling Our Passion for Jesus"* journey, the first of the *Rekindling Series*. Thanks for traveling with me. Oh, and by the way, if this is a new beginning, rather than a rekindling, that's even more joyous for me to share in with you.

TABLE OF CONTENTS

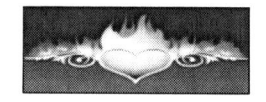

Introduction	Invited to Experience Intimacy ix
Chapter 1	Passion or Preoccupation? ...15 *"Who or What Do You Really Love?"*
Chapter 2	Got Jesus? .... 34 *"Realizing & Embracing Our Need for a Savior"*
Chapter 3	Married or Mistress? .... 60 *"Experiencing Real Intimacy with Christ"*
Chapter 4	No Other Gods! .... 79 *"Ridding Ourselves of the Spirit of Legalism &Condemnation"*
Chapter 5	God Bless "My" Plans .... 103 *"Seeking God's Agenda, Not Our Own"*
Chapter 6	Taming the Tongue .... 124 *"Understanding the Power of Words"*

Chapter 7	Passion Equals Position......147	
	"Finding the Place of God's Richest Blessings"	
Chapter 8	Go Light Your World 169	
	"The Power of Giving Jesus to Others"	
Chapter 9	Focus On Forgiveness.........191	
	"Whew... this is a tough one... Pardoning the Unpardonable"	
Chapter 10	Contagious Gratitude.........217	
	"Making Every Day... Thanksgiving Day"	
Chapter 11	More than Conquerors 238	
	"O, Mighty Captain, Prevail in Our Lives"	
Chapter 12	Enjoying the Journey 262	
	"Embracing the Abundant Life Jesus Provided"	

1

PASSION OR PREOCCUPATION?
"Who or What Do You Really Love?"

PASSION. *Have you ever really thought about what that word means pertaining to your relationship with Jesus?* I grew up learning about Him, teething on church pews. Maybe you did too. We learned all the *how to's* — you know, the *do's and don'ts* in religion. We met the *Holier Than Thou's* who were quick to *condemn* others by their *personal convictions* and *interpretation* of what God hated. We learned what sin was and how to repent and ask Jesus into our hearts. We even learned the importance of following the Lord in baptism. All so we could make it to heaven. However, somehow along the way there was not a lot mentioned about ***passion***. There were not many people mentoring others on this topic. There were few courses to take, or Sunday School classes being taught about *how to fall in love* with Jesus.

Let's expand our understanding of what ***passion*** really means. Passion is: fervency, zealousness, zestfulness, vivaciousness, gusto, emotion, feeling, animation; Being passionate means to have spiritedness, vigor, enthusiasm, fanaticism, mania, obsession, craving, thirst, hunger, yearning, longing, desire, affection, and compulsion. It also means willingness to endure pain, suffering, agony, even martyrdom.

Now as we consider these words that define passion, can we honestly say that they are descriptive of *how we feel about Jesus, how we serve Jesus, or how we share Jesus with others?*

WHAT REALLY MOTIVATES YOU?

What is your true passion in life? Have you ever contemplated seriously what you are genuinely passionate *about?* Have you placed causes or issues, money and possessions, career advancements or promotions, family and fortune, fame or applause, community or cultural needs, sports, or politics before God? If you have, then where does God fit into your picture of life? Could it be that your life is preoccupied with everything *but Him?*

What really motivates you? What do you really love? What gets you up and going in the morning besides *Starbucks* or *Folgers?* Are you passionate about life or are you just existing? Are you preoccupied with everything but that which is eternal — new cars, motorcycles, homes, clothes, toys and trinkets, a better job, more money? In reality every passion in life is short-lived. Fun and stuff only last for a season; the games, the entertainment, the vacations, the things that we accumulate, all the earthly pleasure is fine, even pleasurable, but none of it is lasting. There is certainly nothing wrong with enjoying life; Jesus said that He came to *"give us life and that more abundantly."* John 10:10. However, when we use things for the purpose of ultimately bringing us lasting joy or to fill a void in our hearts, then things become temporary fixes for a much deeper spiritual need that gnaws at us. We're trying to be happy, to fill the void, but soon we're looking for more and more, or something different to satisfy.

Emptiness in our hearts is caused by a deep hunger that God actually placed there, on purpose, when He created man. He knew that no-thing or no-one would ever be able to satisfy or fill that void except Jesus. You may be thinking about many things that satisfy. So rather than ask, *"what?"* I would ask *"for how long?"* Try as we might, everything we will experience, do, or have, eventually ends. It lasts but a moment. A good example of this is found in planning of a wedding. Months, sometimes years go into it, not to mention the finances, and in about forty-five minutes, or less, it's over. The happy couple cruise off in ecstasy and elation while the family is left to clean up. Oh, they are happy too, but the celebration is over and reality sets in. They may be left feeling empty and happy, but also a little sad. Why? It ended. Of course it's just the beginning for the newlyweds, but the party is over. Celebrations end. Then we find ourselves right back at the planning board scheduling something else that might bring us joy, purpose or fulfillment.

Obviously, life is about love and happiness—relationships, family and friends. Soon the days, months, and years roll by and before we know it our children have children, their children have children, and we're much, much older. Life has been great. Good. Not so good. Terrible. The message is this: Though life is made up of a myriad of experiences—times of joy and sorrow, times of feast and famine—still **everything about it should be wrapped up in Christ Jesus.** He is the core and center of all that life is. In the midst of our love, involvement, and focus on our family, our church, our work, and our community, what we cannot forget is *who* we are really living for. The questions we need answers for are:

Why are we here? Who are we living for?
What is our real passion in life?

What is our motivation for getting up every morning and trudging on? Why do we allow everything else to have preeminence over the one who is supposed to *be* our life? Jesus is the one who keeps our world rotating on its axis. Nothing functions properly without Him in His rightful place.

Everything in life is temporary. Scripture says that life itself is a vapor; here for a moment and then, poof, it vanishes. James 4:14. Everything is temporary *except God* and His plan. So the great news is that all that pertains to God is eternal.

This is an irrevocable truth. *We weren't born to just aimlessly pursue all the stuff that life is about, and get all we can — we are here to love God and pursue a personal, passionate, intimate relationship with Jesus.* Our love and passion for Him is the only thing in life that has eternal value.

HUMOROUS PASSION

People have countless *passions*. Shopping is at the top of the list for most women. There is something rejuvenating about going to the mall, or outlet stores, or even *Goodwill*. It gets our minds off the stress making life a little more tolerable.

There is a humorous story about a woman who woke up one morning quite depressed, knowing the perfect prescription for her sadness was of course — shopping. She informed her husband that she was going downtown to shop. His response was the same as most men, "Fine, go look, window shop, but don't spend any money, you know it's not in the budget. In fact, if you even get the least bit tempted to buy anything, I want you to say, 'get thee behind me satan'." Out the door she went with her husband's words ringing in her ears.

As she arrived downtown she noticed lots of "Sale" signs in the shop windows. In the heart of town was a lovely furrier salon. She entered the store and since she lived in the cold northeastern part of the United States, she had always dreamed of owning a full-length mink coat. Lo and behold, these coats were 50% off. She found a gorgeous sable her size and carefully put it on. Wrapping it around her she felt warm, confident and beautiful. The more she looked in the mirror, the more she desired it. Naturally, the sales clerk was even more convincing as she said, "Oh, honey that is you!" Not being able to control herself with the amount of money she would be saving, she slapped the credit card on the counter and made the purchase.

When she arrived home with the unbelievably expensive coat, her husband absolutely hit the roof! "I can't believe you did this. Why, buying was one thing, but a mink coat — have you lost your mind? I told you if you even got tempted to say, 'Get thee behind me satan.'" The woman looked at her husband as only she could and responded sheepishly, "Why, honey, I did, and he said it looked just as good from the back."

Oh, don't get me wrong, I'm at the front of the line to shop at times. Though I've used this humorous story, could it be that often we are more passionate about things that really don't amount to a hill of beans rather than things that are significant? One of my girlfriends had a favorite coffee cup. The writing on it said, *"There are only two things in life I really want, thin thighs and world peace – and I really don't care that much about world peace."* Might these trite words be, in a sense, more realistic than we want to admit? Our passions are often focused on the ridiculous rather than on things that matter… eternal things. Are we so preoccupied that we miss the main purpose for living?

WHAT SHOULD MOTIVATE US?

What then should we be passionate about or preoccupied with?

> *What we are passionate about is precisely what we will be preoccupied with.*

Our time, energy, and attention will go into our passions. When we're preoccupied with everything but God, motivated by everything but Him, our priorities are not in sync with God's Word. Life becomes a rat race, filled with stress and anxiety. But when we are motivated by God, to do God's work, God's way, in God's timeframe, nothing remains the same. He has a definite design, a destiny plan to walk out daily with joy beyond compare. Yes, we will still have challenges. Roses, as beautiful as they are, still have thorns. As wonderful as life can be, it will still have adversity, but we will be able to face it victoriously when we allow our passion for Christ to be primary.

If we sincerely desire a blessed life rather than one of heartache, then we become motivated by love for Jesus. We become passionate about Him. Passion for Christ puts all that pertains to life in perspective. The results are focus and purpose. Rather than trying to fill the emptiness with *everything but Him*, we begin to fill the void in our lives *with Him*. We become captivated by the *living water*. Our thirst changes from natural desires to supernatural desires. Each day we experience less thirst for the world, and more thirst for Jesus, the living water. I John 2:15-16. Matthew 5:6. Yes we are in the world, with obligations, jobs, and commitments. Though we are *in* the world, we are not *of* the world. Life takes on a totally different perspective as we embrace the truth that we are of Christ. We belong to Him.

THE LIFEBLOOD

Passion is our lifeblood. Without it, we just exist. God created us to have passion. Everyone, depending on their personality will express or demonstrate passion different ways; however, it has to be *focused*. As we focus our passion to more deeply love Jesus, the true meaning for living will unfold.

Lifeblood in the physical realm provides life. Without blood, there is none. We cannot live without blood flowing through our veins to arteries in our heart, then through our body and brain causing us to live and breathe. It doesn't take a lot of blood — just six quarts — but what powerful quarts. Life is in the blood.

The same truth applies in the spiritual realm. Without blood, *the blood of Jesus*, we can't experience life with or *in* Him. We won't experience the abundant life or be unable to embrace or fully understand real meaning *in* life. Neither will we be able to know eternal life when our human bodies die. A personal, passionate, intimate relationship with Him is the only way to be fully alive. The blood of Jesus cleanses us from all sin, I John 1:7. He gives us meaning in life, hope and a future. Jeremiah 29:11. No blood — no life.

Passion Or Preoccupation?

For 12 years I was in sales and management with a Dallas, Texas based company, *Home Interiors & Gifts*. It was a Party Plan business with an incredibly beautiful line of decorative accessories for home and office. Mary Crowley was the Founder and President. May I say that she was a phenomenally anointed, vibrant, woman of God. Every person she met was touched by her passion for Jesus. She taught us that bookings were the lifeblood of our business. Why? Without them we wouldn't *have* a business. There would be no women to touch, no lives to change, no homes to make beautiful, and no money to be made. There would be no *blood flowing through the veins of our work without bookings*. The last two years in management our team was in the top fifty out of over eight hundred groups in the nation. My goal was to lead by example—holding shows, booking, selling and recruiting. That made it easier for me to identify with their challenges at our sales and motivational meetings.

People booked shows with me. Why? Well, first of all because I had dedicated this business to the Lord from the very beginning, asking Him to bless it and enlarge my territory. Secondly, because when you're passionate, it's contagious. This was a great job. Home Interiors was a company one could believe in and rely upon. I was consumed with our lovely line of accessories. Women wanted what I had because I was blessed by God to be gifted with decorating skills and had applied myself to study—the passion was the icing on the cake. I was so convinced that others too believed. Women recognized that there was not a superior quality product on the market or one more beautiful anywhere.

Guess what? This same truth applies to our passion about Jesus. We have to be convinced that there is nothing that compares to Him. We have to be so consumed, so confident, so passionate about Jesus that others will see there is no greater relationship in the world than one with Him. So they also, won't want to live—can't possibly live—without Him. Passion makes all the difference. Passion makes us intentional. We know who we love and why. We focus on giving ourselves to that passion for the sake of Christ. It's a choice.

Without passion *for* Him we are probably not going to be very effective in our work *with* Him. Until we have this lifeblood flowing through our veins—in this case passion for Jesus, then our message of hope won't be vibrant, we won't see lives to touch, or hearts to mend, or wounds to heal. *Who in the round world would want what we have if we aren't passionate about Him ourselves?* People will desire what we have if they believe it's real. If they see it's worthwhile and if they are convinced that we are convinced and believe in what we're doing for the cause of Christ. We can say we *know* Jesus, but are we making a difference because of our passion for Him? Or are we just going through the motions? We go to church, read our Bibles occasionally, and pray when we feel like it. But are we hungry to know Jesus more deeply? Are we excited to have answers to life's problems? Our passion for Christ should be so vibrant that it compels people to desire this Jesus we know and serve.

HIS GAME PLAN

I personally really enjoy NFL games and the Pittsburgh Steelers are my favorite team. But when quarterback Ben Roethlisberger passes the ball and a team player catches it to run across the goal line and score, fans by the thousands stand and cheer as if there is no tomorrow. That's when reality sets in for me, *"What has that guy or this team ever done in my behalf, for my life, or for my country?"* Yet I will scream my lungs out; practically lose my voice by the end of the game, and for what? **For the love of the game.** *Why is it that we can't seem to muster up at least the same measure of passion for Jesus?* I once heard a preacher ask why we get so excited at football games, standing up and cheering like crazy people, yet we're subdued and reserved in our worship. Why? At least in church if someone jumps up and shouts, you won't get beer spilled all over you. If we can get so excited for the love of the game — can't we get equally as passionate for the love of our Savior?

Yet our passion for Him is so often reserved. We have little or no emotion. God's game plan is for us to fall so deeply in love with Him that we are not ashamed or afraid to show it. We wouldn't hesitate for a moment to tell someone who our favorite team is, would we? We wear sports memorabilia of all kinds — hats and sweatshirts, socks and shoes, carry umbrellas, and have bumper stickers on our cars. Are we that passionate about telling others who our Lord is and what He's done in our lives?

God has had a *game plan* and it's not to win in the last 2 seconds with a 50 yard field goal. It's the ultimate game plan for life that rescues us from a sinful, losing state. It's been on His *slate* since time began. He made a way for us to win every time in life, not just in the closing moments of it. This plan gave us Jesus who scored the winning touchdown for all eternity. Now it's time for us to get passionate about the game and decide who we're playing for.

LOVE CHANGES EVERYTHING

Genuine, heartfelt passion for Jesus and preoccupation with Jesus transitions how we view life. It transforms what we see from temporal to eternal. Passion changes us from just doing the things we think we have to do, or what we want to do, to doing what we *love to do.* But here's one of the most important aspects about passion.

> *Passion changes everything,*
> *because passion stems from love*
> *and love changes everything.*

It's impossible to be passionate without love. Try and convince me that you have never felt what love can do in your life. Love is the most powerful force in the universe. Love was created by God. Love makes men and women do things they never thought they could or would do. You know what I'm talking about—laugh, if you will. It makes you spend money you don't have, go places you wouldn't normally go, wear clothes you wouldn't have otherwise been caught dead in. Love will cause you to listen to songs or styles of music you once thought was atrocious, move across country to live—leaving a home and location you thought you'd never leave, and reach out in ways that once seemed impossible...all for love. Love is the strongest, most transforming force we will ever experience. Whether sinner or saint, love moves people. Love changes people. Love instills joy in people. Love gives hope. Love creates a glow on faces that were once in despair. ***Our passion for Christ is a direct reflection of our love for Him.***

I loooove chocolate. I love Coca-Cola. I love blackberry jam with seeds, and pumpkin bread, actually anything pumpkin. You notice a pattern of my love for such *healthy* food. Actually those loves have dramatically changed since writing of this book. My true love now— Isagenix Products. Healthy nutritional cellular cleansing! This has totally transformed my life. It has given me new passion for helping people find the miracle of God's created human body, which heals when given pure nutrition releasing fat as a marvelous side benefit. Contact me for more information.

I love music. I love singing. I love writing. None of these loves love me back (except Isagenix). Nor, can these loves ever compare with the love I have for Jesus. Why? Because nothing we love on earth; silly, insignificant, temporary things can compare to Jesus. He *is* the ***real*** thing. He loves us back. His love is beyond comprehension. His love is, unending, purposeful, unconditional and irreplaceable. **He first loved us. Not only did He love us, He showed how much.** John 15:13. *"Greater love has no one than this, than to lay down one's life for his friends."* Excluding maybe a parent or spouse, has anyone ever loved you first? No one has ever or will ever love like Jesus. That's reason enough to fall in love with Him—to allow passion to grow.

We cannot, however, fall in love with Jesus until we invite Him into our lives. Sounds kind of like a real relationship, doesn't it? He longs for a personal relationship with us, but He will never push His way into our lives. He is a Gentleman. He shows up by invitation only.

FORSAKING OUR FIRST LOVE

In Revelation 2:2-4, Jesus addresses the most incredible, vibrant on-target-doing-every-thing-right-church with a little hint of displeasure—the Ephesians. This is what He said. *"I know your deeds, your hard work and your perseverance. I know that you cannot tolerate wicked men, that you have tested those who claim to be apostles but are not, and have found them false. You have persevered and have endured hardships for my name, and have not grown weary. Yet I hold this against you: You have forsaken your first love."*

These people were righteous, hated sin, embraced others in love. They carried out the teachings of the church ambitiously. But Jesus told them He still had a problem. They had lost their first love, their ***passion***. They were preoccupied with doing all the right stuff, mindlessly performing the duties of the church. But their passion, their love for Him was gone. Jesus said this to a church, it's not a matter of *doing*; it is a matter of *being*; loving God with all of our hearts; passionate about the gospel.

Could He be saying the same to us today? *"I have somewhat against you; you have left your first love."* You have forgotten or forsaken what it means to **love me.** Not church work, not the church building, not church related activities or meetings; not even church people; but loving me.

Passion that stems from love cannot be experienced because we faithfully attend church or because we sing in the choir, or on the praise team, or serve on committees or boards. This passion is experienced as we fall more deeply in love with Jesus every day, spending time with Him—time in prayer, time in His Word, time just sitting at His feet. I love the chorus written by Mike Murdock: *"I love sitting at Your feet, I love hearing what you say. I love knowing Your desires; I'm so pleasured to obey. Your favor is like sunrise, driving, all my doubts away, I love sitting at Your feet, every single day."*

PREOCCUPIED & PASSIONATE ABOUT JESUS

I had the privilege of singing in a large church choir in Charlotte, NC. One Wednesday evening during rehearsal I was sitting on the piano bench with the pianist rehearsing a solo I was to sing with them for a future Sunday morning service. Afterwards, the two of us sat talking about how long she had served this church as the pianist. I complimented her on her incredible talent and how awesome it was that she had devoted so many years to serving the Lord. She smiled and responded kindly, "Well, Regina, I have been playing here for over 25 years, but I have not served the Lord all those years. For many I simply played because it was my job. Week after a week I showed up. I played. I performed as I had been taught to do." I looked at her a little confused, wondering how she could have heard so many sermons, so many invitations, yet had never given her life to Christ. She said, "I didn't recognize that I was lost. I was a good person. I didn't see a need. I didn't know what it meant to have a relationship with the Lord. Then, one Sunday morning the light came on. At that moment I realized *my* need to commit *my* life to Jesus."

From that day on her focus changed from playing the notes; it being a job, to becoming her ***passion.*** A genuine commitment changed everything.

This kind of passion isn't experienced by going through religious rituals, ceremonies or prayers. It isn't found by living a good life. It doesn't become real by being in church, anymore than being in a garage makes a person a car. It is found by seeing our need for, and falling in love with, Jesus.

How do we do that? How do we fall in love with Jesus?

First: We realize we are sinners. We have to be forgiven and cleansed from sin. Romans 3:23 *"For all have sinned and fall short of the glory of God."* Once we realize our need, then

Second: We ask Jesus to forgive us; to cleanse us from every sin. We invite Him to come into our lives and be our Lord and Savior. Romans 3:24 *"Being justified freely by His grace through the redemption that is in Christ Jesus…"* Lord is different than Savior. Lord means He is Master, *the boss* — so to speak — in a very good way. Savior means Redeemer, forgiver of sins. We invite Him to be both. Once we have established that,

Third: We follow the Lord in baptism. Fundamental, Evangelical, Full Gospel or Pentecostal and Charismatic churches everywhere will immerse you into Christ. We ask Him to fill us with His Holy Spirit.

Fourth: We find a church home to attend regularly for corporate worship; one that teaches and preaches the Bible - the *whole* Bible. There's strength in the community of like believers. We spend time with people we love. We go to their house to visit. We show our love for Jesus in the same way. Because we love Him, we want worship in His house.

Fifth: We spend time talking to Him, which would also be known as ***prayer.*** Spend time listening; He will speak if we're listening. John 10:1-4 *"And when He brings out his own sheep, He goes before them; and the sheep follow Him, for they know His voice. Yet they will by no means follow a stranger, but will flee from him, for they do not know the voice of strangers."* *"My sheep hear my voice, and I know them, and they follow me."* John 10:27.

Sixth: We spend time reading and studying God's Word, His love letter to us. Have a journal ready, or paper to write on, He has much to say and show us.

Seventh: We spend time privately with the Lord. That means, when no one is looking, when we are alone; we spend time with God, in His presence. A love relationship in the natural requires alone time. It's no different in the spiritual. Our greatest growth in Christ comes from the moments we spend with Him - just Him and us. Praying, loving Him, singing, dancing before Him, whatever you feel comfortable with personally. This time is crucial for spiritual growth, and parallels in importance to studying God's Word.

PASSIONATE SINCE CHILDHOOD

For some reason, even as a young child, I loved Jesus. Maybe it came from the fact that I was conceived in the womb of a Mother who really did not, at that particular time in her life, want me. Mother told me this story herself sitting in her beauty salon many years ago, while she was coloring and cutting my hair.

When she found out she had conceived, those nine months were not good ones for me, or her. She had previously experienced 2 miscarriages and was not emotionally or physically prepared. After my birth, she was still challenged having a new baby around.

For almost 2 years I had a constantly runny nose. I remember she would grab my nose, so weary of the watery fluid that was always there, tearing at it with a handkerchief, saying, "I am so tired of this snot, why do you have this?" Finally, reluctantly, at her wit's end she took me to the doctor. He just so happened to be a Christian. He asked my mother, *"Are you constantly on this child about something; are you angry with her?"* Her response was *"Yes, I guess I am."* Inwardly, she was still wrestling with the thought of having me and the doctor simply told her that my condition was completely emotional. There was nothing wrong with my health; there was nothing he could prescribe. If she would just love me, hold me and accept me, I would get well.

Mother followed his advice. Within a brief time the runny nose was gone. From then on she went out of her way to show her love for me. She proved through the years to be a very strong *positive* and in *some ways negative* influence in my life. Mother had a dominate personality. There were things that had to be done her way, and her way was the right way. But most importantly she taught me to deeply love Jesus. That He deeply loved me. In church, she would sit me on the piano bench beside her. She would wrap her arms around me at the altar when we knelt to pray. She took me to church *all the time*. Not just Sundays and Wednesday nights, but any time there were special revival meetings or healing services. If Mother asked, I was eager to go.

She instilled within me, as Daddy did, what it meant to have a relationship with Jesus. He had a special plan for my life. That truth made a huge impact. I came to realize that He was my Savior and friend. I remember sweeping my floor at nine years old talking to the Lord, singing to Him. There was already an acute awareness of who He was and what He had done. He heard me when I prayed, or talked to Him. Though I couldn't see or touch Him, He always there.

My passion for Jesus has grown through the years, not because I was born a preacher's kid and went to church every time the doors were open, (sometimes when they weren't) ☺ but because I learned at a very young, impressionable age about the genuine love of Jesus. That He was real. This transpired because of the precious, intentional teaching and guidance of Godly parents. I understood and embraced those truths. The Holy Spirit, who dwells in me, has never let go, nor have I.

PASSIONATE BECAUSE OF ETERNITY

When our earthly life ends, and we can rest assured it will; we will all come to the end of our journey. We will be transported into an eternal destiny to one place or another. Life does not end in death. It is simply a change of address. We will transfer into another life called eternity.

It may sound crazy, but we were born with an eternal soul that is *immortal*. It lives on forever and we will live joyously in heaven with Jesus. Or we will find ourselves in another very real place of everlasting torment called hell. When God created man, He created a soul that never dies. You just thought you wanted to be a vampire and live forever; well, you are going to, we are going to. Not be vampires, but live forever. What we have to decide is where it's going to be…eternal joy or eternal torment?

I would ask, what can passion about everything else in life but Jesus do for you when it's time to change your address from this world to the next? Oh, yes, there is of course the temporary pleasure experienced. But other than that, what can anything you have ever been passionate about or preoccupied with do for you when you breathe your last breath? What will you have accomplished on earth that will have had lasting, eternal value or positive eternal consequences? Will what we have devoted our time, our talents, our lives to, or been so passionate or preoccupied with matter? Did any of it have eternal value? *"What does it profit a man if he gains the whole world and loses his own soul?"* Matthew 16:26.

"Jesus said unto him, 'You shall love the Lord your God with all your heart, with all your soul, and with all you mind. This is the first and great commandment." Matthew 22:37

With all of our HEART - 1 Samuel 16:7 *"But the LORD said to Samuel, 'Do not look at his appearance or at the height of his stature, because I have refused him. For the LORD does not see as man sees:*

for man looks on the outward appearance, but God looks at the heart." I'm thankful that God always sees our heart; another great attribute of God, so unlike man's.

Matthew Henry's Commentary noted that "The heart is the root, the language is the fruit. The heart is the fountain, the words are the streams. The heart is the treasury, the words are the things brought out of the treasury. It is the character of a good man, that he has a good treasure in his heart, and from thence brings forth good things." Saint Matthew said it before Matthew Henry, *"Out of the abundance of the heart, the mouth speaks.* Matthew 12:34b. Unless the heart is transformed, the life will never be totally reformed.

Out of the heart come the *issues* of life: Love, hate, anger, pride, peace, joy, grief, jealousy, passion, tenderness, compassion, bitterness, hardness, forgiveness, and unforgiveness. Everything in the natural and spiritual realm is connected or interwoven to the heart. Without a pure heart; we cannot love God. Out of an evil heart come evil living, evil words, and evil intentions. Evil cannot love God. Our hearts must be pure, whole, and properly functioning, if we are to love God with all of it. Jesus is the one who cleanses, transforms, and even replaces an evil heart. We can't give ourselves a pure heart, but as we submit to the Lord and ask, it will happen. The process is a constant one. Hearts can easily become hardened and embittered, filled with sin. We just come back to the cleansing blood of Jesus. All we have to do is ask Him to keep our hearts holy and pure — tender, as we keep a constant watch, diligently guarding them.

With all of our SOUL - That is the *supernatural-God-breathed* portion of man, the part that never dies. Since God gave us life through His breath, and God is eternal, this is the part of us that is eternal. The soul is the seat of our personality. It is where we perceive, reflect, feel, desire. We might think it comes from our mind, but thoughts actually are birthed from the soul of man. This is described in biblical commentaries as the seat of the *sentient element* in man or the place of perception. It's imperative for us to know whether or not our soul, the spiritual part of us loves God or loves the devil. We cannot love both. When we love Jesus with all of our soul, we can be confident that He will see us through all of life's adversity into victory; and that we will spend eternity with Him.

With all of our MIND – *"Casting down arguments and every high thing that exalts itself against the knowledge of God,* ***bringing every thought into captivity to the obedience of Christ."*** 2 Corinthians 10:5. Our minds are our greatest battlefield. If we can conquer the mind's doubts, prejudices, lusts, wrongful thoughts, and evil imaginations; we will grow more deeply in our passion for the Lord and love Him. But to conquer mind's battlefield it takes prayer. We rely upon the power of the Holy Spirit's work in us. He's the only one that can heal and restore even the most troubled mind. We ask. We yield. He heals.

We also win this battlefield by continually filling our minds with the right stuff. Pouring garbage into them will never manifest healing or purity of mind. If we allow garbage in, then the thoughts we have will be garbage. Garbage stinks. It's nasty. It's not something we want to hold in our hands, so why would we want to hold it in our minds. We keep our minds stayed on things that are good, pure, holy, righteous. Philippians 4:8; *"Finally brethren, whatever things are true, whatever things are noble, whatever things are just, whatever things are pure, whatever things are lovely, whatever things are of good report, if there is any virtue and if there is anything praiseworthy – meditate on these things."*

For some, maybe even many who are reading this book, the greatest mind-battle you have might be tormenting memories of your childhood. It would be horrific to know the exact number of children who are molested in their lifetime. We wouldn't even want to know, but God knows. This battle of the

Passion Or Preoccupation?

mind is a spiritual warfare. As we take every thought captive through the power of Christ allowing the Holy Spirit to heal and transform then we will overcome and experience peace of mind. In Chapter 9, I share a powerful teaching on spiritual warfare prayers. This will help in the prayer of healing and release from harmful memories. Always hold tightly to truth. God is mighty. We do our part, He does His. We cannot ask or expect God to heal us if we continue to dwell on or entertain thoughts that we need to release to Him. Nor can we expect Him to heal our minds if we continually fill them with filth.

When we embrace a genuine love for Jesus we will experience great passion for Him. Ultimately the passion and preoccupation we have for Him determines an abundant life now and a glorious eternal life with Him in the place He is preparing for those who love Him.

NO LOVE... NO PASSION
LITTLE LOVE ... LITTLE PASSION
GREAT LOVE ... GREAT PASSION

2

GOT JESUS?
"Realizing & Embracing Our Need for a Savior"

*D*id you ever imagine that in our lifetime everything would be so influenced by advertising and image? As ranchers in the old west used branding to distinguish their livestock from another's, modern society now uses the term to make products, enterprises, and even people more recognizable. *Branding* enhances image and makes it more visible with specialized logos and portfolios. The industry is exploding. Packaging compels people to respond in a positive way—to purchase or participate. From automobiles to investments, from some miracle sinus-allergy decongestant to shampooing with a magic formula that will make one's hair lustrously silky and shiny; billboards strategically positioned on superhighways and Interstates scream *"look at me."* Radio and television commercials entice viewers to transform their lives—guaranteed with the use of their product. And whatever you do, don't wait. Do not delay. Get your credit card and purchase today. Don't pass up this once-in-a-lifetime opportunity to experience a *life-changing* new product.

I love the Chick-fil-A marketing ad that was used a number of years ago with this witty Holstein cow writing on the billboard, "*Eat Mor Chicken.*" Another one that caught my eye asked the question, **Got Milk?** Most often some celebrity or well known personality would have a huge mustache of milk on their upper lip, smiling as though *milk* was the end-all answer. Okay, so this billboard honestly did capture my attention. In the whole scheme of things, milk really doesn't make a huge impact on our quality of life. Yes, it's refreshing when it's cold and tastes great with cookies; but can our lives function without it? Well, except for babies, of course. And let's not forget calcium is great for our bones, so we need to drink it for that—unless of course we're lactose intolerant. My, doesn't one thing lead to another?

But wouldn't it be exciting when traveling through cities in America to see huge billboards capturing our attention with the most joyful expression of contentment on people's faces and a picture of the pearly gates of heaven in the background or some beautiful, lush, peacefully green meadow with this question, **Got Jesus**? Nothing in life—not milk, not food, not material goods, or anything we *got* will ever begin to compare to Jesus. There is no nothing more necessary and no one else to be more passionate about.

Got Jesus? More than any refreshing drink, more than calcium for our bones, Jesus not only makes life worth living. He is life. **People everywhere need Jesus**. Life without Him is mundane, empty and meaningless. People are searching for answers everywhere except where they can be found. **Jesus is the answer**. He has every solution to every problem or question we will ever have.

WHEN WE ARE THIRSTY - Jesus is the water of life, the living water. When we drink of Him our spiritual thirst will be quenched. We will no longer desire worldly things that we once craved because He satisfies thirst like nothing else can. Isaiah 55:1. *"Lo, everyone who thirsts come to the waters..."* John 4:14 *"But whoever drinks of the water that I shall give Him will never thirst. But the water that I shall give him shall become a fountain of water springing up into everlasting life."*

WHEN WE ARE HUNGRY - When we are hungry for spiritual food, for the inner craving to be filled, He satisfies with His Word and through Himself. There is emptiness in the soul of every man. Jesus is the bread of life. He fills the hungry. *"And Jesus said to them, I am the bread of life. He who comes to me shall never hunger..."* John 6:35. *"For He satisfies the longing soul, and fills the hungry soul with goodness."* Psalms 107:9.

WHEN WE ARE WEARY - When we feel completely spent from life's daily demands and difficulties; when we've gone beyond the call of duty, utterly exhausted; He is the giver of rest. Jeremiah 31:25. *"For I have satiated the weary soul, and I have replenished every sorrowful soul." "Come unto me all you who labor and are heavy laden, and I will give you rest."* Matthew 11:28. *"For we who have believed do enter that rest. For He who has entered His rest has himself also ceased from his works as God did from His. Let us therefore be diligent to enter that rest."* Hebrews 4:3, 10-11.

WHEN WE ARE IN NEED - He promised that He would provide for our needs; spiritually, physically, financially and emotionally, if we would ask and believe. Philippians 4:19 *"And my God shall supply all your need according to His riches in glory by Christ Jesus." "Therefore I say to you, whatever things you ask when you pray, believe that you receive them, and you will have them."* Mark 11:24. *"I have been young, and now am old; yet I have not seen the righteous forsaken, nor his descendents begging bread."* Psalms 37:25.

WHEN WE ARE DISCOURAGED OR DEPRESSED - Jesus is the great encourager and the lifter of our heads. In moments of deepest despair He will fill our hearts and spirits with assurance. He will deliver, heal and comfort us. Psalms 34:17. *"The righteous cry out, and the LORD hears, and delivers them out of all their troubles."* 2 Corinthians 1:3-4. *"Blessed be God, even the Father of our Lord Jesus Christ, the Father of mercies, and the God of all comfort: Who comforts us in all our tribulation, that we may be able to* *comfort those who are in any trouble, with the comfort we ourselves are comforted by God."*

WHEN WE HAVE LOST HOPE - Of all the range of human emotions there's none as significant as hope. When we have hope, the promise of something better to come, we have the ability to face any adversity. Hope is one of the most important elements for having joy and for knowing peace in the midst of turmoil. Jesus is our hope. Romans 5:5. *"Now hope does not disappoint, because the love of God has been poured out in our hearts by the Holy Spirit who was given to us." "Now may the God of hope fill you with all joy and peace In believing that you may abound in hope by the power of the Holy Spirit."* Romans 15:13.

WHEN WE ARE FEELING LONELY OR FORSAKEN – There's nothing like His presence. There's nothing to compare with knowing that He will never leave us or forsake us. We are never alone when we know Him. Hebrews 13:5 *"For He Himself has said, I will never leave you nor forsake you."* Psalms 27:10. *"Fear not; for I am with you, be not dismayed: for I am your God. I will strengthen you; yes, I will help you, yes, I will uphold you with the right hand of My righteousness."* Isaiah 41:10.

WHEN WE FEEL WEAK - He becomes our physical and spiritual strength whenever we need it. All we have to do is call upon Him. His resources never diminish. 2 Corinthians 12:9 *"And He said unto Me, My grace is sufficient for thee: for My strength is made perfect in weakness."* 2 Chronicles 16:9 *"For the eyes of the Lord run to and fro throughout the whole earth, to show Himself strong on behalf of those whose heart is loyal to Him."*

WHEN WE ARE WORRIED – Worry is like a rocking chair. It gives us something to do, but gets us nowhere. Worry is truly one of the most futile efforts of our existence. It robs us of our peace, steals our joy and accomplishes nothing. Isaiah 59:1 *"Behold, the Lord's hand is not shortened, that He cannot save; neither His ear heavy, that He cannot hear."* Romans 4:20-21. *"He (referring* to Abraham) *staggered not at the promise of God through unbelief, but was strong in faith, giving glory to God. And being fully persuaded that, what He (God) had promised, He was able also to perform."*

WHEN WE NEED DIRECTION - All we have to do is ask Him to show us the way. After we have asked, we listen for His response for direction. Then we receive and obey. Jeremiah 33:3 *"Call unto Me, and I will answer you, and show you great and mighty things which you know not."* Proverbs 3:5-6 *"Trust in the Lord with all your heart, and lean not on your own understanding; in all your ways, acknowledge Him, and He shall direct your path."*

GOD'S DIRECTION IN BUSINESS

I remember during one of my years as a Manager in Home Interiors our team had grown immensely. God blessed this business that had been consecrated to Him. My constant prayer was for divine direction and wisdom in leadership to build a successful team.

Sales were good. Recruiting was good. Our team had expanded from one to sixty-five representatives. But we had reached a plateau — almost a stagnant place. We weren't progressing or regressing. We were holding our own. I knew that wasn't the best place to be. Businesses aren't successful and stagnant. I focused on planning sales meeting that were topic oriented, creative, fun, and informative. I asked the Lord for wisdom and creative genius, so the training would be infused with success driven ideas for their home show presentations; booking, selling and recruiting. I ran contests with great prizes for high achievers. But still *something* was holding us back.

We began the meetings with the pledge of allegiance, a devotional, and a time of opening prayer — giving everyone an opportunity to share a need or express praise. But things were not moving forward. I began to seek the Lord more fervently for divine intervention. *"Lord, please show me what's wrong? What do I need to do? What's the solution? What are we lacking for continued growth? What can be implemented to bring in more bookings and higher sales? What needs to be changed or corrected? I need your help, your guidance."*

I asked and He gave me an answer. I would admonish you to keep this in mind whenever you say a prayer of this nature. God will always give you the answer, but it may not be the one you want to hear. The Lord clearly communicated that I needed to be ready spiritually for what would transpire from my request. It wouldn't be easy. In fact it would be impossible in my own strength. But, if I would prepare myself in His presence—even fast—then as I followed His instructions I would see the necessary change for growth come to fruition.

What the Holy Spirit led me to do was: On a date in the future, at the end of a sales meeting, allow the displayers an opportunity to share in an open session. Let them tell me how they felt I could be a better leader. Give them a chance to express what changes might be beneficial; what they didn't like, or ideas to bring about positive impact for greater success as a team. The meeting would be open to whatever they felt they needed to express.

Okay. I asked God for direction and He gave me a decisive plan, even precise details as to how to prepare for it. He answered. I listened. I obeyed. Little did I know how very, ***very*** difficult it was going to be. Many complaints and negative thoughts echoed through the room. The meeting proceeded for over an hour. I spoke not a word. No excuses. No justification. No recourse. I listened with open heart and open ears to the myriad of criticisms. No positive statements.

At the conclusion most left smiling, feeling good about being able to air their opinion of my leadership (or lack thereof). It could have been devastating for me **but for God**. It was a mystery as to how this team had been so successful, or had accomplished as many goals as we had. Everything just felt negative. For over an hour I literally laid on my face on that floor weeping, *"Oh Lord, how can I measure up? How can I ever be what they need or expect? I am such a failure."* At that moment the Holy Spirit again spoke clearly to me. I will never forget what He said. His words carried me through one of the darkest times of my life. *"Regina, you have obeyed. I am with you to uphold and strengthen you. Go forward in faith and in continued repentance and prayer. Pray especially for your team. My Spirit will give you peace and joy, and heal you from the brokenness you have experienced today. Take to heart all that you've heard, and follow through with the words spoken by these women. Consider the source of each statement. You will see changes and blessings begin to unfold. My strength is made perfect in weakness and my gifts are bountifully given to the obedient and humble of heart."*

Within one month, praying a lot, remembering the words of the team members, and of the Holy Spirit; changes in my leadership began to transpire. The business dramatically improved in the most unbelievably positive way. The team grew. The camaraderie was vibrant. That year we were among the top 50 in the nation. There were 800+ teams. We reached one million dollars in sales. Those figures were wholesale. We sold over $1,450,000.00 in retail. (That's a whole lot of candlelight and wall sconces.) We had become a million dollar power house. *How?*

First I had to acknowledge that there was a problem, and much of it pertained to me. Second, I needed the Lord's healing, His help and His direction. I didn't have a clue without supernatural intervention. **Third, I asked Him to show me what to do and was willing to submit myself in obedience** to His instruction, even though it was probably the most difficult thing I had ever done. **Fourth, He answered my prayer, instructed me with a specific plan, and I obeyed.** Not later, but right away, as I prayed and fasted. He gave me the assurance that I was spiritually equipped to handle what would transpire. We must be prepared spiritually for these kinds of tests. If we aren't they could affect us in a detrimental way, pushing us away from, not closer to, the Lord.

Did you know that even *delayed obedience* is disobedience? God's divine direction without obedience results in absolutely nothing. No change. No transformation. Situations in life cannot change, nor will we, until we are obedient, allowing the Holy Spirit to transform us and our circumstances.

HE IS EVERYTHING WE NEED FOR EVERY NEED

Got Jesus? He is all we will ever need, for every need, whenever we are in need. Look no further. The lyrics to *"I AM"* written by Rusty Goodman say it perfectly:

> *When it was dark in my heart,*
> *You brought light to me,*
> *A child of darkness became a child of light;*
> *And when my soul was dry,*
> *Oh, and I needed a drink,*
> *The water of life, You became for me.*
>
> *I Am, I Am, You said to me,*
> *I am the Bread of Life, just take and eat.*
> *I Am, I Am, You said to me,*
> *I'll be what it takes to meet your need.*
>
> *You were the widow's cruise of oil,*
> *Old Elijah's meat,*
> *You were shelter for Brother Noah,*
> *A shepherd for the sheep.*
> *And in the fire, You were the fourth man,*
> *And a cloud by day,*
> *A fire by night for Your little children,*
> *To lead the way!*
>
> *I Am, I Am, You said to me.*
> *I am the Bread of Life, just take and eat.*
> *I Am, I Am, You said to me,*
> *I'll be what it takes to meet your need.*

HOW DO WE FIND JESUS?

So let's discuss now what it means to *find Jesus*. Is He lost? When using that term I don't literally mean *finding Him*. No. He isn't lost. We are. But we cannot pursue Him until we first come to the realization that we are in need of Him. Once we understand how desperate and empty our lives are without Him, then we are able to see the need of inviting Him into our lives; finding Him in a sense. He comes only when we invite Him. It's also important to understand that this invitation from us to receive Him cannot be in response to a *head knowledge* we've embraced, or from a fear of going into eternity without Him. Rather, it must be motivated from our hearts; a genuine desire to commit our lives to Him from an evident need within us. That is a powerful thing. It's definitely a heart issue. When we give Him that, we are saying *"Lord, this is not just a matter of soothing my conscience. It's finally a reality! I am totally aware, for the first time in my life of my need for Your forgiveness — my awareness of the emptiness, the meaninglessness of life, without You. Cleanse me of my sins make me a brand new "creation" in You. There is no longer a desire to keep living life as I always have. There has to me more to it than I have been experiencing. My life needs meaning and purpose that only You can give. I need You Jesus."*

When Christ comes into our life, even if we think we're already a good person, we begin to see an immediate change in our lifestyle. 2 Corinthians 5:17 says *"Therefore if anyone is in Christ, he is a new creation; old things have passed away, behold, all things become new."* There is newness in your spirit that comes with a genuine conversion. A *passion* for Jesus is born. We don't want to go to the places we used to go, participate in the things we once did or say things we once said. The blood of Jesus has cleansed us. The process of change is being manifested in our lives with this brand *new heart* experience. True passion for Christ cannot unfold in one's life until we have experienced *finding Him*, receiving Him as Savior, accepting His forgiveness. Then, continuing to grow cultivating a genuine desire to know Him more intimately. It may take time for old habits to go completely, and even the desires to leave. For some it happens instantaneously—for others, it's a process. But the change will be obvious as we continue to walk with Christ and allow His cleansing blood to completely set us free from our old sinful nature. We are being sanctified daily—set apart from the world, as we make conscious choices to live like Jesus. As our relationship with Him continues to deepen and mature.

We all come to Christ in our own way with our own private issues, sins and needs. Romans 3:23 says, *"For all have sinned and fall short of the glory of God."* Romans 10:9 *"If we confess with our mouth the Lord Jesus, and believe in our heart that God has raised Him from the dead, we will be saved."* That is truth. We never have to wonder about that! Never doubt your salvation experience. But here's the real question, *"Is that all you want?"* If that's all you want, then that's all you'll get. You have received salvation. But there is so much more. So much more that God has for us in Him.

Some years ago I was attending a Tuesday morning prayer meeting with a few other girlfriends. I was spiritually hungry for more of God in my life—to see Him begin to do the miraculous. About once a month we would enjoy having lunch together after the prayer time. We had chosen a little Mexican restaurant with a nice atmosphere and a reasonably priced, very tasty luncheon menu. I am, at times, quite the creature of habit. And, as usual, I ordered my favorite, Item #6—Speedy Gonzales. This meal included a taco, an enchilada, and Mexican rice. We visited, enjoyed our lunch said our goodbyes, and went our separate ways until the following week.

Fastening my seatbelt, starting the engine, the Lord spoke to me as only He can. In my spirit I heard these words, *"Regina, my sweet daughter, you are so boring."* Now mind you, He wasn't condescending, or reprimanding, or even being negative toward me. God doesn't do that. You can rest assured He is always on your side, ready to build up and encourage.

But He also imparts wisdom and revelation. His words were simply matter of fact, not a big deal. My instant response was, *"What makes you say that Lord?"* He responded, *"Because you always order the same thing."* My reply was of course, *"and why do you care about what I order in a restaurant."* *"Because that's exactly what so many of my children do week after week at My table – always ordering the same thing when I have so much more for you to partake of."* There's **so much more.** But we never ask. We never seem to even think about it. We often don't see *the trees for the forest.* We are creatures of habit. Boring. We have permission to ask for our needs but Jesus has so much more. 1 Corinthians 2:9 *"But it is written, Eye has not seen, nor ear heard, nor have entered into the heart of man the things which God has prepared for those who love Him."* I don't believe that verse is just referring to Heaven. It's also speaking of the here and now. The verse goes on to say, *"but the Spirit has revealed them to us."* So we have had a foretaste, a revelation. Yet we rarely or meagerly tap into the greatness of our God or His deep riches and blessings, the miracles that can be ours because we don't seem to desire them or even think to ask.

The initial *passion* pertaining to life that we have, to a great degree, has been there since birth. It is evidenced by what we presently really like, love or even hate. If we hate something, we want to do something to change it, to make a difference. This gifting or passion was placed within us at conception. It is the inborn God-given ability, genius, capacity, knack or skill for specific things. What kind of world would it be if God didn't put within people the innate desire and nature to become scientists, doctors, lawyers, preachers, teachers, dentists, chiropractors, engineers, surgeons, naturopaths, dancers, to serve in the military, construction workers, mechanics, chefs and restaurant owners, authors, musicians, speakers, poets, singers, actors, entertainers, politicians, newscasters, sound and studio technicians, computer geeks? Well, the list could go on and on, but you get the drift. Some have a passion for the medical field. I couldn't be a nurse or doctor if my life depended upon it. I faint at the sight of blood, get sweaty palms when I walk into a maternity ward, and almost become nauseous when I'm in hospitals for any length of time around illness. I can visit and I can pray—but I could not make a living in a hospital. Not to ignore the fact that science wasn't one of my best subjects. That's why God blesses others, (lots of others) with a love, skill and aptitude for holistic products and medicine. There are innumerable vocations we could discuss, but the point is this; out of *that passion or gifting*, people focus or invest time and education into what often becomes their life's chosen work—which is indeed God's purpose so that we will enjoy our labor, rather than just tolerate it.

Our marvelous Creator also gave us learning skills, mental capacity or IQ to pursue our gifts. I have a cousin who really was (he is now in heaven) a rocket scientist. He built missiles for NASA. Gary always had, from the time we were children, an interest in space. He had the brains to go with the love. God gifted from the inner soul.

Unfortunately, we aren't born with a love for Jesus like we were given other passions or skills. He could have done that too—instead, He placed a *vacuum*, a God-sized emptiness in us that only He can fill. He chose to create us as free moral agents with the right to make our own decisions pertaining to Him. Choosing Jesus is one decision we will have to make entirely on our own. We don't reach an intimacy with Him through osmoses. The best scenario is to have parents who teach us from birth, so we can grow up learning about Him, loving Him and knowing who He is; then the chances of understanding our need for Christ and inviting Him into our lives will be far more likely. But, often that is not the case.

Many people reach adulthood with little or no knowledge or exposure to church or Jesus. At some time or another we have to be introduced to Him, and then come to an understanding of who He is, and why we need Him. There are so many variables involved in a person making a commitment to Christ. Often it takes far more than just being invited to church or someone witnessing. Hardened hearts, abuse, broken spirits, people who have been exposed to the occult

Rekindling Our Passion For Jesus!

or demonic world, those addicted to drugs or alcohol, or who have been in gangs, people who have been involved in false religions or even those who have just simply never known anything about God — probably won't easily see or accept the path of Christianity. These are the ones we *"pray for without ceasing,"* believing that the Holy Spirit will supernaturally intervene and show Himself miraculous in their behalf.

Once a heart is touched by the Holy Spirit, and the eyes of the unrepentant heart have been opened to the truth of God's glorious gift of Jesus, and how He can change our lives and bring an awesomeness to living we have never known before — then passion can begin to grow in our hearts for Him and He will become far more than just a mere acquaintance. He will give meaning and purpose to life.

Until we want this life-changing, transforming experience, a relationship with Christ will find little priority in our lives. Until passion burns in us like a fire, by the Holy Spirit, we will be of the mindset that we've got things to do, places to go and people to meet — God... well, He's always going to be there. Kind of like the World Trade Center buildings. *Surely nothing could ever take them away?* But something did. And guess what, God is always going to be there, but we may not always have the opportunity to **call on Him.** Life is precious and can be snuffed out in a millisecond. Or we may think, *"He's God and He understands that I'm busy making a living. I just don't have time to really spend with Him. But it's ok. He doesn't really need me. There are a lot of other people who have more time than I do. He's God so He understands."*

Oh yeah, He understands alright. But the issue goes deeper. If we have accepted Christ and yet seem to have no passion, then maybe we need to sincerely pray, asking Him to fill us, to pour into us His Spirit, so that we will no longer be lukewarm in our relationship. Ask Him to stir up His fire in our hearts so that our passion for everything else won't be stronger or seem more important than Him. *"Oh Lord, may we feel passion from You, to give You first-place in our lives."*

Becoming passionate about Jesus actually comes down to more fully understanding His purposes. This is so amazing; **God created us to have fellowship with Him.** As unlikely or even crazy as that sounds, the reason He created us was because HE desired our company, our worship, our praise and to be with us. His existence wasn't dependent upon us. He wanted us. He longed for companionship. He wanted to be loved and praised for who He is. God is completely self perpetuating, self sufficient, and perfect. He is Omnipresent, Omniscient, Omnipotent and Immutable. He's everywhere, all knowing, all powerful, and unchangeable. Superlatives more incredible than any super hero man could ever dream up! Yet He chose to create human beings from dirt; fashioning us in the likeness of the Triune Godhead, Father, Son and Holy Spirit. God breathed into us His breath of life. He gave us free-will and a voice with which to curse and deny Him; to praise and worship Him. Among all of His creation, we alone can speak His name and give Him glory. That is why we were created. To worship, honor, and glorify God. That truth is amazing. Often we miss the mark or fail to embrace our need for Him. And guess what, the other amazing thing is that if it weren't for Him — we wouldn't even be here. We wouldn't exist.

So, why in the world wouldn't we understand our need for Jesus? Why wouldn't we worry about finding Him for ourselves? Or does it really even make a difference anyway, in the whole scheme of things? Here are a few questions to ponder:

1. Do *we* have anything to do with being born in the first place? Do we feel life is just about us; our our desires, our happiness, and our choices? Who created us? Who gives us the very breath we breathe each day; a functioning mind, the ability to live, walk, talk, see, hear, and breathe, to use our hands? Who allows us to live, move and have our being?

2. What value or purpose can we really place on life? Other than money and possessions, when we're gone will it have mattered that we ever lived? What kind of a legacy are we leaving our children?

3. Who do we call on or what do we do when sorrow or tragedy, sickness or death occur? Who do you feel gives you comfort during these times? Isn't it ironic that even in our nation when there's a serious situation everyone is called to pray?

4. If there was no money or possessions, what objectives would there be in life for goal setting if we weren't pursuing *things?* What would our other goals be?

5. If we feel that we are a *good* person, who is good except God, and if we do not know God, how can we truly be good?

6. What about joy, what do we feel can bring true, lasting joy in life?

7. What about eternity? Will we take anything with us that we now possess when we leave?
Can we know for certain where we will spend eternity? Is there any merit or meaning to life without hope for a future or life after death?

KNOWING JESUS

If someone were to ask you if you knew Jesus, what would you say? Would you be able to tell them stories about what He did? Would you say He was a mighty prophet, sent from God? That He worked miracles during the thirty-three years He was on earth; opened blinded eyes, healed the sick, caused the lame to walk, opened deaf ears; He was a Redeemer? Or could you really tell them who He is to you, personally?

Got Jesus?

A number of years ago I met a naturopathic doctor who believes in Jesus, yet he actually worships another man who came long after Jesus—another *prophet* of sorts. Not someone from Biblical times, but much later; who he claims is *his* messiah. This person is his perfect example of a pure, sinless life. How can someone be your messiah if he is not capable of taking away your sins? Messiah literally means *He who takes away the sin of the world.* How can one improve on Jesus who is perfection to the nth degree? I don't believe earning forgiveness or doing penance counts. If that were the case we would be saving ourselves by works. Jesus is the Messiah who truly forgives and pardons through His death on the cross. Furthermore, if his messiah was born a man, not deity, how could he be a savior at all? A human cannot atone for sin—he is sin. Neither could any human being accomplish the supernatural. Why is it that people continue to search for *another* messiah? Because they are blinded by satan and cannot perceive or receive truth.

Jesus didn't come to force people to accept Him contrary to what some may believe. He came in obedience to the Father to offer Himself as the sacrificial Lamb—the final payment for sin. He was sent from God, conceived by the Holy Spirit, born of a virgin, crucified on a cross, and raised the third day thus proving that He not only conquered death, but that He fulfilled all that the Father commissioned Him to do. He is now sitting at the right hand of God ever making intercession for us. He is the only way to God. John 14:6 says *"Jesus said, 'I am the way, the truth, and the life. No one comes to the Father except by me.'"* There is no other name, no other prophet, no other holy man or person, whereby we can or ever will be saved. Acts 4:1 *"Nor is there salvation **in any other**, for there is **no other name** under heaven given among men by which we must be saved."*

Oh, I know, this truth is not socially acceptable, nor politically correct. Regardless of what the world dictates as acceptable, one day every knee will bow and every tongue confess. Philippians 2:9-11 *"Therefore God also has highly exalted Him and given Him the name which is above every name, that at the name of*

Jesus every knee would bow, of those in heaven, and those in earth, and of those under the earth, and that every tongue should confess that Jesus Christ is Lord, to the glory of God the Father." In that day it isn't going to matter what kind of beliefs we have programmed into our mental computers. Truth will prevail and all other doctrines, traditions, cults, false teachings and beliefs will bow and confess that there is only one given—His name is **Jesus.**

One of the most ironic things about *false religions* is that their *holy* teachings all came from...guess where? That's right, the Word of God. The *good stuff* Jesus wrote they duplicate, except of course the most important truth, the death, burial and resurrection of Christ. False religions never come up with original truth or righteousness. The moral or integrity issues, purity, kindness, brotherly love, honesty, compassion and so forth, are copied from the greatest teacher who ever lived, Jesus. They are His original teachings. John 1:1-3 *"In the beginning was the Word, and the Word was with God and the Word was God. The same was in the beginning with God. All things were made by Him and without Him was not anything made that was made."* He created everything, including the Word. The devil has copied, counterfeited, quoted and used God's word for deception since his inception. Remember that false religions also have the absurd, even corrupt teachings. Those include idol worship or pagan rituals, inflicting bodily harm or punishment to others as payment for sin, self-inflicted pain, abuse, penance, torture and even death, just to name a few. All of these servitudes came from yet another source—satan; the one who *"comes to kill, steal and destroy."* John 10:10a. This automatically bankrupts and cancels out every false religion. Man cannot worship God & satan. Jesus is the only way to God. Looks crystal clear, don't you think? Why be tempted by the devil's counterfeit, empty, bankrupt, false religions of the world that ultimately lead to an eternity in hell, disguised as godly religion.

THIS IS HOW WE FIND JESUS

FIRST: WE HAVE TO *WANT* TO FIND HIM: We find something or someone by going to where it is, or they are. Jesus is as close as the mention of His name. We can just speak His name... Jesus and He'll be there. He's easily reached, so easy to talk to. Or, if you're not comfortable doing that, you could go to a church, or call a person you know is a Christian—tell them you want to know Jesus. Whew, would that ever make their day.

Once we've invited Jesus into our lives, we make Him our Savior. He becomes our Redeemer—and more, we ask Him to become our Lord. He's in charge. Now what I mean by that is that we don't continue living life as we always have, because we have taken on a new nature, His nature. Our desires begin to change—we won't want to keep doing the things we used to do—pertaining to sin, or the things or lifestyle of the world. If this hasn't happened in you then take inventory—making sure you have truly committed your heart to Christ because you want Him in your life. This decision has to be more than a mind decision; it has to be a heart transformation. Begin asking the Holy Spirit to live through you, making you a Godly person. Ask Him to cause you to be more ethical in your work, in your lifestyle, in everything you do. Ask Him to give you the want to—the desire—to know Him more passionately.

Discuss with God the decisions you need to make or direction for your future! He desires to be the Lord of everything pertaining to life. Lanny Wolfe's song *"Jesus Be the Lord of All"* says it well:

> *In my heart are kingdoms of,*
> *A world that's all my own,*
> *Kingdoms that are only seen,*
> *By myself and God alone.*

In the past when I, tried to rule my world,
It just seemed to fall apart.
So please Jesus, be the Lord of all —
The kingdoms of my heart.

Jesus, be the Lord of all,
Jesus be the Lord of all,
Jesus be the Lord of all,
The kingdoms of my heart.

Cause if You're not Lord of everything,
Then You're not Lord of all.

It's so important to realize that all that pertains to life is interwoven, linked together; the links get really tangled up when we compartmentalize. Nothing can function properly if we separate God from our work, church, home, family, entertainment, vacations, play and then — oh, yes, let's don't forget to keep a compartment for God. God not only cares about everything that pertains to life — He is the most important part of life. If He's not preeminent, nothing will ever be right. Life functions with proper perspective and purpose as we honor Him, for who He is; seek His will in everything. He is Lord. He loves us. Who better to be in charge of our lives than the all wise, all knowing, perfect, loving God?

If we include Him only in *spiritual things* then we are excluding Him from all the other important issues pertaining to life.. We are not giving Him Lordship. We're still driving. He's just riding along. As we keep Him in the driver's seat, we will begin to grasp life from His perspective. We will experience joy, peace and direction. He certainly knows far better than we, where we need to be going. He always makes the right decisions. We will know such peace because we are walking obediently, not having to experience difficulties we might have had, outside of His Lordship.

SECOND: GET PASSIONATE ABOUT HIS LETTER: Can you imagine how your girlfriend or boyfriend, or spouse would feel if you never read their emails or letters? If we say we love them then our actions will show it. If we say we love Jesus, then our actions will show it. We will read His Word daily. We will get to know Him better in those pages, and ask Him to speak to us through His Word, and open our eyes to truths we have never seen before. God's Word has such depth and meaning we won't scratch the surface of its power in our lifetime.

The Bible is not just another book of history. It is God's love letter and roadmap for life; A *Rand McNally* that will never be obsolete. There aren't any new roads to be added. They've all been traveled and accounted for, the best route, the only way and the perfect way. Everything required for a successful journey in life is spelled out perfectly. Our part is to read it. Ask the Holy Spirit to illuminate it to our minds and to our hearts. Only then will it accomplish the purpose God intended. It will be a *"lamp unto our feet and a light unto our path."* Psalms 119:105.

There isn't a need we have, a problem we face, or a question we ask, that God's Word won't meet, solve, or answer. All that we will ever encounter on this spiritual journey is addressed in the pages of this incredible book. Get passionate about His letter—it was written out of His love for us.

THIRD: LIVE PASSIONATELY ACCORDING TO HIS WORD: Reading God's Word can sometimes be challenging—even difficult to understand and apply. I would encourage you to find a version that speaks to you. I remember as a little girl reading King James and becoming so frustrated with trying to understand it. One day I ran downstairs to the kitchen where Mother was, slammed the Bible down on the table and vented quite loudly, *"I'm not reading the Bible anymore. It's just too hard to understand."* Now Mom didn't rush to the nearest Christian Bookstore to buy another translation. But she did look at me lovingly and say, *"Honey, just ask the Holy Spirit to reveal to* *your heart what He wants you to know. He'll help you understand what you need for today."* So, I did, and He did. Now that may or may not be the answer for you. But in order to get passionate about God's Word, we can't just read it out of guilt, or under duress. We *gotta wanna* read it, to have a hunger and thirst for it. The only way to live by His Word is to read It, and then, hide it in our hearts.

It is one thing to read the letter — even hide it in our hearts, or put it to memory; but quite another to **live by it.** That's what matters. Don't just read it, devour it, digest it. Live by it and you will find an abundant, satisfying, marvelous life. If you don't have a desire to read the Bible, ask the Holy Spirit to do some supernatural surgery on you. Ask Him to place a hunger in your heart; to make you crave *spiritual food* just as you do natural food. God's Word is more intriguing and mysterious than any novel. The most amazing thing is that every verse and chapter is ***still new.*** There's no other book in the world like it. If you've ever doubted that it is the inspired, inherent Word of God ask yourself: after thousands of years, how could a book still be completely relevant and as applicable as it was when it was written? How many books can we say that about?

FOURTH: SPEND TIME DAILY IN PRAYER. SIT IN HIS PRESENCE: Spending time in prayer every day is what equips us for service. It is what causes us to really ***know Jesus*** and indicates to Him our true commitment. Prayer changes things. Prayer changes people, circumstances, and life. Without prayer, we will never know intimacy with Christ, or real passion for Him. Neither will we walk in victory or see the miraculous. Prayer is the air we breathe in our relationship with Him. We can't survive, let alone thrive without prayer. Ephesians 6 talks about *the whole armor of God* that we put on to be able to stand against the attacks of the enemy. Verse 18 gives us the most significant piece of the entire covering, *"praying always with all prayer and supplication in the Spirit, being watchful to the end with all perseverance and supplication for all the saints."* We can wear everything else, but prayer is the *glue*, if I can use that term that secures and holds it all in place—so it will protect and provide us with the victory.

When we pray we also need to *"Be still and know that He is God."* Psalms 46:10. Prayer is not meant to be a monologue where we do all the talking and God never has a chance to respond. As we spend time in prayer we also need to just be quiet and listen. We don't treat God like He's some big Santa Claus in the sky. He tells us to make known our needs and requests to for Him. Then we believe for an answer, because He is God. It seems that we all too often keep asking, failing or forgetting to praise Him. Thank Him. Adore Him. And listen. Waiting on Him to speak to us, to respond and give us instruction.

During our prayer time it's so important that we focus and block everything else out. Give God our undivided attention during a specific time of the day—time that is **only** His. We need to honor Him without interruption, just as we would anyone we're talking to. People who say they can't find time for the Lord would soon realize when they make time there will be ample left for everything else they need to accomplish. God's mathematics isn't like ours. He can multiply our time as we honor Him. He multiplies our finances when we obey Him with our tithe. He can do far more with 90% when we give, than we could have with 100%.

Women have mentioned in Bible studies I've lead, or at conferences, that they just don't know *how* to talk to God. It's really pretty simple. Just talk to Him as you would any friend. You don't have to speak some fancy *King James* lingo, or necessarily use perfect English. Praying is the one place you can just be yourself; after all, God is all-knowing and we can't hide anything from Him anyway. Be transparent and honest with Him, revealing your true heart in every way. E.M. Bounds tells us *"Prayer is not acting a part or going through religious motions. Prayer is not official nor formal nor ceremonial, but direct, hearty, intense. Prayer is not religious work that must be gone through, and that avails much because it is well done. Rather, prayer is the helpless and needy child crying to the compassion of the Father's heart and the bounty and power of the Father's hand. The answer is as sure to come as the Father's heart can be touched... and the Father's hand moved."*

One last thought on prayer. There's no special posture that matters to God. One can pray sitting, standing, just about anywhere any time; however, again, it's important that we give the Lord our total focus daily for a time of prayer. Don't just talk to him while peeling the potatoes for dinner or driving kids to a soccer game or in the shower. Remember He wants to talk to us too, and it's a little difficult to write down what He might be speaking to us, if we are never in a place to do that, so keep that in mind too. I love the humorous, yet mind provoking story Ken Davis shares in his book *Jumper Fables* about prayer.

"Every morning I run around the lake, and as I run, I talk to God. Some mornings I say, 'God thank you for the wonderful morning! Thanks for the trees, and the leaves, and everything else you've made. It's just so great to be alive' Other mornings I pray, 'God I feel terrible. Where are you anyway? I don't feel you near me. My life's a mess, and I don't know what to do.' And I pray all of this out loud... which keeps other people from jogging near me.

A woman once asked me, very critically, 'Don't you kneel when you pray?' 'No I tried it once, but I only made it halfway around the lake. It hurt so bad!'"

The question isn't really whether we kneel when we pray, or whether it's okay to pray out loud in public and freak people out. The question is: How honest are we with God when we pray? When I'm angry with God or when I'm feeling lousy, I let Him know it. "God, I don't think it's fair! God I feel like you let me down. God I feel absolutely miserable."

I've heard people say, "That's sacrilegious. You shouldn't talk to God that way." But how do you think God wants us to talk to Him? Do you think He wants us to lie? Isn't that what we're doing when we say, "God I'm feeling good today; glad to be here." When in reality we're angry or afraid or discouraged? We're afraid to tell Him the truth. We're afraid it's a sin to feel that way.

But David, the great King, the shepherd boy, never worried about that when he prayed. In the Psalms he was about as honest with God as he could be. He said things like: "I am feeble and utterly crushed: I groan in anguish of heart" Psalm 38:8 and "My God, my God, why have you forsaken me? Why are you so far from saving me? I cry out day by day but you do not answer." Psalm 22:1-2.

Prayer is pure, honest, sincere communication with God. Yes, He wants us to grow in Him. He desires for us to mature in Him; to see obstacles and challenges as but stepping stones to a higher intimacy. But in the process, He wants us to be purely honest in our communication. After all, He already knows the intent of our heart and every thought we have. Luke 5:8, 22; 9:47, 1 Corinthians 3:20. What would make us think we could hide anything from Him? He is God.

FIFTH: FIND A PLACE TO WORSHIP: A church that preaches and teaches the entire Word of God and only the Word of God Find one that worships Him in spirit and in truth, one that ministers to your spiritual needs—where you feel you can also contribute your gifts and talents to be a blessing.

We need the fellowship of family, of the community of believers in the body of Christ. We cannot live victoriously just with CD's, radio, Christian television and Christian music. We must have a place—a church that we identify with and love and those who make contributions to financially, physically and spiritually. It will be quite difficult to become more passionate in our relationship with Jesus without a family of like faith! The Bible exhorts in Hebrews 10:24-25, *"And let us consider one another in order to stir up love and good works, not forsaking the assembling of ourselves together, as is the manner of some, but exhorting one another, and so much the more as you see the Day approaching."*

After a few of the usual Sunday evening hymns, a Pastor slowly stood up and walked over to the pulpit. He gave a very brief introduction to his childhood friend who was visiting whom he had asked to share in testimony. With that, an elderly man stepped up to the pulpit to speak.

"A father, and his son and a friend of the son were sailing off the Pacific Coast," he began, *"when a fast approaching storm blocked any attempt to get back to shore. The waves were so high, that even though the father was an experienced sailor, he could not keep the boat upright, and the three were swept into the ocean."* The old man hesitated for a moment, making eye contact with two teenagers who were, for the first time since the service began, looking somewhat interested in his story. He continued.

"Grabbing a rescue line, the father had to make the most excruciating decision of his life. To which boy would he throw the other end of the line? He only had seconds to make the decision. The father knew that his son was a Christian. He also knew that his son's friend was not. The agony of his decision could not be matched by the torrent of waves.

As the father yelled out, 'I love you, son!' he threw the line to his son's friend. By the time he pulled the friend back to the capsized boat, his son had disappeared beyond the raging swells into the black of night. His body was never recovered."

By this time, the two teenagers were sitting straighter in their pew, waiting for the next words to come out of the old man's mouth. He continued. *"The father knew his son would step into eternity with Jesus. He could not bear the thought of his son's friend stepping into an eternity without Jesus. Therefore, he sacrificed his son. How great is the love of God that He should do the same for us."*

With that, the old man turned and sat back down in his chair as silence filled the room. Within minutes after the service ended, the two teenagers were at the old man's side. *"That's a cool story,"* one of the boys expressed politely. *"But I don't think it was very realistic for a father to give up his son's life in hopes that the other boy would become a Christian."*

"Well, you've got a good point there, son." the old man replied, glancing down at his very worn Bible. A huge smile broadened his narrow face, and once again he looked up at the boys and said: *"It sure isn't very realistic, is it? But I'm here today to tell you, that story gives me a glimpse of what it must have*

been like for God to give up His Son for Me. You see, I was the son's friend."

GOT JESUS?
Don't face another day without Him!
Jesus is all we will ever need,
For everything we will ever need,
Whenever we are in need.

3

MARRIED OR MISTRESS?
"Experiencing True Intimacy With Christ!"

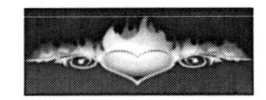

Sound like a strange chapter title for a Christian book? Maybe; but you'll soon see the reason behind the idea. You'll understand more clearly as we go along. My prayer is that you will perceive the picture as clearly as the Lord has revealed it to me. And yet, perception itself can often be completely different for each person.

A man who was playing *Frisbee* with his dog in a park that had a large pond. He threw the Frisbee across the lawn and it landed in the water. The dog ran to the edge of the water, put one paw in, then, literally walked across the water, retrieved the *Frisbee* and took it back to his master. The man was completely stunned. He threw the circular toy again waiting to see how his incredibly gifted pet would respond. Once again, the dog repeated the exact routine. Reaching the edge of the pond he walked across the water, grabbed the *Frisbee* with his teeth, and carried it back to his owner. Totally amazed the man decided to ask someone else to watch. He needed to know if anyone else would see what he was seeing. He needed perception, just in case he was hallucinating or imagining what was happening.

He located a guy sitting on a park bench reading a newspaper. Tapping him on the shoulder he politely asked the man if he would mind observing the dog's trick and then describe to him what he saw. The stranger consented. The owner tossed the Frisbee once again into the water and watched as his dog, for the third time, repeated the exact same amazing antics.

"Sir, asked the dog's Master, what do you think? What did you see? "Well Mister," the man responded, "looks to me like — well honestly, Sir, it looks to me like you got a dog that just plain can't swim."

My, my; what we see or perceive can be so different from what another sees. My heart's desire with each chapter is to communicate the truth of God's word. For each reader to see it for what it really is—truth. *The man didn't have a dog that couldn't swim — he had one that could walk on water.*

In the beginning, God not only created man—He also created woman. He realized that it wasn't good for man to be alone. As we read in the first few chapters of the book of Genesis it's noted that after God created each thing He saw that *"it was good."* It was complete—finished, good—until Genesis 2:7. *"And the Lord God formed man of the dust of the ground, and breathed into his nostrils the breath of life; and man became a living soul."* When He created man, He then realized that it was not good: *"And the Lord God said, 'It is not good that man should be alone; I will make him a helper comparable to him.'"* Genesis 2:18. Man wouldn't be complete or good without a woman. Okay guys, when you have any doubt whatsoever, there it is in black and white, in the Holy Bible.

God created man and woman for each other. They were to become one flesh, to love, honor and cherish one another and to become life-long companions and friends; and, of course, to have children to enjoy, to repopulate the earth carrying on legacies for generations to come. We are living souls. Only mankind was created by God with a living soul. Look no further fellow citizens, we will live forever.

There is a parallel between earthly marriage and in our relationship to God. Not, of course, in the physical sense, but in the spiritual realm. The correlation has to do with His desire for us to also have an intimate, personal, relationship with Him—to cherish, honor and adore Him. To worship only Him and keep ourselves only to Him as long as we live.

Please be aware as you read through this chapter that I will be addressing some topics that are quite controversial. For too long Christians have watered down the truth of the gospel in an effort to be more *seeker friendly*. We've tiptoed and pampered people into a comfort zone in an attempt to not offend. Jesus never worried about offending people with truth. He implores us to boldly speak the truth in love. If you feel angry while reading this, good; that's my intention. Anger can awaken people to take serious inventory; to stop living lukewarm lives being comfortably lulled to sleep in a society that continues to say that SIN is okay. *"If it feels good, do it; it's your body."* No. It is not okay. God is holding His church responsible to confront sin with truth. Knowing and living truth sets people free. If we agree with the world—condoning and tolerating sin—then we are not only living *in* the world, we are *of* the world. 1 John 2:15; *"Do not love the world or the things in the world. If anyone loves the world, the love of the Father is not in him."*

Yes, we live in the world. But while we're living here, we don't have to live like the world, or according to its standards. We should not embrace the worldly mindset or love things (get wrapped up in or consumed with) anything that distracts us from loving God first—in a sense holding us captive to the temporary rather than to the eternal. In Romans 12:2 Paul reminds us, *"And do not be conformed to the world, but be transformed by the renewing of your mind, that you may prove what is that good and acceptable and perfect will of God."*

Renew means to *revive, refresh, rejuvenate, refurbish, renovate, recondition*. Our minds need this more often than we realize. Our minds are *shoulder computers* needing defragmented daily. There is way too much input of junk and not enough important, life-changing data being downloaded. The renewing of our minds brings transformation. Renewing our minds by the word of God is critical to understanding what this whole personal, intimate, passionate relationship with Jesus is all about; the *Jesus* mindset or way of thinking.

GETTING ACQUAINTED

Can you imagine marrying a person after your first date? You go out to dinner and the next day you get married. Reminds me of that crazy commercial where a guy is sitting at a table with a girl he just met. He tells her that he's bypassing all the delays. He hands her a ring, has the wedding planned, reservations for their honeymoon, how many children they will have and will help her move into his house tomorrow. Not just corny—completely absurd. How could anyone make a decision that affects his or her entire life without a reasonable amount of time to get to know the person? It takes an ongoing relationship to discover whether this is someone you would want to spend the rest of your life with; to decide if you're even compatible. It could take more than one date to find out if one has a desire to even pursue the relationship; let alone instantly consider life-long commitments.

And so it is with our relationship with Jesus. It has a beginning when we come to know and accept him personally into our lives. Then it becomes an everyday, ongoing, beautiful, intriguing, exciting life of companionship. Or at least that's what He desires for it to be—not a relationship out of fear or obligation that becomes drudgery. Rather, a love-relationship because we want Him to be preeminent in our lives. Now the huge difference in this relationship is that He is God. From the very beginning of time He desired companionship with every living soul. It's amazing, isn't it, that God sees the heart of man, and loves us in spite of our faults and imperfections or even our annoying personality traits, and wants to have fellowship with us?

Having this relationship with Christ doesn't mean that it will be easy or perfect. He will often require of us things that go completely against our nature. After all, He's infinite,

Rekindling Our Passion For Jesus!

we're finite. He's perfection, we're imperfection. He's knows all things, we barely know our own name at times! But we can be confident that He will be patient and give us room to grow. *You know why?* Because He formed us in our mother's womb, and He already knows what makes us tick. He understands and can relate to whatever we feel or will ever face in life. He's already faced rejection, death, physical pain of the worst kind, the loss of loved ones, temptation, His Father saying no. He felt the sorrow and disappointment of His friends betraying Him and even denying knowing Him. He was arrested and beaten. Every possible thing we can face, He faced it first. Hebrews 4:15; *"For we do not have a High Priest who cannot sympathize with our weaknesses, but **was in all points** tempted as we are, yet without sin."*

He's not just someone we should call on when there's something tragic or earth shattering happening in our lives, or if we have a particularly serious need — you know, like a genie in a bottle. Nor is He One we should ignore when things are going grand. Rather, He is a constant, ever-present, loving friend — a companion. Deuteronomy 31:6. *"Be strong and of good courage, do not fear or be afraid of them; for the* LORD *your God, He is the One who goes with you. He will not leave you nor forsake you." "And the* LORD, *He is the one who goes before you. He will be with you. He will not leave you nor forsake you; do not fear nor be dismayed."* Deuteronomy 31:8. Friends even family may at some time disappoint, hurt or even leave us — God never will. Our relationship with Him is secure, unlike most human relationships. He isn't an on again, off again God.

HOMOSEXUALITY & SIN

It has been tragic to watch our nation fall away from God. Legalizing things that would make our forefathers turn over in their graves. Not to mention what God Himself thinks about our promiscuity, evil living, greed, abortion and so many more blatant sins. If God destroyed cities because of homosexuality, what makes us think we can rename it, or scientifically justify it?

Marriage is a covenant. It is a covenant instituted by God between one man and one woman—not two women or two men. He created Adam and Eve, not Adam and Steve. Sarcastic but true. Homosexuality is absolute blatant sin. At one time everyone believed this, even those who didn't consider themselves Christian, but not anymore. It now has been renamed. We call it an *alternative lifestyle* posing as some marvelous act of benevolence, when in reality we have given people a license to write their own death sentence. Homosexual marriage has now been legalized in five states and Washington D.C. recognizes marriages performed in other states. Change the label all you want, call it tolerance, but God will indeed have the final say. He destroyed Sodom & Gomorrah because of homosexuality. God does not change. *"I am the Lord, I do not change; therefore you are not consumed, O sons of Jacob."* Malachi 3:6. *"Jesus Christ is the same yesterday, today, and forever."* Hebrews 13:8. Because He is merciful, we are not consumed. He continues to give us the opportunity to accept Him and turn from sin. God does and always has hated homosexuality. Leviticus 18:22 states, *"You shall not lie with a male as with a woman. It is an abomination."* *"But the cowardly, unbelieving, abominable murderers, sexually immoral (fornicators, adulterers, homosexuals & lesbians), sorcerers, idolaters, and all liars shall have their part in the lake which burns with fire and brimstone, which is the second death."* Revelation 21:8. *Does God, or should we, hate the person who is involved in this kind of perversion?* No. But we are never to stop hating the sin. Jesus came to set those who are bound by satan's evil schemes *free.* When Jesus sets us free we are free indeed. Whatever tactics satan has to use to take people to hell with him, he will use. He has always been in the business of deception. If he can, for a moment, make people feel good, loved, cared for, even in some false perverted totally anti-God way, he will do it, and claim their very souls.

Would not the epidemic of AIDS be a sure sign that homosexuality is sin? Is not God trying once again to get the attention of mankind telling us we cannot live any way we choose for sexual pleasure? He has designed a way, and we know that way. When we ignore the rules, there will always be consequences to face. *"For the wages of sin is death."* Romans 6:23. When we work, do we deserve a paycheck? Do we receive wages for our hire? And does that check reflect the hours of work we've done—what we've earned for our labor? So it is in the spiritual realm. There is a paycheck coming for choosing to live a blatant, intentional life of sin—these are the wages given for such a choice! God's Word tells us it is death. Maybe not today, maybe not even tomorrow, but eventually if we don't accept the *gift of God* we will never experience the eternal joy He has prepared for us.

Death in this context means total separation from God and everything holy, death to abundant life now and eternal life with Him in heaven. The wages of sin means death to everything beautiful and meaningful—eternal punishment and banishment from God. If we chose to live for satan on earth, we will also choose to live with him and his demons throughout eternity in a world of more intense pain than one can ever imagine. Matthew 13:41-42 *"The Son of Man will send out His angels, and they will gather out of His kingdom all things that offend, and those who practice lawlessness, and will cast them into the furnace of fire. There will be wailing and gnashing of teeth."*

Now, speaking of AIDS, of course there are innocent children and adults suffering from this horrible disease because of an accident or from no cause of their own. Blood transfusions from contaminated blood or the infected blood of a parent can transmit the disease to the innocent. There are many things that cause it to be transmitted from one person to another who in no way deserve it. But where did it originate? Do the research. It will be enlightening. The introduction of this horrifying disease into society came from illicit sexual acts with animals.

There are also deadly consequences in perverse heterosexual relationships as well—adultery, fornication, incest. Any kind of sexual intimacy outside of God's design creates pain and repercussions bringing ruin, devastation and death—very real, lasting consequences. It's not a matter of tolerance. Please. God makes it clear in His Word. He does not, nor will He ever tolerate sin. Sin can and is forgiven, but not tolerated. He does not ignore it. He will not bless a nation that continues to sanction or endorse sin. God hates murder, and adultery. He despises gossip, lying, and backbiting. God can't stand deceit or deception. He grieves and weeps beyond belief at abortion.

SIN SEPARATES UF FROM GOD

God's mind hasn't changed because we have advanced in technology with computers and the world-wide-web. God's thoughts toward sin remain the same even though people can have sex-change operations and become who they think they were really meant to be. I believe He knew who we were meant to be. God does not make mistakes and He does not change. Therefore what was sin will remain sin. And sin separates us from relationship and companionship with God. Oh, a person can say, *"It's my life, I'll live it the way I choose, and it's none of your business."* Yes, you're right. God was gracious in giving us the freedom of choice; we are not puppets. But ultimately it is my business because I care about where you are going to spend eternity. It is even more His business. One day we, every single person, will stand before Him. That's when we will totally find out how much it is God's business. He ultimately has the final word. But then it will be too late.

What He desires is for us to turn from sin—all sin. Confess, repent, and receive Christ. Begin experiencing companionship with Him. But we must see the reason we no longer desire to live the way we are living and then let go, and let God. We have to become miserable and empty. We have to reach a place of desperation, seeing our need of forgiveness. We have to realize that we have need of a constant companion who will nudge us away from sin and to the Cross where everyone stands at the same level of need. Maybe we have to reach the end of ourselves. We have to come to a place where we are completely sick of life as we know it. We are searching for something more. Once we choose Jesus, we can begin to experience a passionate relationship with Him; realizing that life without Him is empty, void and unfulfilling.

MARRIAGE

Being married is a wonderful thing for many people. For others, being single is a wonderful thing. For yet others, they aren't quite sure either is wonderful. I read once that *"love is blind... marriage is an institution for the blind."* Sometimes that is a really answer for this thing called marriage. Once you share those vows, try to be blind. There will be things, habits, even personality traits that will drive you a little crazy. So make sure you're blind, in one way or the other, when you say I do.

A woman asked her husband, *"Honey, will you still love me even when I'm old and gray?"* His reply, *"I don't know why not sweetheart, I've loved you through five other hair colors."*

I was emailed a true story about a Minneapolis couple who had planned a vacation trip to Florida. Unfortunately their jobs dictated different times for their flight departures so they decided the husband would go ahead of his wife and check in to their room, and prepare for her arrival on the following day. After getting all settled he decided to email her. Inadvertently he emailed it to the wrong address.

At another place in the United States a minister had passed away. His funeral had just concluded. The widow decided she would take a few minutes in the office to check her email in case any of her friends who had been unable to attend the services had contacted her. As she read the message she collapsed in the chair. Her son, waiting in the car became somewhat concerned at her delay. He went back into the building to the office, somewhat frightened as he found his mother slumped over in the chair passed out. He looked up at the computer screen to read the following message:

To My Loving Wife:
I've just been checked in. Everything has been prepared for your arrival here tomorrow. Looking forward to seeing you then.
Your devoted husband
P.S. It sure is hot down here!

Oh, the joys of love and marriage.

OR MISTRESS?

God is the creator of not only man, but marriage; the joining of man and woman to become one flesh. He strategically and sovereignly designed this. In fact, He believed so much in *family that* **He, by the Holy Spirit overshadowed** a young virgin, named Mary, so that she would conceive and bear Him a son. **He wanted a son. Even God wanted and needed a family.** We know that the purpose in Jesus being born was two-fold; but right now let's talk about the desire God has for intimacy.

He created us to be *needy* human beings—*very needy*. We have innate desires to be loved, to love, and to have companionship. Most people don't like being alone.

God also longs for intimacy. He created man to have companionship with Him. The truth of the matter is that no other love can take the place of God's love. Nothing else and no one else can replace His love for us or, our love for Him. He desires first place. In a sense, He longs to be treated the way He purposed for us to treat our *spouse*—the one we have pledged ourselves to—faithfully giving Him a portion of each day with our *undivided attention*. It might sound strange that God desires to be with us that much. The truth of the matter is that it is actually more about us than Him. In His great wisdom God knew that the only way we would ever be able to face life victoriously, the only way to have answers for life trials and troubles, was to have an intimate relationship with Him. We understand this in the natural realm. Family and friends become dearer to us the better acquainted we become. The same is true in the spiritual realm.

> The more time we spend with the Lord,
> The more we read His Word,
> The more we draw from His strength,
> The stronger we become to face the battles of life,
> And, the greater our joy in the midst
> Of life's uncertainties and challenges.

But how often do we spend time with the Lord? I'm not referring to corporate worship. I want you to think about time that just you and God spend together alone, in prayer; in communion. Isn't it true when a married couple stays intimate with one another, with open and frequent communication, there seems to be a closeness that gets them through the difficult times? *Are we honestly treating God as though we are married, honoring and cherishing Him, or is it more like a mistress relationship?*

Do we treat Him as though we're just fooling around—a little tag on extra—giving him a once-in-a-while moment or hour? We have little or no genuine commitment or real consecration—kind of like a mistress? We say we love God, but do our lives attest to that? Would our husbands or wives believe we loved them if we showed the same amount of passion or gave them the same measure of time that we do the Lord? Would they believe we loved them? How would they feel if we never gave them our undivided attention, or acted as though we cared whether or not they were even around?

Can you catch this picture that the Lord revealed to me? We often treat Him exactly that way; as though He were no more important to us than an extramarital affair, a mistress. Let me bring this a little closer to home. In your most intimate moments as a couple would you even consider stopping at a time of intense passion, look at her or him and say, *"Honey, I really need to make a few phone calls that are weighing on my mind right now. I'll be back in a little while, just give me a few minutes, it won't take long!"* Sound ridiculous? Or, *"You know sweetheart, this is so nice, but I didn't get to finish cleaning the kitchen tonight after dinner so I really need to get that done and I'll be back, we can pick up where we left off then, ok?"*

Sound outrageous, absurd? *Yet how often, do we do this to our Lord?* We may be in the very midst of a very special quiet, intimate time we have set aside to love and be with Him. Somehow during these intimate moments our minds are wondering and racing. We are thinking of all the things that need to be done. The *to do* list is simply more important; we are preoccupied. We are absorbed with every-thing *but* Him. After all, He understands, He's God. He knows we have pressures and time schedules to keep. So, it will be ok. Will it?

How often do we set aside time each day, besides the blessing over the food or a hurried three minute devotion on our way out the door? Better yet, just read the scripture plaque. When do we give our **undivided attention to just love Him?** Love Him.

"Well, you know Regina, I pray every day. What do you mean, love Him?" Sounds almost foreign doesn't it? Are we really passionate about Jesus, like He is the love of our lives and our true companion? Or are we conveniently going through the motions, meeting with Him like some extra little fling on the side when we feel like it?

What are some ways a mistress might be treated? Could this be the way we are treating Jesus?

1. Stolen time, moments here and there, but never given priority.
2. Left-over portion of the person, no genuine focus, mind wandering ridden with guilt.
3. No promise of a lasting relationship or commitment.
4. An act of selfish gratification to help us through difficult or lonely times.
5. A secret relationship — too ashamed — can't tell anyone.
6. No complete, total giving — because the person belongs to someone else.

7. Sinful state—it makes God sick, both in the natural realm and in the spiritual.
   He told us He would rather we be hot, (really serving Him) or cold (totally away from Him), but never lukewarm.

Being lukewarm in our relationship with the Lord is just like having an affair. All caught up in everything but God. We dabble with Him on the side, call on Him occasionally, or when we are selfishly in need. His Word says if we are lukewarm He won't tolerate it. Revelation 3:16 "*So then, because you are lukewarm, and neither cold nor hot, I will spew you out of My mouth.*"

THE RESULTS OF WRONG RELATIONSHIP

Most people know what the end result is in any affair—misery, guilt, family ruin, loss of trust, anger, brokenness. Nothing good comes from one. Without a genuine relationship with the Lord we will not see His blessings. We will not experience His provision or His plan for our lives. Then, we get mad at Him. As though it's His fault we never give Him our complete love. Jesus gave His all, He wants our all. Not just a small part of our lives. Not just the left-over's, or whenever it's convenient, but preeminence. He wants us to be *married* to Him in the sense that He is our central focus above all else. He's not a tag on little extra, *I'll try to make time for you*, affair.

Many treat Jesus this way: "*I want you to be in my life, but I'm still going to stay married to all the other things I love even if you don't like them. I'll come home when I need you, or when I'm lonely, or when I need answers. I want you to be there. I'll spend time with you, when I have it, but only if I have some left over. I know we've made this commitment to one another, but I still want to run around and see other people and do what I want when I want. Oh, I do love you, but on my terms.*"

This is *not* what God's intention or plan for a relationship. Yet many Christians are living this way. They know him. In many cases they've even accepted Him. But there is no passion or intimacy, or even a desire to know Him more deeply, to spend time with Him, or to put Him first in any way. What will it take for us to understand what it means to love Him, to talk to Him, to experience true intimacy?

Jesus is our faithful, constant, intimate companion. He knows us better than we know ourselves. He is one we can talk to anytime, anywhere who never judges us wrongly or severely. He has never desired a *convenient* relationship. He will never say He's too busy or doesn't have time for us. Think of it. He has time for us. We can call on Him anytime. He is always available. He won't put us on hold or make us leave a message on voice mail. *What if He wasn't always available?* Reminds me of an intriguing email I received. I shared it with some slight revisions:

What if God decided to install voice mail? Imagine calling on Him and hearing this response: "Thank you for calling My Father's House. Please select one of the following four options: Press 1 for requests. Press 2 for thanks. Press 3 for complaints. Press 4 for all other inquires."

What if God used the familiar excuse: "All attending angels are assisting others right now. We are a little shorthanded. Please, stay on the line. Your call will be answered in the order in which it was received."

Can you even imagine getting these kinds of responses when you wanted to call upon Him: "If you'd like to speak to Gabriel, press 1; for Michael, press 2; for any other angel, press 3; if you'd like David to sing a Psalm for you, press 4; to find out if a loved one has been assigned to Heaven, enter his or her Social Security number. For reservations at My Father's House, press the letters J-O-H-N followed by the numbers 3-1-6. For answers to nagging questions about dinosaurs, the age of the earth, and where Noah's Ark is, wait until you get here!

Our computers show that you have previously called today. Please hang up immediately. This office takes only one call per day. If you are trying to reach us on a Sunday, please call back on Monday after 8 a.m. We are closed for worship. Heaven's choir is singing and Heaven's orchestra is playing."

Thank the Lord for a real relationship. One in which we can communicate as often as we want or need to. We only have to call upon Him. What a marvelous friendship. Isaiah 58:9 *"Then you will call and the Lord will answer; you will cry for help, and He will say, Here am I."*

Family is about love. Relationships are about love. Marriage is about the most beautiful of all loves—unconditional love. The kind of love Jesus desires for us to have with and for Him. Having an *affair* is about selfishness and self-gratification, not to mention it is SIN, and sickening to God. Marriage is about giving; having a *mistress* is about taking, living a completely unGodly lifestyle. *Which would you say fits your relationship right now with the Lord?*

LOVES PERFECT EXAMPLE

Jesus is our perfect example especially when it comes to love. Jesus is our perfect example about giving. John 3:16 says *"For God so loved the world that He gave His only begotten son that whosoever believeth in Him should not perish, but have everlasting life."* To think that this is all that God desires from us—for us to embrace His giving love and keep ourselves only to Him. He knows in our doing so, life will unfold in a marvelous, abundant way. There will be hardships and challenges, adversity and pain, but He will most certainly carry us through victoriously.

Jesus mirrored every attribute associated with love. We read a good list of what real love is in I Corinthians 13. I want to share it with you from *The Message*. It is beautiful. *"If I speak with human eloquence and angelic ecstasy, but don't love, I'm nothing but the creaking of a rusty gate. If I speak God's word with power, revealing all His mysteries and making everything plain as day, and if I have faith that says to a mountain, 'Jump,' and it jumps, but don't love, I'm nothing. If I give everything I own to the poor and even go to the stake to be burned as a martyr, but I don't love, I've gotten nowhere. So, no matter what I say, what I believe, and what I do, I'm bankrupt without love.*

Love never gives up.
Love cares more for others than for self.
Love doesn't want what it doesn't have.
Love doesn't strut,
Doesn't have a swelled head,
Doesn't force itself on others,
Isn't always "me first,"
Doesn't fly off the handle,
Doesn't keep score of the sins of others,
Doesn't revel when others grovel,
Takes pleasure in the flowering of truth,
Puts up with anything,
Trusts God always,
Always looks for the best,
Never looks back, but keeps on going to the end.

Love never dies. Inspired speech will be over some day; praying in tongues will end; understanding will reach its limit. We know only a portion of truth, and what we say about God is always incomplete. But when the Complete arrives, our incompletes will be cancelled.

When I was an infant at my mother's breast, I gurgled and cooed like any infant. When I grew up, I left those infant ways for good.

We don't yet see things clearly. We're squinting in a fog, peering through a mist. But it won't be long before the weather clears and the sun shines bright. We'll see it all then; see it all as clearly as God see us, knowing Him directly just as He knows us.

But for right now, until that completeness, we have three things to do to lead us toward that consummation: Trust steadily in God; hope unswervingly, love extravagantly. And the best of the three is love."

Though we may never feel like we can measure up to this kind of love, that's our quest. This is the hope set before us: To love Jesus as He loves us, unconditionally.

It is not so difficult to love Him when life is good; when things are running smoothly in our households. But when the enemy brings on the adversity, well then, we wonder why God doesn't show up more quickly. *Where are you Lord, if you love me so much?* Love is made stronger through hardships, not necessarily through happiness. Sometimes, hardships test our love. Do we love Him for what He does for us? Or, do we love Him because of who He is? Would we love Him more if He gave us more? Or will we love Him more just because of who He is? **We know His heart.** Many years ago on *Focus on the Family* I heard Dr. James Dobson say, *"When you can't trace God's hand, trust His heart."* There are times when it seems His hand is against us; His hand is bringing anything but favor. But in those times, no matter how it seems, or looks, the heart of God is always lovingly holding His children. Even today, while working on this book a phone call came that could potentially be financially devastating for me. A sizeable miracle that I thought for sure was on the way may not come to fruition. At first I was broken, crying out to the Lord with the financial needs for Seasons of Hope Ministries. There is studio time to pay for recording the daily broadcasts. There is a network time expenses due daily for airing. There are printing bills and other ministry office expenses. We continue to walk by faith everyday believing God for provision, favor, and direction. And in the midst of all the many obstacles that seem to potentially hinder or thwart this blessing we know that God is still God. We trust His love. He loves me. He loves you. He will not allow one door to close without opening another. We trust His faithfulness. Though there is corruption in our government, in business, with individuals, even in the church, God is holy and will never allow the devil to win. No matter what he might try to do to sabotage God's divine plan, satan loses. We hold on tenaciously to the Lord's promises and love. Maybe this is just a test to see if I will indeed trust His heart even though presently His hand seems shortened. His love cannot fail. His love will not fail. He in turn never wants us to waiver in our love for Him.

In the city of Chicago, one cold, dark night, a blizzard was setting in. A little boy was selling newspapers on a street corner, the people were in and out of the cold. The little boy was so cold that it was quite difficult to concentrate on getting people to make a purchase. He walked up to a policeman and said, "*Mister, you wouldn't happen to know where a poor boy could find a warm place to sleep tonight, would you? You see, I sleep in a box up around the corner there and down the alley and it's awful cold in there, of a night. Sure would be nice to have a warm place to stay.*"

The policeman looked down at the little boy and said, "*You go down the street to that big white house and you knock on the door. When they come to the door you just say John 3:16 and they will let you in.*"

So he did. He walked up the steps to the door, and knocked on the door and a lady answered. He looked up and said, "*John 3:16.*"

The lady said "*Come on in, son.*" She took him in and sat him down in a split bottom rocker in front of a great big old fireplace and left the room. He sat there for a while and thought to himself, "*John 3:16 — I don't understand it, but it sure makes a cold boy warm.*"

Later she came back and asked him "*Are you hungry?*" The boy replied, "*Well, just a little. I haven't eaten in a couple of days and I guess I could stand a little bit of food.*"

The lady took him in the kitchen and sat him down to a table full of wonderful food. He ate and ate until he couldn't eat any more. Then he thought to himself. "*John 3:16. Boy, I sure don't understand it, but it sure makes a hungry boy full.*"

She took him upstairs to a bathroom to a huge bathtub filled with warm water and he sat there and soaked for a while. As he soaked he thought to himself, "*John 3:16... I sure don't understand it, but it sure makes a dirty boy clean. You know, I've not had a bath, a real bath, in my whole life. The only bath I ever had was when I stood in front of that big old fire hydrant as they flushed it out.*"

The lady came and took him to a room, tucked him into a big old feather bed, pulled the covers up around his neck and kissed him good night, then turned out the lights. As he lay in the darkness and looked out the window watching the snow fall on that cold night he thought to himself. *"John 3:16 – I don't understand it, but it sure makes a tired boy rested."*

The next morning she came back up and took him down again to that same big table full of food. After he ate she took him back to that same big old split bottom rocker in front of the warm, cozy fireplace and she took a big old Bible and sat down in front him. She looked up at him and asked. *"Do you understand John 3:16?"* He responded. *"No Ma'am, I don't. The first time I ever heard it was last night when the policeman told me to use it."* She opened her Bible to John 3:16, and began to explain to him about Jesus. Right there in front of that big old fireplace one little, homeless, cold, lonely, forsaken boy gave his heart and life to Jesus. He sat there with tears in his eyes and thought— *John 3:16 – don't understand it, but it sure makes a lost boy feel safe."*

You know I will never understand this love Jesus has for me, but what I am beginning to understand more everyday is that His love is so great that there's nothing it leaves out. He is a faithful, true and constant companion. He is always there, an incredible caregiver. That is what He longs for us to be with Him; a faithful, loving *bride* that will never treat Him any other way than with honor, respect, and adoration.

What do you want your relationship with Christ to be from now on in your life? Total commitment, or just a part-time, once in a while *mistress – an affair* kind of relationship?

Do you want to experience the ecstasy and fulfillment of a life totally committed to Christ, or the misery of guilt? Do you want the companionship of a life-long relationship and all that goes along with a God that is there, or just a God of convenience for when you need some selfish favor or answer to prayer. *Hot for Christ, or lukewarm?* Sold out? Are you ready to faithfully and passionately love and commit to Him? Or do you just want to fool around in your relationship?

MARRIED or MISTRESS?
There's really only one choice,
God will never just fool around.

4

NO OTHER GODS
"Ridding Ourselves of the Spirit of Legalism & Condemnation"

*H*ow can we even begin to identify or elaborate on all the gods that people can and do worship in our world today? The scripture is so clear pertaining to this. God is a jealous God. He is jealous over us. *"For I, the Lord your God, am a jealous God..."* Exodus 20:5b Yes, one of God's attributes is a *holy* jealousy. Exodus 34:14; *"For you shall worship no other god, for the Lord, whose name is jealous, is a jealous God." "...For I am jealous for you, with Godly jealousy."* 2 Corinthians 11:2. When it comes to worship, He wants us to worship Him, and Him alone. God didn't create us to worship anyone or anything else. He created us to focus our greatest passions on Him. Pretty amazing isn't it that our Holy, Almighty God of the universe wants and needs our worship? May I remind you again that we are created in His image, in His likeness, and ultimately the plan is for us to be *just like Him*? I love the lyrics to Phillips, Craig and Dean's song made popular in contemporary Christian music a number of years ago entitled, "I Want to Be Just Like You."

He climbs in my lap for a good night hug,
He calls me Dad and I call him bud,
His faded old pillow, bear name Pooh,
He snuggles up close and says,
"I want to be like you."

I tuck him in bed and I kiss him good night,
Tripping over the toys as I turn out the light,
I whisper a prayer that someday he'll see,
He's got a Father in God,
Cause he's seen Jesus in me.

Lord, I want to be just like You,
Cause he wants to be just like me,
I want to be a holy example,
For his innocent eyes to see.
Help me to be mirrored by the Lord,
That my little boy can be.
I want to be just like You,
Cause He wants to be just like me.

I got to admit I've got so far to go,
Make so many mistakes
And I'm sure that you know,
Sometimes it seems no matter how hard I try,
With all the pressures in life
I just can't get it all right,

But I'm trying so hard to learn from the Best,
Being patient and kind,
Filled with Your tenderness,
'Cause I know that he'll learn
From the things that he sees,
And the Jesus he finds will be the Jesus in me.
Lord, I want to be just like You,
Cause he wants to be just like me,
I want to be a holy example

> *For his innocent eyes to see.*
> *Help me to be mirrored by the Lord*
> *That my little boy can be.*
> *I want to be just like You,*
> *Cause He wants to be just like me.*
>
> *Right now from where he stands*
> *I may seem mighty tall,*
> *But it's only 'cause I'm learning*
> *From the best Father of them all."*

Oh, how Jesus wants us to desire to be like just like Him, and to worship Him and Him alone. He said He would have *"no other gods before Him."* Exodus 34:14. He is the one true God—from everlasting to everlasting. *Why would we look for or even want to worship any other God*? Why do we continue searching for answers when they are blatantly in front of us? Are we; blind, stubborn, ignorant, rebellious, self-sufficient and prideful? Here are three primary reasons that God requires **no other gods**.

    #1. BECAUSE HE IS THE ONE AND ONLY TRUE GOD
    #2. BECAUSE HE CREATED US TO WORSHIP ONLY HIM
    #3. BECAUSE HE CREATED US TO LOVE AND OBEY HIM

WHAT DO YOU MEAN BY OTHER GODS?

If we are to ever fulfill God's destiny plans for our lives we are going to have to completely, unreservedly worship Him. Not His Word, not His church, or His ministers. We cannot worship anything or anyone else. Not the gifts of His hand, not the gifts He's given us, not His miracles, nor His creation. Ironically, this *no other gods* jealousy applies to even making *religion,* or having a *religious spirit,* or *legalistic spirit,* a god. These *spirits* are connected to *knowledge* we have acquired pertaining to our interpretation of scripture. The Pharisees are a prime example of these spirits. They were consumed with the *letter* of the law, but they *ignored* the *love*. Why is it that sometimes Christians feel we have the right to position ourselves in an arrogant, prideful manner—*acting as though we are God* in judging others according to our interpretation of holiness or sinfulness? The Word of God is crystal clear concerning sin. Make no mistake, it's plainly spelled out. Even *sinners* know what sin is. That's not what I'm addressing. Rather, it's the issues pertaining to man-made rules and interpretations that are contrived and given by man, not God. Matthew 15:7-11 says, *"Hypocrites! Well did Isaiah prophesy about you saying: 'These people draw near to me with their mouth, and honor me with their lips, but their heart is far from me. And in vain they worship me, teaching as doctrines the commandments of men. Then He called the multitude and said to them,' Hear and understand: Not what goes into the mouth defiles a man; but what comes out of the mouth, this defiles a man.'"*

HERE ARE SOME OF THE "OTHER GODS" WE'VE IDENTIFIED:

Worshipping **THINGS, CREATION, OR PEOPLE** making them a god
Worshipping **FALSE GODS** associated with other religions, or idols
Making **RELIGION ITSELF** a god, creating in people a religious, legalistic, or judgmental spirit

Yet another *god* mankind worships is *SELF*. If you have an inward belief that man himself possesses a *god* power of greatness, that belief elevates you above God. Within ourselves we are nothing. *"For in Him we live and move and have our being, as also some of your own poets have said, 'for we are also His offspring.'"* Acts 17:28. That means that we get our very life from God, not ourselves. The Bible tells us there is none good but God. Matthew 19:17; *"So He said to him, 'Why do you call me good? No one is good but One, that is God.'"* Anything of greatness we have came from Creator God. We certainly did not give them to ourselves. Without Him there would be nothing.

No universe. No heaven & earth, or planets. No people. It's true that God allows people, in or out of Christ, to possess special gifting because the world could not function without them. It's imperative to have people with capabilities, skills and genius to meet the needs of society. Things would not run smoothly and successfully without them. But, that's the way life is because of God. He chose for people to be born whether they choose Him or not. The world remains and continues functioning properly, successfully. This *new age movement* that is rampant in the world today isn't new at all. It's as old as time. This so called religion began in the heavens when a beautiful angel of light, whom God had created, got an attitude—an arrogant, prideful, evil attitude—that boasted he was as great and powerful as God. So **Almighty God** cast him out of heaven. Wouldn't that be a wake-up call? However, he got really angry, and ugly, scorned and spurned, God allowed this demon to become the prince and power of the air. This once beautiful angel now had a new home, his own *heaven* – except God named it hell. He became satan, intensely corrupt and more sinful than any other, with a deeply wicked and perverse mission: to deceive everyone he can, anyway he can, into eternal hell. So much for *being or becoming as god;* he became one all right—the god of hell.

What does it mean to have other gods?

Anything or anyone that a person loves more than God, or that they give themselves to or focus their attention on more than God, can become a god. Something or someone a person tends to *worship: money, work, play, people, possessions or places*. Of course one doesn't bow down to these *gods*, or *idols*…like someone would a statue, but rather people are driven, focused, or have an almost abnormal affection for something…it consumes their time, thoughts and actions. A car could be someone's *god*. If it is treasured or adored more than the Lord…if more time is spent with it or caring for it than a person would God...then it is *in a sense being worshipped... becoming a god.*

EVEN A PET COULD BECOME ONE'S GOD

I have a close friend who loves Akitas. He had a male named Kuma, and the dog accidentally died from ingesting toxic flea shampoo while being groomed. After a year, he decided to purchase another one.

He located a kennel with pure-bred-show-dog-quality Akitas. They are really beautiful dogs, great companions, and make sweet pets. They are originally from Japan, bred for two specific reasons: hunting bear and being caretakers to babies and children. What a contrast. He chose the female pup he wanted out of the litter, and she was a beauty. He named her *Sheba*. She was quite the queenly female with perfect lines, beautiful hair, and a perfect build. She carried herself, even at that age, like a champion. He'd decided to develop, train, and groom her for dog shows. Every free minute would be given to her. Every week-end, which meant Sundays for many months out of the year, would be focused on dog shows and traveling so Sheba could compete. One day after having her only for a few weeks, he came home from work around noon for lunch. She greeted him happily, as they went outside for some brief exercise and her duties. After lunch and a few more minutes of play time for Sheba, he put her in the small laundry room, a temporary place until he could purchase a cage. He made sure there were no rugs or any toys she could be harmed by or destroy. He loved the dog and I could see he was becoming more and more consumed with her beauty and champion bloodline.

That evening when he arrived home and opened the laundry room door, Sheba was nowhere in sight. Then as he looked around the small room he knew the door had been tightly closed and no one else had been in the house—she couldn't have possibly gotten out. He pulled the washer away from the wall and found Sheba wedged there. She was not breathing. Somehow, pushing her way behind the washing machine, her strong body forced the machine plug away and had connected her to the 220 plug. She had been electrocuted. It was horrible and so sad. He was more than brokenhearted; he was devastated because he already was so attached to Sheba. He was consumed with giving all of his extra time to her and focused on competition to show her off.

Is it a sin to own show dogs? Not in the least. God created dogs—every species, breed, and gender. There are few things as entertaining to me as a great dog show. Obviously, if a person is outside the faith, God doesn't hold those people accountable to put Him first. They don't even claim to know Him so why would He expect them to honor Him? They obviously would put their dogs before Him. To others, they love their animals, but it's a fun hobby and they are not necessarily consumed with it. But in this particular situation, for this particular person, maybe, just maybe—and this is simply an observation on my part—but He was a new Christian at the time, and maybe the Lord knew that he was going to give first priority to this gorgeous new female Akita show-dog. Missing Sunday services every week would have hindered his spiritual growth and taken his focus away from where God wanted it to be. Obviously it could have simply been a freak accident, and it just happened. On the other hand, God is capable of intervening and saying, *"No, not this time. This is not going to happen because I love you too much to see you take your focus completely off me and give it to _____ whatever you want to fill in the blank with."*

This story is heart breaking, but a few days later I talked him into going back to the kennel and purchasing another Akita. He had the cage, the toys, the food, everything, but the dog. Since he missed Sheba so much, he decided that would be the best antidote for his grief. But this time, there was only one puppy left in the litter. She was adorable, but not in any way show quality. She was butter-ball fat, and not the least bit pretentious. The last female in the litter, unwanted by any other buyer, but she became a loving, adorable companion for over 14 years. Guess what? He had Sundays to attend church and finances to give that he would have spent on the dog. Sheba went to doggie heaven, where he'll see her again—God stayed in His rightful place of priority.

If you ever wonder whether there are other *gods* in your life, look at your checkbook, take inventory on the amount of love, time, priorities, and money that is being spent more on things other than your family or God. You'll definitely have a clearer picture of what you're the most passionate about, and if there are **Other Gods**.

A RELIGIOUS SPIRIT, LEGALISM & CONDEMNATION

Another area that has become an issue within the church pertaining to the sin of *other gods* is known as a *Religious Spirit, or Legalism & Condemnation*. Why would these be considered gods, and how do you know when a person practices this kind of worship?

There are preachers and lay people who have become so enamored by their own interpretation of scripture and doctrine, that *it* becomes their god. Much of it pertains to holiness—teachings that emphasize *works* rather than *grace*. Legalism embraces a number of things that are unscriptural, among which is bondage and guilt. It also dictates sinless perfection in order to be accepted, forgiven and used by God. After all, God wouldn't and couldn't use someone who has sinned. Oh, but my friends, that's what grace and mercy is all about!

I love the story of **Seabiscuit**. If you haven't read the book or seen the movie with Jeff Bridges, who plays the role of Charles Howard, it's a great flick. They used the Lord's name in vain, which I disliked immensely, but the story overall was just phenomenal. There are some incredible lines—wake you up and shake you up lines. All the characters are broken, scarred people, even the horse, Seabiscuit, has been deeply wounded, almost ruined from of life of abuse. They are injured, struggling; unlikely to ever become anything great in life — and certainly not the fabric that would make World Cup Winners.

A few lines said by Seabiscuit's trainer, Tom Smith played by Chris Cooper really struck a chord in me. The horse-whisperer had pitched a tent in the woods behind a huge horse auction that was being held. He was basically homeless. He'd come upon a horse farm some miles back and found them getting ready to shoot a mare that had a broken leg. He stopped them. Said he wanted her. They told him she was worthless, needed to be put down. He said he'd save them a bullet. So, they finally let him take the horse. He had been nursing her back to health. Charles had seen him earlier in the day, and asked another man who he was. The guy just answered, *"he used to be some big-time horse trainer, but now, he was just a wanderer, a nobody taking care of horses no one else wants."* Tom Smith would get odd jobs at traveling circuses training horses or working with those that were lame to *"heal them"* — horses no one had any use for any longer. Charles made his way through the bushes and came upon him at his camp. He asked if he could visit with him, Tom said, *"Sure, have a seat."* Charles sat down on the ground. Tom offered him coffee...but told him it was awful. Mr. Howard asked, *"Are you always this honest?"* Tom answered, *"Yes sir, I try to be."* Then he asked him about the mare — was it going to race. He responded, *"No not this one, but it will make someone a good riding horse or nice lead pony, and besides, she's just nice to look at."* *"So why did you go to all the trouble of saving it?"* Charles inquired. Tom answered, *"Because I can, and* **because you don't throw a whole life away just because it's banged up a little bit."**

Later in the story, the jockey, Red Pollard, played by Toby McGuire, loses the race for the Santa Anita cup. It wasn't because of anything Seabiscuit lacked that they hadn't won. Red didn't see Rosemont gaining on his left side to take the lead. He couldn't see. Of course Tom was livid, screaming and hollering. *"What in the world were you thinking? I told you to watch out for Rosemont."* The jockey responded with tears welling up in his eyes, *"Because I can't see out there, I didn't see the horse gaining on me." "What do you mean you can't see? He was in plain sight, right on your heels." "But I couldn't see...I couldn't see him, I'm blind in one eye!"* The jockey had been in all kinds of prize fights, fighting to live — in more ways than one — he'd been hit so hard on the left side his face that his eye sight had been permanently damaged. He had told no one.

About that time Charles Howard came walking up to see if the jockey was okay and he hears this exchange of heated words. Tom Smith looks at Charles and tells him with strong conviction, *"He lied to us. He lied to us. Do you want a jockey that lies to us? He lost the race because he's blind, he can't see in his left eye. He never told us."* Charles responded, *"It's fine Tom, it's fine." "It's fine?"* yelled Tom. *"Yes."* Charles said. Then Charles placed his hands on the shoulders of his horse trainer and repeated what he heard the wise Tom Smith say only a few years before, **"Remember... you don't throw a whole life away just because it's banged up a little bit."**

Tragic things have happened in all of their lives. They continue to happen throughout the story, yet still, with courageous effort and resolve they rise again and again above every adversity and obstacle. Against all odds they become winners; believing in each other — encouraging one another being there for one another, cheering each other on, every step of the way.

JESUS CHOOSES THE IMPERFECT

That is exactly what Jesus taught. He continues to teach us the same truths today. Look at the people God should have never considered useful — beginning Cain. Though he was the first murderer and alienated from his family, he traveled to the land of Nod where he founded the first city. He became the ancestor to the earliest musicians and metalworkers. This is all recorded in Genesis 4. Then, there was Moses, a Godly man, a chosen leader, who couldn't even speak well. Yet God used him mightily. Even the great Abraham who completely missed God's will in the birth of Ishmael, and nations have continued suffer and be at war to this day. How about Joseph's brothers? What a clan — genuine siblings love. Out of jealousy they pushed him into a pit, felt guilty so they sold him into slavery, fabricated a blood stained coat, and lied to their own father to cover their deceitfulness. We won't mention in-depth the children of Israel, God's chosen people whom He freed from bondage only to have to put up with their forty laboriously long years of whining and wandering. Yet He chose them. Are we getting the picture? David, a man after God's own heart committed adultery. If that wasn't enough, he had Bathsheba's husband, Uriah, placed at the front lines of battle so he would get killed. That plan left Uriah's adulterous widow for David. She was pregnant with David's child.

These are just a few examples from the Old Testament. How about the New Testament? Oh, Paul would be a glowing example. In Acts, Chapter 7, as Stephen was cast out of the city and was being stoned, he was calling on God. Chapter 8, verse 1 describes Saul as *"consenting to this great man of faith's death."* Then in Acts 8:3…"*As for Saul, he made havoc of the church, entering every house, and dragging off men and women, committing them to prison."* In Chapter 9 God asked Saul why he was persecuting Him. There is also the account of Ananias saying *"he had heard from many about him how much harm Saul had done to the saints in Jerusalem, with authority from the chief priests to arrest all who call on the Lord's name."* That's some serious hatred. Among the twelve that Jesus called His very closest friends, His disciples: Judas betrayed, Peter denied, and the rest slept while He prayed in the Garden of Gethsemane. Then they all forsook Him when he was arrested. These were the very men who saw His miracles, heard His teachings, laughed with Him, traveled with Him, even ate fish with Him along the seashore. Yet all of them were so far from being perfect. But, **"you don't throw a whole life away just because it's banged up a little bit."**

If Jesus were looking for perfect people to call Him Lord, He would have no worshippers let alone ambassadors. If God would have thought for a moment we could have lived perfect lives or become sinless people by our own efforts, then God would not have had to provide the final atonement for man's sin. Jesus would not have had to shed His precious blood — His death would have been in vain. Grace would have never be the most important part of the story.

GRACE BY FAITH – VERSUS THE LAW

Paul is clear in his teachings about the *law* versus *grace*. Grace does not give us a license to willfully sin or live in sin. What grace does is take away the heavy burden of trying so hard ourselves to atone *for* our sin. We confess. He forgives. He paid the price so we no longer live under the law. We live under grace. Those who have embraced a Religious Spirit, or Legalism, have a completely wrong interpretation of what sin is. Many are still caught up in keeping the law — earning their salvation by the works of the law. Galatians 2:18 says, *"knowing that a man is not justified by the works of the law but by faith in Christ Jesus, that we might be justified by faith in Christ and not by the works of the law; for by the works of the law no flesh shall be justified."* Verse 21, *"I do not set aside the grace of God: for if righteousness comes through the law, then Christ died in vain."* Galatians 3:1-3 continues with more emphasis on the gift of grace. *"O foolish Galatians! Who has bewitched you that you should not obey the truth, before whose eyes Jesus Christ was clearly portrayed among you as crucified? This only I want to learn from you: Did you receive the Spirit by the works of the law, or by the hearing of faith? Are you so foolish? Having begun in the Spirit, are you now being made perfect by the flesh?"* There's so much here, let me share just a few more scriptures concerning "Grace, by Faith — versus the Law" Galatians 3:11-13, 19, 21 *"But that no one is justified by the law in the sight of God is evident, for the just shall live by faith. Yet the law is not of faith, but the man who does them shall live by them. Christ has redeemed us from the curse of the law having become a curse for us....What purpose does the law serve? It was added because of transgressions, till the Seed should come to whom the promise was made; and it was appointed through angels by the hand of a mediator. Is the law then against the promises of God? Certainly not. For if there had been a law given which could have given life, truly righteousness would have been by the law. But Scripture has confined all under sin that the promise by faith in Jesus Christ might be given to those who believe. But BEFORE FAITH (that is faith in the grace and blood of Christ) came, we were kept under guard by the law, kept for the faith which would afterward be revealed. Therefore the law was our schoolmaster to bring us to Christ, that we might be justified by faith. But after faith has come, we are no longer under a schoolmaster."* I've quoted enough but in Chapter 5 Paul goes on to tell the Galatians to stand fast in the liberty wherewith Christ made them free. They were not to take again that *yoke of bondage,* but be led by the Spirit because they were no longer under the law. Bondage, that's what living by the law of works, is all about. Jesus came to set us *free* from bondage. This may seem like a lot of scripture pertaining to the law and how Jesus did away with it, but this is such an important part in the process of Rekindling Our Passion for Jesus.

So many people may have never accepted Jesus because they feel it is just too difficult. They constantly feel condemnation because they don't measure up, or can't be good enough. That's exactly what a religious spirit or legalism says. If one isn't living a perfect enough or holy enough life, according to their standards (and of course, these standard are also supposedly scripturally based), then they wouldn't give the time of day to you. Legalism basically says *"my way or the highway. You're not worth even being around; I might get soiled."* That teaching, or action, is completely contrary to the teachings of Jesus or how He lived. Yet they claim to propagate this in His name. How one can ever consider themselves Christian and have and anti-Christ spirit or attitude toward others? Surely it must sadden the very heart of Jesus. It must grieve the Holy Spirit.

Let's clarify or give definition to the word LEGALISM:

LEGALISM: *Control or manipulation over another to dominate or dictate a certain set of rules, beliefs or regulations for people to adhere to. In the Christian realm, these laws, rules, or regulations are supposedly taken from the Bible, but are interpreted by people who feel they are an authority or have a greater insight into scripture. They seek to manipulate or force a specific lifestyle on others, all in the name of God. When not adhered to, the legalistic entity then continues to dominate and control through criticism and condemnation. In the world of Christianity, legalism actually takes on the cloak of holiness and uses scripture out of context to hold guilt over people when they do not live up to the standards that they have contrived, and will often treat those outside of their religious venue with disdain and contempt. This behavior is also known as a religious spirit. Legalism is excessive adherence to a man-made law or personal interpretation of scripture carried out with strictness, pettiness, narrow-mindedness, hairsplitting, quibbling, nitpicking and contentiousness.*

This does not sound like Jesus. This is such an important issue to address. People spend much of their time condemning others for not living the way they interpret the scripture, rather than by what the Word of God actually says. It's all about rules, regulations and laws. Measuring up to a standard that man dictates. It's nothing about **grace.** We know how God felt about *the law.* He realized it would never work. It couldn't work. He loved man and knew that man was too far from deity. He replaced the law with His Son. No one would or could ever be perfect enough to keep the law. God knew that it was impossible. So Jesus came, fulfilled the law, and replaced it with The New Covenant called **grace** *through faith* to all who would believe and receive it. He took away the guilt and pain of man's imperfection. He replaced it with His final payment of perfection.

There is conviction of sin from the Holy Spirit to mankind that compels us to the cross. It reveals the awfulness of sin and what it's consequences. But conviction is not meant to cause unbearable guilt. Its purpose is to bring us to repentance. That is entirely different than accusing guilt for mistakes, failure or worst of all, sin.

Many who have a religious spirit or legalistic condemning approach are often caught up in ultra-conservative teachings that include a dogmatic approach to outward appearance, and proving our holiness by extremely conservative dress, especially for women. Women are holier with long hair. Men with short hair and clean shaven faces. Without reservation I am a strong believer in appropriate dress and modesty. However, modest attire doesn't secure my salvation; any more than dressing immodestly will send me to hell. Falling in love with Jesus brings change in a person's life. When the Holy Spirit resides, He begins His work of convicting and transforming hearts. Sound biblical teaching and mentoring is also very important—nurturing new Christians in their walk of faith. But judging others as to their relationship with God based on non-conservative clothing is a harsh man-made law causing many to be deceived into believing that's real Christianity. **True Christ-likeness—being like Jesus—goes far deeper than the clothesline.**

Divorce is also a huge issue among legalism; that, of course, is the ultimate *unpardonable* sin. If you divorce and remarry, you are doomed for life. You are no longer fit for kingdom work. Amazing how none of this has anything to do with Jesus. It actually cancels out His work on the cross for us. He provides total atonement and forgiveness. Actually, this religious mindset is exactly what *false religion* is all about. It's about being holy by our own works, in ourselves, still *"keeping the law" – in a sense, negating what Christ has already done in our behalf.* We can't be holy—not on our own. It's impossible. It's not in us. Only the Holy Spirit's work in us can bring true holiness. We will never be good enough, no matter how hard we try, or even how perfect we try to live. Whose perfection is it anyway? How do we measure that? Yet this spirit of *legalism* demands that we have to be *good enough* for Jesus to accept and love us. This god of *"legalism and condemnation"* is taking the world by storm. It comes in all shapes, colors and kinds. It's about people, preachers, and churches who are caught up in *condemning* people into their realm of holiness. Here's what my Bible says about *condemnation* ... yours probably says the same depending on your translation.

"There is therefore now no condemnation to those who are IN Christ Jesus, who do not walk according to the flesh, but according to the Spirit. For the law of the Spirit of life in Christ Jesus has made me free from the law of sin and death. For what the law could not do in that it was weak through the flesh, God did by sending His own Son in the likeness of sinful flesh, on account of sin: He condemned sin in the flesh, that the righteous requirement of the law might be fulfilled in us who do not walk according to the flesh but according to the Spirit. For those who live according to the flesh set their minds on the things of the flesh." Romans 8:1-5b. This scriptural reference describes legalism in a nutshell. This is the very same mindset the Pharisees had — thinking that through their own abilities, they could be good enough and keep the law. But who are we to go against what God Himself has provided and established? Regardless of what we do, WE will never be good enough. All we have to offer that is good enough is our repentance and acceptance of Jesus and HIS grace. Isaiah 64:6. *"But we are all like an unclean thing, and all our righteousness's are like filthy rags; we all fade as a leaf, and our iniquities, like the wind, have taken us away."* Matthew 23:27. *"Woe to you, scribes and Pharisees, hypocrites. For you are like white washed tombs which indeed appear beautifully outwardly, but inside are full of dead men's bones and all uncleanness."*

In essence, these scriptures were chosen to remind us that it is not about *our* holiness. It is not about how righteous we may look or seem on the outside or our ability to keep certain rules and regulations that matters to God. When we try to *do* all of this, we are continuing to hold on to what Jesus came to set us free from: the law. Worse than that — we are making ourselves god. The Spirit of life in Christ Jesus sets us free from all the legalism that caused man to continually strive to be good enough and look good enough. Jesus took all of that on Himself, telling us to quit striving, just receive Him. Accept His finished work on the Cross. It is more than enough. When we live according to the Spirit, then it's all about Him. He manifests the attributes of Christ through us. That is the real evidence of genuine discipleship.

We do not intentionally choose to live in sin, and justify it by saying, *"Oh, Jesus died for us so it's okay; He's forgiven all sin, so we can live anyway we like."* No. Even the desire to *live in sin* should go when we accept Christ. But living without condemnation means that we allow Christ to do the finished work in us through the Holy Spirit, and quit trying to earn it ourselves by being religious, and feeling guilty if we fail.

Why are there so many who call themselves Christian, miserable? Worse yet, they and make others feel miserable too. They are not free. They are caught up in *legalism and condemnation* — appearing to be righteous. But it is about their righteousness, not God's. Looking holy does not mean one is holy. Going to church doesn't make one a Christian, anymore than a mouse in a cracker box, makes him a cracker. Confessing with our mouth, but not believing in our hearts is the crux of the matter. When our lips are filled with vile communication, (I'm not referring to profanity), but condemnation, treating others wrongly, as though they have a contagious plague. Vile communication is speaking evil of another. *"There is now (presently and forever) no (that means none, zero) condemnation to those who are in Christ Jesus, who do not walk according to the flesh, but according to the Spirit."* Romans 8:1. We repent, turn from sin, and go forward serving the Lord. We walk after the Spirit. We desire to please the Lord and serve Him. When we are grafted into Him, regardless of the mistakes we've made, the wrong choices, the wrong paths we taken, all the stuff in our lives, the divorce, the abortion, the adultery, and the lies, anything that was or is contrary to God's Word, if we have repented, then we are forgiven. Free to pursue God's plan for our lives without punishment. Oh, there will be consequences for our sins. But we can, nonetheless, walk in newness of life and experience the blessings of God on a future in Him—without condemnation.

There are legalistic people who still believe if you've ever been divorced, you are living in sin if you are remarried. If God's Word says *"there is now therefore **no** condemnation"* isn't that what it means? And John 8:36 *"Therefore if the Son makes you free, you shall be free indeed."* Galatians 5:1 *"STAND fast therefore in the liberty by which Christ has made us free, and do not be entangled again with the yoke of bondage."* If we are walking in the Spirit, that means we have entered into a new covenant of forgiveness, righteousness and freedom in the Lord. We have repented. We are forgiven. End of discussion. God's Word is final. There are no ifs, ands, or maybes about it. If Jesus does not forgive, restore, and send out—*then is there any merit to God's Word at all?* **Was His blood not enough? If our sin cancels out the power of His atonement, then the blood of Jesus was not an adequate payment. What heresy.**

Some legalistic people believe that it's imperative to reconcile a marriage if there's been a divorce. What then, if a spouse has already remarried or they themselves have remarried? One cannot go back and unscramble eggs. In most cases it's impossible to put a divorced couple back together. Someone else will get hurt, and think about it; that would be yet another divorce and re-marriage. Let it go. Either we believe in the cleansing blood of Jesus or we don't. Unbelieving is probably the greatest sin of all. Revelation 21:8 *"But the cowardly, unbelieving... shall have their part in the lake which burns with fire and brimstone, which is the second death."* Embrace truth. God's forgiveness surpasses man's ability to comprehend it. Man will not be our final judge, God will. His Word is clear as to where He stands, and we need to stand, pertaining to sin. It's forgiven and forgotten by God, when we repent and turn from it.

THE GIFTS AND CALLINGS ARE IRREVOCABLE

My brother, David, was a called, charismatic, anointed man of God; a student of the Word with a powerful servant heart. He went to be with the Lord in 1996. David and his second wife and two step daughters attended a Baptist church in North Carolina. The Pastor and Elders of the church would not allow him to participate in any leadership role, including carrying a communion tray, teaching a Sunday School class, or even taking up the offering. Why? Because he was *divorced*. He was the innocent party. His wife left him for another man. Without any choice of his own, he was served with divorce papers. Do I believe God wants to heal and restore marriages? Absolutely, without question, that's His perfect will. But when it doesn't happen—when circumstances are such that two people cannot reconcile for whatever reason, I believe if either of them has a desire to continue serving the Lord they should be restored in love, by the church, and given every opportunity to walk in their calling, as long as they are living for the Lord.

Are the gifts and calling of God *for us* forever? That's what the Word says. *"For the gifts and the calling of God are irrevocable."* Romans 11:29. King James says *"they are without repentance."* God never repents that He has called us, no matter what happens in our lives. So if God's Word is true, and we know that it is, does God take away our gifts because of a *divorce — or any other sin for that matter?* Does He slap us on the hand and say, *"Sorry — oops, I made a mistake, you're not perfect, you've failed me, you're damaged goods — you're not good enough to be used by me anymore?"* Oh my, there's a whole lot of explaining God would have to do if that were the case, because He cannot lie. Take a look into scripture and see again and again that he restored every single time someone failed and put them right back on course. **God never takes back what He's given us**. Oh, but man does. Man has now elevated himself in so many aspects to a level greater than God. They can make those kind of decisions and say, *"You can't serve, you're a failure, you sinned."*

Yet week after week ministers stand behind pulpits, imperfect, with sin in their own lives, but justified because no one knows about the sin in their lives, or they aren't *divorced*—the big D word, the greatest of all sins. Sin is sin the eyes of God, whether it's a lie, and a lie is a lie in every sense, if you've made a promise you didn't keep it's a lie. Consider the scenario in which you're standing in a room and the phone rings and your child answers. If it's someone you don't want to talk to and you whisper *"tell them I'm not here,"* is that not a lie. You bought a new outfit, but don't want your husband to know so you put it in the closet for two weeks, take it out to wear and he says, *"Oh, honey is that new?* And you say, *"Oh no, sweetheart, I've had this for weeks."* Could that be a lie? We are all sinners saved by grace. Daily we must come before the Lord and say, *"Lord Jesus, cleanse me, forgive me, help me, make me more like You."* We cannot condemn others, when we ourselves stand guilty. *"It's me, it's me oh Lord, standing in the need of prayer. Not my brother, not my sister, but it's me oh Lord – standing in the need of prayer."*

LIVING UNDER GRACE

The beauty and freedom of living under **grace** and not **the law** is to know, understand and embrace the powerful, completed work of forgiveness that Christ accomplished on the cross. Amazing how even before Jesus gave His life He practiced the very forgiveness He came to give. He came upon the men stoning the woman caught in the act of adultery. Kind of strange that the gal was being stoned don't you think? Where was the guy? Still in bed, it seems, not being held accountable of the same sin. *What was that about?* So Jesus looked out at those with stones in their hands, ready to throw at her, John 8:3-6 *"Then the scribes and Pharisees brought to Him a woman caught in adultery. And when they had set her in the midst, they said to Him, 'Teacher, this woman was caught in adultery, in the very act. Now Moses, in the law, commanded us that such should be stoned. But what do you say?'"* "*This they said testing Him, that they might have something of which to accuse Him. But Jesus stooped down and wrote on the ground with His finger, as though He did not hear."*

Could it be that these very spiritual people were being used by satan? He is after all the *accuser* of people. Have you ever thought about what Jesus might have written in the sand? Something made these guys from the Sanhedrin take off. Maybe He wrote the very sins of the men who were stoning her. You see, He didn't care what they were saying with their lips because He *knew* the condition of their hearts. Jesus knew even the *hidden* sins of these men, yet they stood condemning another.

Accusation is a spirit that comes from satan. If you doubt my statement, here's a scripture to substantiate it. Revelation 12:10; *"Then I heard a loud voice saying in heaven, 'Now salvation, and strength, and the kingdom of our God, and the power of His Christ have come, for the accuser of our brethren, who accused them before our God, day and night, has been cast down.'"* Sounds like, looks like, reads like, he's the real deal accuser. The devil will one day be cast down forever. *"So when they continued asking Him, He raised Himself up and said to them, 'He who is without sin among you, let him throw a stone at her first.' And again he stooped down and wrote on the ground. Then those who heard it, being* **convicted by their conscience,** *went out one by one, beginning with the oldest to the last. And Jesus was left alone, and the woman standing in the midst. When Jesus had raised himself up and saw no one but the woman, he said to her, 'Woman, where are those accusers of yours? Has no one condemned you?' She said, 'No one, Lord,' and Jesus said to her, 'Neither do I condemn you; go and sin no more.'"* John 8:6-11. He used an active verb: Go. The literal translation means **"now go and fight for the good life."** Do My bidding because you are forgiven, you do *not have to work* to have your sins forgiven, that was what the law said — earn everything yourself, be righteous in your own strength and prove how worthy you are of Me, how holy you can *seem*. But now I say, the work is a completed and perfect work. You do not have to *prove* yourself perfect to Me, or serve a penance. It's not about what you do; it's about what I have already done. I forgive you. Forgive yourself and don't let others spew guilt upon you or cause you to feel you that you have not been forgiven.

If others accuse you, know where it comes from and the spirit that must dwell in them who bring accusation against you. Basically what He told her was, *"I not only do not condemn you, but I am calling you and sending you out."* What gives a person the right to think they have more authority over the forgiveness of sin than Jesus Himself? *Who among us has no sin?*

NO FISHING SIGN

The glorious message of the Gospel is that Jesus forgives sin. You can say hallelujah right here. He not only forgives sin, but after that, *"For as the heavens are high above the earth, so great is His mercy toward those who fear Him; as far as the east is from the west, so far has He removed our transgressions from us."* Psalms 103:12. That means **never** to be remembered against us again. His word says He casts our sins into the sea of forgetfulness. Micah 7:19 *"He will again have compassion on us, and will subdue our iniquities. You will cast all our sins into the depths of the sea."* I like to put it this way: After Jesus throws our sins into the deepest part of the sea, that's the depths of the ocean in parts that can never be reached. He then posts a *"**No Fishing**"* sign. If we even take a deep sea fishing boat out, and try to fish things up or if someone else does, Jesus will say, *"what sin, what are you talking about, I don't remember that sin, it's forgiven and washed in the blood. I can't see anything that's been washed in my blood."* Washed clean. Our sins are not covered in the blood of Jesus they are washed in the blood of Jesus. When we pre-spot clothing, you know that tasty, once quite delicious spaghetti sauce that ended up a stain on our clothing? We use our miracle working pre-spot, then wash it with dirt defying laundry detergent in *cold* water and it's gone – gone. We might remember where it was, but we can't see it any more. Well, most of the time, but you get my drift. The powerful cleaning blood of Jesus' is a sure thing every time for the stain of sin. *Once He washes it, there are no longer traces of anywhere unless we choose to go back and commit the same sin again.* So, if Jesus completely and totally forgives, what in the name of heaven gives people — imperfect, human, falling-short-of-God's-greatness human beings — the right to bring up and condemn others of sin that has been forgiven and forgotten by God Himself? Newsflash — He is God; we are not. No matter how holy we might think we are, we can point a finger at others about their sin, and see 3 other fingers and a thumb pointing back at us. There is none good — only God. There is none perfect — only God. If we don't begin to embrace this truth, we may find ourselves falling far short of the gospel message we are preaching. Is this not the story of redemption, forgiveness and healing? Was it not written to provide hope and a future? The New Testament emphatically communicates the message of grace; the atonement for sin through the precious, spotless, blood of Jesus.

How many parents reading this book would even consider the possibility of their son being crucified on a cross for sinners? What, are you kidding? Trying to even comprehend, or imagine how much God loved us is almost humanly impossible. He gave up His only begotten Son — for sinners.

Yes, it's true. Many of our sons and daughters lay their lives on the line every day, serving in the military, or as law enforcement officers, and firemen; for our freedom, protection and safety. That's purpose. Obviously we pray that God will protect them, kept from harm's way, and bring them safely home to their families and friends.

But God offered up Jesus, cognitive of the ultimate outcome. Jesus would be falsely condemned, severely beaten, spat upon, reviled, and pierced. A crown of thorns pushed violently upon His head. His feet and hands nailed to a cross. He was forsaken. Jesus knew what He would have to endure. The *man-part* of Him cried out in the Garden of Gethsemane asking His Father if it was possible *to let this cup pass from Him.* Yet God still required His death, because of His love for us. *Can we grasp the possibility that God possibly loved us more than His own son?* Think about the depth of that love.

But no matter how perfectly God orchestrated, planned and presented this, ultimately it was still up to Jesus. He had to willingly surrender His life for wretched, unconcerned, apathetic, almost blasphemous human beings. Then, as time went on, many more would reject Him, than would receive Him. *Think about it. Why wouldn't we want to embrace Jesus and love Him passionately for all that He willingly suffered and sacrificed for us?* How can we continue to ignore or be oblivious to the truth—Jesus finished the work, so we wouldn't have to. All we have to do is believe and accept. He gave everything. God—the only God sent His Son, who became sin for us, so we could become the righteousness of God in Christ. He is the only God we worship.

NO OTHER GODS
HE is the ONLY GOD
HE ALONE is WORTHY of our WORSHIP

5

GOD BLESS "MY" PLANS
"Seeking God's Agenda, Not Our Own"

A love letter read:

Dear Jane,
   Words cannot express how much I love you and need you in my life. I feel incomplete and empty when you are not with me. Each day I anticipate more our wedding day, and becoming one with you. There is nothing I wouldn't do for your love, climb the highest mountain, weather any storm, swim the deepest ocean, just to feel your arms around me and touch your soft beautiful face. I miss you and love you more than words can say.

John

PS. If it doesn't rain Saturday **my plan** *is to come and see you.*

Let me ask you a question. *We say we love God, that we want His will for our lives, but do our actions communicate that?* It so easy to get up every morning, check our calendar, see what the schedule is for the day, say a quick prayer over breakfast, eat, and run out the door ready to meet the world. Oh, yes, and we read the scripture plaque hanging on the wall on the way out. *"I can do all things through Christ who strengthens me."* Philippians 4:13

OUR PLANS, OR HIS PLANS?

*Is life actually about God blessing **our** plans or **His**? Do we even ask Him what He wants to accomplish through us on a daily basis; Or for that matter allow Him to interrupt our schedule, to show up during our daily activities and surprise us with something that's in **His schedule**, rather than ours? Do we, even on occasion, anticipate an intervention of something miraculous that He planned to happen?* Not accidentally or being at the right place at the right time kind of thing, but a real God-ordained incident. That's my passion. To begin living everyday with the anticipation that there is, small or great, some kind of miracle awaiting me during the upcoming 12-15 hours of being awake that I will experience before laying my head on the pillow that night. What a difference that can make in the *abundant life* that we know. It could be an everyday occurrence or even weekly. Regardless of how often, it's the idea of living with expectation, looking for miracles and allowing God to sovereignly carry out His plans daily in our lives. That, to me, is the beginning of experiencing the abundant life, and having a passion for Him that exceeds anything we could ever imagine.

It's great to go to church. That's His plan. Praise and worship, fellowship with like believers, *the assembling of ourselves together,* anticipating a blessing, being a blessing and finding encouragement for the week to come are very important in our relationship with God. But, ultimately, God's greatest plan isn't inside the four walls of a sanctuary. It's outside those four walls.

We, for the most part, live to ourselves. General speaking people are private. We go through our daily routines, associate with the friends and loved ones we have, occasionally we will make new acquaintances. It's becoming more prevalent in our society. The truth of the matter is that is not God's plan. Unfortunately, to some extent, *sin* has dictated such

God Bless "My" Plans

behavior because of the actions of truly *sick* individuals. God, however, never intended for us to be an island. He didn't plan for us to live selfish lives, but in a sense we often do it out of protection. We don't trust people so much anymore—and rightly so. God's ultimate perfect plan was, and is, for us to win the lost; to present Jesus to a lost, dark world. We are to be salt and light. Yet we so often feel uncomfortable, even unsafe doing this. We live our lives and get through our agendas and plans that we've made, seldom influencing another with acts of kindness, let alone the Gospel. Weeks, months, and years go by and many of us have trouble counting on *one hand* how many we've even talked to anyone about Jesus. I personally feel convicted. *"Oh, Lord, let our lives count for You so others will find Jesus."* Why? *Why does it really matter?* It matters because if we love God we're supposed to love people, all kinds of people. The Word says in Mark 12:29-31. *"Jesus answered him, 'The first of all the commandments is; Here, O Israel, the Lord our God, the Lord is one. And you shall love the Lord your God with all your heart, with all your soul, with all your mind, and with all your strength. This is the first commandment. And the second, like it, is this; You shall love your neighbor as yourself. There is no other commandment greater than these."*

It matters because people matter! It's rather hypocritical to say I love my neighbor if I don't even care if they know Jesus, or where they will spend eternity. We embrace our *circle of friends*, and our families, but outside that how often do we even see the needs of others? Not necessarily even their physical needs. Looking into their eyes, do we see emptiness, a longing, a hunger for something? And if we do, does it matter? Do we care? Are our plans so crucial that we never take time to see—to really notice others who desperately need Jesus?

Another reason it matters, for me, is because I don't want to *just make it* into heaven. I remember at the age of five, tugging on my Daddy's coat after knowing I had accepted the Lord, yes I knew, asking to be baptized. Dad's first response was, *"It's ok, baby, you have plenty of time."* I said, *"No, Please Daddy, I want to be baptized now. I want Jesus to be with me. I want* *to serve Him **all of my life**. I don't want to wait."* So Dad baptized me. My brother and sister had already been immersed so they, along with Mother, witnessed this *life changing* event. Dad didn't ask me to wait until Sunday; he immersed me immediately. It was a joy to know I belonged to Jesus, that I was following His example and command for baptism—that He was going to use my life for His glory.

Have I lived for Jesus all these years? Yes. Have I been perfect? You've got to be kidding. No. Far from it! Not in any way. Have I ever failed Him? Yes... so many times. Just as Paul said, *"For I know that in me (that is, in my flesh) nothing good dwells; for to will is present with me, but how to perform what is good I do not find. For the good that I will to do, I do not do; by the evil I will not to do, that I practice. Now if I do what I will not to do, it is no longer I who do it, but sin that dwells in me. I find then a law, that evil is present with me, the one who wills to do good."* Romans 7:18-21. Ok, the NKJ is a little difficult to embrace, so let me share it from "<u>The Message.</u>" This is awesome. *"Yes, I'm full of myself—after all I've spent a lot of time in sins prison. What I don't understand about myself is that I decide one way, but then I act another, doing things I absolutely despise. So if I can't be trusted to figure out what is best for myself and then do it, it becomes obvious that God's command is necessary. But I need something more. For if I know the law but still can't keep it, and if the power of sin within me keeps sabotaging my best intentions, I obviously need help! I realize that I don't have what it takes. I can will it, but I can't do it. I decide to do good, but I don't really do it; I decide not to do bad, but then I do it anyway. My decisions, such as they are, don't result in actions. Something has gone wrong deep within me and gets the better of me every time. The moment I decide to do good, sin is there to trip me up. I truly delight in God's commands, but it's pretty obvious that not all of me joins in that delight. Parts of me covertly rebel, and just when I least expect it, they take charge."*

Unfortunately this is the reality of humanity; we have a tendency to fall short. But, in the midst of my shortcomings, my heart remains repentant, humbled, and most thankfully, forgiven. Here's one thing for certain sure. Serving the Lord

God Bless "My" Plans

has always been the most important aspect of my life even when I've miserably failed Him and even after experiencing deeply painful rejection and brokenness. Somehow there's a passion that never leaves my spirit; a gnawing hunger for my life to count for Christ. I don't want to just make it into heaven—you know breathe a sigh of relief when my name is called from the Lamb's Book of Life. I want sheaves to lay at the feet of Jesus. This is huge. How about you? Life is so much more than accumulating things and taking vacations. Our legacy matters. What we are doing must count for eternity, for Jesus matters more than anything. The lyrics to a song that has stayed with me through the years rings again in my ears even now— with yet another reminder that life passes so swiftly. What we do for Christ is the only thing that will last for eternity.

It matters so little how much we may own,
The places we've been or the people we've known.
It all comes to nothing when placed at His feet,
It's nothing to Jesus, just memories to keep.

Only one life, so soon it will pass,
Only what's done for Christ will last.

The days pass so swiftly the months come and go,
Years melt away like new fallen snow,
Spring turns to summer, summer to fall,
Autumn brings winter, and death comes to all.

Only one life, so soon it will pass,
Only what's done for Christ will last.

Written by Lanny Wolfe

HIS PLANS... OUR CALLING

Do you know that the gifting or calling you possess is directly connected to the things you really love or really hate? I hate poverty. It rips my heart out to see a hungry or homeless person. I have been blessed to be able to share in feeding and clothing some of them through World Vision, Rescue Missions, Shelters, and even personally. God has a calling on my life to love and care for the homeless. Why? I hate poverty. God hates poverty. It breaks His heart. The more we fall in love with Jesus, the more we will love and hate the things He loves and hates. The clearer His plans will become to us.

I hate—HATE—the devil. I hate sin and what it does to people's lives. It destroys, ruins, and devastates. Sin often looks so appealing—like fools gold it can shine like the bright lights in Vegas; they look so pretty, but they're only lights. When the power goes off, there are broken, shattered, and empty lives. The enemy of our souls makes people think he has such great plans for them—bright lights, bright futures—when ultimately it's death and destruction. In Luke 4 we learn that Jesus was tempted by the devil. Verse 1 is one to contemplate; it says, *"Then Jesus, being filled with the Holy Spirit, returned from the Jordan and was led by the Spirit into the wilderness.* Luke 4:2-13 *"Being tempted for forty days by the devil. And in those days He ate nothing, and afterward, when they had ended, He was hungry. And the devil said to Him, 'If You are the Son of God, command this stone to become bread.' But Jesus answered him, saying, 'It is written, Man shall not live by bread alone, but by every word that proceeds out of the mouth of God.' Then the devil, taking Him up on a high mountain, showed Him all the kingdoms of the world in a moment of time. And the devil said to Him, 'All this authority I will give You, and their glory; for this has been delivered to me, and I give it to whomever I wish. 'Therefore if You will worship before me, all will be Yours.' And Jesus answered and said to him, 'Get thee behind Me, satan. For it is written, you shall worship the Lord your God, and Him only you shall serve.' Then He brought Him to Jerusalem, set Him on the pinnacle of the temple, and said*

God Bless "My" Plans

to Him, 'If you are the son of God, throw yourself down from here. For it is written:' 'He will give His angels charge over you to keep you and, in their hands they shall bear you up, lest you dash your foot against a stone,' And Jesus answered and said to him. 'It has been said, you shall not tempt the Lord your God.' Now when the devil had ended every temptation, he departed from Him until an opportune time.'"

Just as he tempted Jesus making promises he couldn't keep, satan continues to deceive, lure, and tempt mankind. Crazy isn't it that the devil thought he could give Jesus what God already owned? Talk about the ultimate deceit attempt, nothing he offered to give Jesus even belonged to him. He may temporarily have some say-so in the *"dominion of the air"* status, but he certainly didn't, nor does he, *own* anything (except one's soul who sells out to him). Psalms 24:1 *"The earth is the Lord's, and all its fullness, the world and those who dwell therein."* Always has been, always will be—God's. Wasn't it kind of presumptuous for stupid to think such a ridiculous thing? Deceit is satan's middle name, and even during the temptation of Christ he was completely deceived. Remember the saying, *"Stupid is, as stupid does."*

I love music, probably loved it from conception. God has called me to sing His praises, write music, and play the piano; to use these gifts to glorify Him and bless others. It's my passion. It's His passion. Has it ever really occurred to us that besides our decision to accept and follow Him, God has ***plans, intentions, and a divine destiny for us?*** Or, do we just begin each day with our schedule and say, "Lord, Bless My Plans. Bless My Day? I know you're God, but I've got my agenda, my schedule, my deadlines; but less me today."

Let's look at God's plans that He designed for every person. Specifics for everyone, the blanket plan. This brief list is enlightening. Seven simple, but critical things:

1. TO ACCEPT JESUS AS SAVIOR, INVITING THE HOLY SPIRIT TO EMPOWER OUR LIVES FOR SERVICE
2. TO ALLOW HIM TO BE LORD OF OUR LIVES— THE ONE IN CHARGE

3. TO SPEND TIME WITH HIM AND HIS WORD EVERY DAY, GROWING — PURSUING A PASSIONATE RELATIONSHIP
4. TO WITNESS — WIN THE LOST TO CHRIST
5. TO SERVE AND BLESS OTHERS
6. TO LIVE AND ENJOY THE ABUNDANT LIFE
7. TO GO TO HEAVEN WHEN WE DIE OR JESUS RETURNS AND ENJOY A GLORIOUSLY PERFECT HEAVEN AND

These seven plans are concise, and potent. But if we embrace **only** the first and last items on this list, then we are living out **our plans**, certainly not His. Just accepting Jesus and wanting to make heaven falls far short of what God's agenda. There's so much more. It's about passion pertaining to God's plan in Christ Jesus. *What is life without passion?*

Becoming a Christian and not fulfilling God's plan is like joining the armed forces, yet never being able to fight for your country or freedom. You get through boot camp and go home. Or, studying an entire life-time to become a concert pianist then only playing chopsticks. Or, you've decided to attend college—you advance to medical school to become a doctor. a brain surgeon. You've graduated with a 3.9 GPA, served your internship, but you've chosen a job instead at McDonalds. Sound crazy?

What have we trained for? Why are we Christians? What's the plan, God's plan? We may not have had to invest the same amount of time or money into our training in Christianity, as we did our education, but it is none the less vital. It's important—even more consequential than any other vocation. It's about eternity, eternal life, and eternal rewards or eternal punishment.

NOTHING MORE REWARDING THAN GOD'S PLANS

Isn't it true that life can become a little mundane? The constant repetition, the same ol' same ol', the monotonous cycle of daily living can be boring and even at times trying. That's why seeking God's agenda rather than our own opens up

God Bless "My" Plans

a whole new world, one full of excitement and rewards. It changes the dreary routine into challenge and anticipation by allowing the Holy Spirit to not be just a part of our lives, but to be the center, to actually orchestrate them. There's nothing as exhilarating as His wonderful surprises as He prepares very special interruptions in our daily agenda. Of course, we have jobs with schedules to keep, but right in the middle of making a living, God can pencil in some incredible appointments of His own if we invite Him and trust Him to do so.

In the movie *"Courageous,"* Javier is a young, Christian Hispanic husband and father who is struggling to make enough money to support his family. No matter which way he turns it seems he cannot find and keep a job. After being laid off from his last place of employment, he receives a call one morning and hears reassuring words; a job has opened up at a big construction site and he is to report immediately for work. Kissing his family good-by he rushes out the door walking because their only vehicle's gas tank is on the big E, but still there's great joy in his heart.

Javier had prayed fervently the night before and asked the Lord to take care of his family and to provide him with work. He arrives at the worksite only to hear the foreman tell him that he isn't needed after all. The boss had contacted one too many applicants, so all the workers necessary are already on the job. The young father was in shock—devastated. He stood there for a few moments running his hands through his hair—confused, frustrated, and hopeless. He approaches the site foreman once more, almost begging. Javier's trying to convince him that he can do *any* kind of work in *any* area, *anything*, just show him. But his persistence fails. He walks away dejected. No job. It seemed like a total dead end with no promise of provision for his family. No answers to his prayers.

Javier begins the walk home, but this time with intense conversation to God. Out loud. He was asking what was happening. He reminded the Lord of His promises and of the need he has. *"Lord, am I going to have to tell my family that we will lose our home?"* Then He asks a simple question, *"God what do you want me to do, what do you require of me; just tell me and I'll do it?"* I believe often that's all God is waiting for is our surrender to His will not our own—His plans, not our plans. Little did Javier know that God's plan was unfolding at that very moment? That's the wonder of trusting and believing God for something miraculous. He moving even when we don't think He is. He is gloriously surprising.

In another part of the story a local policeman had been looking for someone to hire to help build a work shed on his property. A fellow officer had suggested a friend whose name is Javier who is a fantastic builder and great with any kind of construction. He was hired to show up that morning at the policeman's home to begin work at the rate of $150.00 per day. With God in charge, every detail was perfectly unfolding.

Our Javier is walking home, still talking to God, standing ironically, of all places right smack dab in front of the policeman's house, facing exactly where the he wanted his work shed build. As Javier is standing, praying, he hears his name. He turns to see a man in work clothes, with building materials, calling him by name. He answers. "Yes?" "You're late. *Are you going to stand there all day or do you want to work? Your name is Javier isn't it?"* "Yes." "And you want to work?" "Yes." *"Then get over here. I'm not going to pay you $150.00 a day just to stand there and do nothing."* The officer's wife approaches quietly, scolding her husband for being so harsh, and his response is, *"This is the first day and he's late, what kind of reaction do you expect me to have?"* as Javier is running toward them.

Javier is once again in shock, but this time it is a glorious shock of *"wow, God you are working, aren't you."* He has no idea how this man knew his name, that he was a construction worker, or that he needed work. He works all day, does great work, and the policeman hands him a check for $150.00, telling him he was pleased with his work and he would see him again tomorrow.

The other Javier has somehow been laid up in the hospital unable to even contact the policeman about not being able to work. In a few short days the two officers are chatting—

discussing what a great job Javier is doing—and he finds out Javier is actually in the hospital. The next scene is hilariously funny as it all unfolds about the prayers, the needed work, and how God answered and provided at the exact right moment. God's plans…not ours.

DIVINE PLANS

There is nothing like divine intervention, divine direction, divine timing, and divine plans. Oh, that we could learn to trust God everyday with our lives and see the marvelous, glorious things He would orchestrate. The doubter would say it's just coincidence or luck, but there are no coincidences and no such thing as luck. Luck is spelled hard W O R K. But when God is given our permission through our prayers and lifestyle to do the planning, then things can turn around in a moment! *"The effectual, fervent prayer of a righteous man avails much."* James 5:16b. Can you recall times in your own life when God miraculously intervened with plans that far surpassed your own? They may have been small miracles—small answers to prayer. Or, on the other hand, they may have been huge. Either way, God manifested His awesome power and His divine plan unfolded for blessing in your life.

There have been many times in my life when I experienced that miraculous power. Some, as they unfolded seemed to be more of a curse than a blessing, but often it was more about the *"working all things together for the good"* that ultimately brought about the greatest miracle of all—learning to wait on Him, and the process of trusting Him with all of it during the time of waiting. That's huge too, being patient for God's timing. Why is it that He always seems to arrive at one minute before midnight? He's never late. He's never early. He's always right on time. He's a punctual, perfect God.

Several years ago I had a *Seasons of Hope Ministries* Board Meeting scheduled which had been on the calendar for over 6 months. There was plenty of notice for all the members to attend, but unfortunately, two were unable, one could only be there for part of the meeting, and another was "iffy" so that left one member and myself attending. Needless to say, that was not a majority. The meeting would have to be rescheduled. I had prepared some light refreshments, including bottles of drinking water. I will admit, my attitude was not good. After all, this board meeting had been on the calendar for six months. Why couldn't it have been given more priority? Wasn't this ministry valuable?

Exiting the meeting room with my revised plan, I decided to leave off the payment for ministry office phone bill across town rather than mailing it in. Now, here's the amazing thing. God had already made some divine plans that I had never even considered. And I can't honestly say I hadn't asked Him, *"What Lord do You have planned for today? Is there some special mission You might have in mind? Someone I need to meet who needs a word of encouragement or might not know You?"*

If somehow we could just chill a little, be more flexible, and realize that sometimes there's a different plan that might need to be carried out. I've often felt that way when traveling when one delay after another causes me to leave far later than originally planned. Maybe the delays are God's way of saying, *"No, you need to leave at this time, not that time, I have my reasons."* Could it be protection or connection? Only He knows for sure.

I took an alternate route due to heavy traffic and I found myself on Central Avenue in Charlotte, once again in bumper to bumper traffic. Looking ahead I saw a car stalled in the right hand lane... smoke pouring out from under the hood. Approaching from the left lane, I thought, wow, their car must have overheated, they need water. Water— "oh, Jesus, you are the water of life." At that moment the Holy Spirit nudged me and said, *"Yes Regina, you're right but focus on the present for a moment. These kids need water, real water.* My response was, "Ok, Lord, great, what shall I do about that?" *"You have water,"* he responded, *"in your back seat."* He was right, as always. I did have water—six bottles of clean bottled drinking water. As I reached the people in trouble, rolling

God Bless "My" Plans

down my passenger window, I quickly, kindly and loudly asked, "You guys need some water, don't you?" The young man responded, "Boy we sure do, got a hose?" I laughed and reached in the back seat to grab the water once intended for my board of directors meeting and said, "no, but I have some bottles of water, will that work?" The guy looked up at me as though it were a bag of gold, and started to take one. "No, no, please, take them all" I said, "you'll probably need all of them to get your car cooled down." He was so appreciative once again I saw how God really does have plans even when we think we have everything planned months in advance. How can He ever accomplish what He desires if we are so set on our own agenda?

That is what Jesus longs for us to experience — a confidence in **His plan**, a relationship so intimate that He speaks and we hear. He speaks and we obey. "Yes, Lord I will follow through with your plans, not mine." God's plans are always the very best. Jeremiah 29:11 says, *"For I know the plans I have for you, declares the Lord, plans to prosper you and not to harm you, plans to give you hope and a future."*

This passion for Jesus is not supposed to be about our own agenda, or should I say it's not supposed to be about "our plans." Passion for Christ gives priority to Him. Of course, in the present world in which we live the mindset of most is anything but that. It's all about us. *"I Did It My Way"* is our theme song. There seems to be more and more focus on self — magazines with that name, people consumed with themselves, their plans, their future, and their lives. Those who love Jesus, and are passionate about their relationship with Him, actually should be checking in with Him about His agenda. We should be asking Him every single day "Lord what is Your plan for today? Bless Your plans. He desires so much that we put Him in the *driver's seat* of our lives. You know that bumper sticker that says *"God is my Co-Pilot."* Is that right? Not. Shouldn't it be, *God is my Pilot*? We certainly don't just want Him sitting beside us in the plane. We need for Him to fly the thing. Why would we think we have more brains or abilities than almighty God does? There is one thing I do know, actually two. There is a God and I'm not Him. Saying yes to God's agenda means; giving the steering wheel over to the Holy Spirit—getting in the passenger seat—traveling His road and arriving at His planned destination; relinquishing control. That's when we glorify Him the most.

Yes, as I mentioned earlier in this chapter, in the real world we have schedules, appointments, jobs, families, kids, activities, school, church, community functions, and so much more; but in the midst of all the things we have to do in life to live life, *remember God's plan, and hand, is intertwined in the midst of it all.*

PLANS FOR A HOMELESS MAN

My plans for this particularly week included a fast for some specific needs in ministry and in my own personal life. But on the third day of *my* fast, God had other plans. I was running errands, passing a Schlotzki's sandwich shop, which just so happens to be one of my favorites. I felt compelled to stop. I wasn't hungry, not even tempted, believe it or not, but the Lord kept nudging me. So with some reservation, I obeyed—not wanting to break my fast, but doing my best to listen. I believe the more often we are obedient to the Holy Spirit's voice, the more often we'll hear Him speak. When we obey, it opens up the doors for more frequent and greater instruction from Him. With each obeyed instruction comes the assurance that He will give us yet another.

I ordered a small sandwich and drink, pulled up to the pay window, got my food and was ready to drive away, still not understanding the purpose of this detour, not to mention the breaking of my fast. As I pulled forward the Holy Spirit spoke again to me and instructed me to park. I hesitated, convinced it wasn't a problem to *eat and drive,* not even really wanting to eat but the impression intensified. As I drove into the parking area, there was a space facing a small strip mall. Placing the car in park, I looked up, and saw, obviously, what

God Bless "My" Plans

the Lord had *planned* for me to see. It was a homeless man digging through a large city garbage can. He was searching for... food. I laid my sandwich down, put the car in reverse and headed over in his direction. I drove up beside him just as he was pulling out a boney, meatless piece of already-eaten-and-thrown-away-chicken-breast. I startled him with my question, as tears began to form in my eyes. *"What are you doing sir?"* He responded with fear in his voice, *"looking for something to eat." "Do you not have a home?" "No, I live behind these buildings in the woods, I am homeless." "Well, please throw that away... throw it away and I'll go buy you something to eat."* He looked at me as though I had asked him to throw back a T bone steak, but he obeyed. I talked him into meeting me over on the curb area by Schlotzki's, asking him what he would like to eat. He said, *"Anything, ma'am, anything at all would be nice."* He was so thin, his clothes were dirty and torn, he was unshaven and he had only a few teeth in his mouth. My heart was broken for this man who had nothing.

I wheeled the car back around to the drive-thru, praying, asking the Holy Spirit to protect me and guide me in this encounter. I ordered again, but this time big — everything big including dessert. The attendant at the window looked at me and said, *"Wow, you must really be hungry today, didn't you just drive through here?"* I replied *"Yes, pretty hungry alright."* I parked again and this time I shut off the car, got out, and took the food with me. I met him at the curb, sat down beside him, handed him his food, prayed over it and watched a really hungry man eat!

Next, I asked him his name, and oh, how I wish I could remember his name, but it's been a lot of years ago — it eludes me. I told him mine. I had a captive audience so I talked to him about his life — how he became homeless. *You know how?* He was born into it! His parents were homeless and they were deceased. He was now alone and homeless. He had never been able to get a job because he had never had any formal education. No home. No telephone. No education. No transportation. So, this was his life and somehow he had survived.

Of course I asked him where he slept, and if he needed blankets, or pillows. How I wished I could have provided a home for him, but it was impossible. I offered to take him to the YMCA or Rescue Mission but he didn't want that; he said he was ok, this was his home.

Then, I asked him about Jesus. I asked him if he knew who Jesus was, and if he'd ever known how to accept Him as his Savior. He said he only knew about Christmas, but nothing else. So I told him all about Jesus — everything I could while he ate. And when I finished and he finished, my face was covered in tears. He looked at me with the most compassionate eyes and asked, *"Regina, why are you crying... why are you crying?"* I told him because he didn't have a home — no place to live and that made me so sad and he'd never heard of Jesus, and that made me even more sad. Then I asked him to pray with me. I told him that should he go into eternity, I didn't want him to be lost, to die without knowing Jesus or accepting him. So, I prayed and he repeated the sinner's prayer after me. Then we both cried.

Many times after that encounter I drove back to the same place, looking for him to feed him. I even took a Bible once, and some supplies, but I never saw him again. There have been times I wondered if it was all a test. Maybe God was just making sure I would respond and obey HIS plan that day. My plan to fast totally became HIS plan to rescue one more lost sheep into the fold.

Isn't that what life is supposed to be about? Well, maybe not meeting homeless people with their hand in a city garbage can, but looking and listening every day for every opportunity to obey God's plan, not our own? Isn't that what makes life filled with so much more than the mundane, monotonous daily routine? I am in awe of all the times I recall Him guiding me, speaking to me. I am so thankful for every single supernatural, miraculous moment. How my life has been deeply enriched by each experience. Some of them required much faith. Normally, they would have seemed unsafe, maybe not even the right thing to do. But God doesn't do normal.

God Bless "My" Plans

Knowing God's voice makes all the difference. With it comes a confidence that *"the angels of the Lord encamp around about those who fear Him."* When He gives us an instruction, He will watch over us and keep us. He always, always, always has. Just as Shadrach, Meshach and Abednego obeyed the Lord—knowing they would be thrown in the fiery furnace. Yet, not a hair on their heads was scorched, and their clothing did not even smell of smoke. Yes, there was a fourth man in the fire with them. So it is in our lives. Where God Guides, He Provides. He gives us everything we need to obey His plan—Protection. Provision. Peace.

GOD'S PLANS... AS WE WALK IN OBEDIENCE

While working on the final draft for this book, the Lord impressed upon me to set aside some days to be alone with Him in the mountains of Tennessee. Kind of wish He would have said a week in Hawaii, ahhh but He didn't. At any rate, He encouraged me to call my dearest friend, more like a sister, who is just a wonderful spirit-filled, dynamic woman of God and invite her to join me for a *"Spending Time to Hear from God Retreat."* I knew she could use some time away, and I needed to hear from the Lord concerning the final editing and writing of this book.

It worked that she was able to take some time and make could make the trip. On the morning we were to leave, since we live in different states, we'd decided about what time we wanted to arrive in Pigeon Forge, leaving our homes at about 6:30 AM so we could meet within a close proximity. I had forgotten she was on Central time which is one hour earlier than mine, but felt peace, and didn't call her until around 9:00 AM. When I got her on the phone she was ready to make the trip, but somewhat perturbed because there had been a tornado watch in her area, and unable to even leave her home, let alone town. She finally began the trip, but then yet one delay after another. I finally told her not to worry anymore. This trip was planned by the Lord—we were on His schedule not ours. We

Rekindling Our Passion For Jesus!

would see each other, regardless of the time, when we both got there. Right after that she came upon an eleven car pile-up involving an 18 wheeler. They were eastbound, and traffic backed up for miles, but she was only about eight cars from the accident and could see everything, even the officers and emergency vehicles on the scene. Was this God's timing? Do His plans matter more than ours? First of all, she may have been one of those eight cars had she arrived moments earlier. The Lord obviously was not ready for her to die. The Holy Spirit spoke to her and put urgency in her heart to get out of the car and approach the officers to see if she could do anything. The policeman asked her if she knew how to pray. Can you imagine? She, of course, said, *"Yes, show me who is alive."* She saw the seriousness of the accident and the officer said eight people had been injured so severely they thought they had already passed away, but two for sure had not. She made her way to where they were, he allowed her to do so, and she prayed with them. They both were able to repent and ask Jesus into their hearts before they died; God's plan. Had she left home a moment earlier or later she would not have been at the right place at the right time. When we ask God to bless His plans, not ours, everyday is an exciting joy-filled ride. What amazing, surprising interruptions the Lord will bring when we are traveling with His plan in hand. She was able to lead two people to the Lord because she was at the scene at the moment — the moment she needed to be there Two people went to heaven. Two lives were spared from eternity without Jesus because of a delay that seemed at first to be a total inconvenience, but turned out to be a great blessing. Both people passed away moments after they prayed. What a huge difference. Big, big… huge mistake when we ask God to bless our plans, rather than finding out what His are; then asking Him to **bless His plans and use us for His glory.**

WAITING ON THE LORD

Sometimes we have to **wait on God's plans** before He can even **bless His plans.** There's always a purpose in the waiting; always a plan, even in the midst of the delay. The waiting process teaches us patience, prepares us for what lies ahead that we may have not been equipped for had we faced it earlier. *"But those who wait on the Lord shall renew their strength; they shall mount up with wings like eagles, they shall run and not be weary, they shall walk and not faint."* Isaiah 40:31 *"Wait on the Lord; be of good courage, and He shall strengthen your heart; wait, I say, on the Lord!"* Psalm 27:14 *"I waited patiently for the LORD; and He inclined to me, and heard my cry."* Psalm 40:1.

One Sunday morning after ministering in a church in Monroe NC, I was making my way back to the product table in the vestibule at the conclusion of the service when a lovely young woman met me in the aisle. Often there are people in congregations who are like *spiritual sponges*, absorbing every word that's being spoken. This gal was like that. It's so awesome when the Lord strategically places a person in the audience who makes ministry seem worth-it-all. We have our moments, when we feel that what we're doing just doesn't matter. In the whole scheme of life, are we really making a difference? But then, God sends one along who really is receiving the Word. She was glowing, and during the service was completely attentive and engaged, but now I noticed her beauty close up. She radiated the love of Christ, but she also had a lovely face, with long, gorgeous eyelashes. We chatted briefly, and then I asked her, as though it would make a difference in mine, what kind of mascara she used. She laughed and told me she bought it at Wal-Mart, — it was a product by *Revlon*. We finished packing all of the sound equipment and product and I jumped into my SUV and headed back to Charlotte. But, on the way, I made a quick stop at — yep, you're right, Wal-Mart. Canvassing the cosmetic section with eyes for detail, I carefully looked for this magic *Revlon* mascara length enhancer. Strangely, I felt someone's eyes glaring at me so I moved a little to the left to make sure she could also see the products. However, when I moved she still didn't move. So after a few more seconds I asked, *"Am I in your way?"* She said no, she said she was just observing me, and how lovely I looked. Well, is there a woman on earth who doesn't like to hear a compliment? You know how this story ended up because I was at a Wal-Mart on a Sunday afternoon in the cosmetic department? It was definitely a *God's plan and timing* scenario. This woman sold Mary Kay. She canvassed cosmetic departments in stores looking for new clients. After several weeks we ended up becoming close friends, and as time went on, it was my joy to be able to share Christ with her and pray for her to be able to conceive; she wanted a baby so desperately. And, guess what? The Lord heard our prayers! She has two beautiful children — a son and daughter. Should we follow our plans or His? More often than not, His plans will seem even strange and rather unorthodox. But never underestimate the power or marvelously good consequences of God's plans. Whether they make sense or not, the ultimate purpose will always bring Him glory, point others to the Cross — and increase our faith.

GOD OUR SOURCE

As we close Chapter 5 there's one last thought the Lord continues to impress upon me about Him — and us — to share with you.

GOD IS THE SOURCE OF EVERYTHING PERTAINING TO LIFE

Do we totally understand that without Him we would not even be able to take a breath, let alone make "plans?" One squeeze of His fingertips on our nostrils and we're history. Of course, that's not how He works, though there have been times, just kidding. It is God, and God alone who created the air we breathe, then allows us to breathe oxygen into our bodies to fuel them and our brain causing them to properly function. From the moment we were conceived, and our little fingers, toes, eyes,

God Bless "My" Plans

ears, mouth, everything inside, every part developing perfectly from brain to toenail is His plan. He created that as well—conception—another God idea. Imagine that. Man. no matter how brilliant he may be, cannot create life *without the seed* that God formed and placed in man and woman.

I heard a story once about an atheist scientist who approached God and said, *"We no longer need you God. We now can create human beings. So, we have no use for you or anything you have contributed to the whole creation process. Man now has everything he needs; all the knowledge, resources and skills."* God responded *"Sounds fine by me."* The man then stooped to pick up a handful of dirt and God said, *"No, sorry, that would be mine too, since I created it. Make your own dirt."* Bottom line, it all came from Him. ALL came from Him. Genesis 1:1 *"In the beginning God created..."* We choose what we're going to be passionate about, often leaving the Lord completely out of the equation. Wouldn't it seem appropriate, even proper to honor the one to whom we owe our lives? Pathetic how seldom it happens; how infrequently people, even Christians, pause to be passionate about their Creator.

You know how there can be real meaning to life every single day you awaken? Give all your dreams and plans to God. Then—ask Him what His plans are for you each morning as your eyes gaze upon His world. Just tell the Holy Spirit you're available—excited and ready for Him to do the planning, for Him to use you. Anytime. Anywhere. Tell Him that you want to be right-smack-dab-in-the-middle of His plans. Thank Him for including you in those plans. That, my friend, is the definition of a passionate, meaningful life everyday in Christ.

"Lord, Bless Your Plans, Not Mine,"
Then get ready...
His plans are totally awesome!

6

TAMING THE TONGUE
"Understanding the Power of Words"

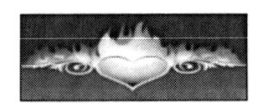

There's little that makes us less like Jesus, or more clearly reveals the condition our hearts in relationship to our passion for Him, than an untamed tongue.

WORDS ARE POWERFUL

James tells us in his writing, chapter 3 verse 2 ... *"For we stumble in many things. If anyone does not **stumble in word**, he is a perfect man, able also to bridle the whole body."* That speaks volumes. Stumbling means to miss one's footing, to slip, totter, tumble or fall. When our feet stumble, the entire body can come crashing down causing major damage. Reminds me of little puppies or toddlers just learning to walk. Their clumsiness is a sure sign of their immaturity. A stumbling tongue can reflect our spiritual immaturity. And, unfortunately, besides tripping ourselves, we often may cause others to stumble.

There is no perfect human being. Even in this context, James is referring to being complete or mature. We are all still in the process of learning how not to stumble in word. He continues with other examples expanding our view of the almost impossible task we face in tempering our tongues. He uses the example of bits in horses' mouths so they'll obey us and we'll be able to turn their whole body. He talks about large ships, even in strong winds, that are controlled and turned by a very small rudder at the pilots' hands. But as he discusses the tongue he says basically it's impossible to tame. It's a little member, yet it boasts of great things. The tongue can wreak havoc. It can set ablaze a forest and defile the whole body. He refers to the tongue as a fire, a world of iniquity. Then he writes this mind-boggling phrase that I'd never noticed before. "It – the tongue - *is set on fire by hell."* James 3:6. Hell is not a place I ever want to be or see. There is certainly nothing there I would ever want to have. So, if anything we possess is in any way connected to hell, we can say without question that it is certainly vile and unrighteous. James 3:8 *"But no man can tame the tongue. It is an unruly evil, full of deadly poison."*

This scripture is extremely disturbing, almost depressing. But, it's a wake-up call. There is great news. The verse tells only half of the story. We are unable to tame the tongue. We can't bridle it, we can't control it, but there is someone who can. His name is Jesus. When we ask the Holy Spirit to take control, He can, if we are willing to relinquish control.

From the beginning, the very beginning of time God spoke all of His creation into inexistence, with words; everything except the creation of man.

The power of words was also demonstrated in the story of the *Tower of Babel* in Genesis 11, when God himself saw that man's ability to communicate was basically unstoppable. Verse 6 says, *"Behold, the people are one, and they all have one language; and now nothing will be restrained from them which they have imagined to do."* Words are so powerful. God knew if He didn't confound the language of man, causing them to be unable to understand one another, that literally nothing would have been impossible for them to accomplish, good or bad. Words create consequences.

Did is a word of achievement, *won't* is a word of retreat, *might* is a word of bereavement, *can't* is a word of defeat, *ought* is a word of duty, *try* is a word each hour, (that means we use it all the time, but it's useless, trying gets you nowhere), *will* is a word of beauty, *can* is a word of power.

Have you ever thought about the importance of words in your own life? There is tremendous power in the words we speak. Jesus said in Matthew 12:34-37 (we know He said it because it's in red), *"Brood vipers!* (These are strong words in themselves) *How can you, being evil, speak good things? For out of the abundance of the heart the mouth speaks. A good man out of the good treasure of his heart brings out good things, and an evil man out of the evil treasure brings out evil things. But I say to you that for every idle word men may speak, they will give an account of it in the Day of Judgment. For by your words you will be justified, and by your words you will be condemned."*

Whew, these are very serious words coming from Jesus. Words are a powerful force. Proverbs 15:23 *"A man has joy by the answer of his mouth, and a word spoken in due season, how good it is."* Then in Proverbs 13:2-3 *"A man will eat well by the fruit of his mouth but the tongue of the transgressor will eat violence. He who keeps his mouth keeps his life."* It seems there isn't much *life-keeping* going on in the world; few of us know how to keep our mouths.

Words; they are a gift. I can't even imagine what it would be like to be unable to talk. Of course some husbands and wives might dream of that being a wonderful reality, at least occasionally. Did you hear the old joke about the preacher who said he could prove from the Bible that there will be no women in heaven? He then quoted Revelation 8:1. *"When He opened the seventh seal, there was silence in heaven for about half an hour."* Very funny.

Sometimes we are totally unaware that our present situation may very well be a direct result of what we are speaking on a daily basis. Yet, we are so careless with our profession, our words, what we say. I've found this to be true in many areas of my own life and in ministry. It's not that we play some game of control with our words; rather it's simply taking truth and applying it to our lives so we can experience a winning life, not a defeated on— speaking words that give life.

SOME *BAD* WORDS

CRITICISM: Words of criticism may not be profane, but they are nonetheless nasty to the ear and detrimental to the soul. *Who exactly are we criticizing?* When we criticize another we are actually saying that God's workmanship does not meet our standards; that we could do better. *When we criticize someone's child, who is ultimately offended? The parent.* This is none the less true with God. He really doesn't appreciate our comments about His creation, nor does He need our opinions; genuine concern or accountability – yes. There's a difference in negative criticism and speaking the truth in love. Wrong criticism more often than not has to do with our own personal opinion of someone or something, rather than trying to mentor someone about Godly principles or living a holy life. Just being critical for the sake of making ourselves feel better, well, that is unacceptable. An addiction to words of criticism is one of the main reasons there is so little light...so little of the glory of God shining forth today. Whenever we criticize someone else we are assuming that we are superior to them. What detriment criticism causes in the lives of others. Even when they don't know negative things are being said, the words are still in the atmosphere causing damage. I have sat in the same room listening to people watching television talk shows or Christian broadcasting, who would literally criticize the Show Host's choice of clothing; and I'm not talking about clothing that was immodest, I'm talking style or color. I've heard comments like, *"Man, look how they've aged, they are sure looking old;"* or *"That guys a tub; look how much weight he's gained,"* or *"That is a just a terrible looking hairpiece, he needs to find the hair dresser that Sean Connery uses." "That dress, why I wouldn't wear that in public if my life depended on it; that's just looks horrible on her!"* This would be referred to as criticism. Please readers, keep in context what I'm saying. We can all be silly at times, teasing, or being goofy when people really do look weird, and in the privacy of our own homes, it is our own business. But how do these kinds of comments affect our children? Or how might other people feel that are listening? And what about the comments we make about people we know well? Or for that matter, some we've met only recently? Do we size them up assuming we really *know* them and who they are? What's that about? If we continually speak negative words, it will be a detriment to our Christian witness; it will also cause us to become bitter, cynical and judgmental — attributes we do not want to embrace or pass on to others.

Why in the world do we do it? Who do we think we are, walking perfection?! Having an opinion, that's fine. But constant accusation and condemnation, that's infuriating! Christians sometimes are the most critical, judgmental people on the face of the earth. *Where are the eyes of Jesus? Where is the heart of Christ? Do we have even a smidgen of the Holy Spirit dwelling within us? What gives us the idea to think that it is all right to be so critical? Was Jesus?* Now, it is true, some styles these days are atrocious and totally immodest. Seems to me there need to be better guidelines for dress in school and in the work place, and church for that matter. If mothers would dress more appropriately, daughters probably would. But here's the deal. We are just as guilty as the person we're criticizing; it's wrong. We weren't put on earth, nor have we become a Christian to constantly give our opinion about how other people look, or to put them down. It is a free country. Often we're expecting sinners to act like Christians. Sinners are just that, *in sin*. Christians on the other hand, well, we need to wake up and take a better look in the mirror, the spiritual mirror, and see how nasty we are on the inside. Check out our own appearance and see how inappropriate our attitude is dressed. We have not been given the credentials to be judge and jury. God only can be that.

Jesus never portrayed this kind of spirit or attitude, nor do we ever read in scripture of Him criticizing people. He was angry at the money changers when they dishonored the temple. But there is never an account of Him being critical or in any way humiliating another person.

That brings us to another word:

PRIDE: Pride causes that which any rational human being (one with any brains at all) should fear most—God's resistance. *"God resists the proud, but gives grace to the humble."* James 4:6. Pride is the precursor to falling. We can depend upon it happening. It's a fact. Become proud and there will be consequences. It might take a while, and we're not talking about God's chastening, or testing to see what we're made of. His word promises that when we embrace a spirit of pride, arrogance, haughtiness; however you want to label it, He will resist that spirit. Buy some band-aids; painful falling is inevitable. Is it just not worth it? First of all, being full of pride is no fun. I like fun. Secondly, being prideful is painful. I hate pain. Honestly, God **hates pride.** Proverbs 6:16-17. *"These six things the Lord hates, yes, seven are an abomination to Him; A proud look..."*

GOSSIP: In a very real since this could be the sibling to criticism; however, the difference is that gossip is always meant to be harmful. Criticism sometimes can be constructive if it's used in the right context, and meant to help not harm. Most of the time gossip is hearsay, meant to hurt and damage. And don't give me that old story when you tell someone something you know is questionable or detrimental to a person's character that you "just want them to pray about it." That's bologna! It is gossip; you both know it and they would be gossiping too if they repeated what you were going to tell them.

Mary Crowley, President of Home Interiors & Gifts, whom I've mentioned in a previous chapter, trained us, as managers, from the book of Proverbs. She touched on gossip often because she knew we were women leading other women. And women have a tendency to make other people's business their business. Here's one of the ways she taught us to guard our lives in the area of gossip. *"Ask yourself four questions before you repeat anything spoken to you:"*

1. **IS IT TRUE?** - Is what I'm about to say true, from the horse's mouth? Do I know that it is true for a proven fact or am I just repeating hearsay?
2. **IS IT FAIR?** - Is what I'm about to say fair to the person it's being said about, and fair to the person I'm telling?
3. **WILL IT BUILD GOOD WILL AND BETTER FRIENDSHIP?** - Is what I'm about to say going to bring about building up the good in another, caring, showing kindness and camaraderie?
4. **WILL IT BENEFIT ALL CONCERNED?** - Is what I'm about to say going to be beneficial or helpful to the person it's about, and to the one I'm sharing it with?

Then she would say, *"If you can say yes to all of the above, go ahead and say what you'd planned on saying. If not, for heaven's sake, keep your mouth shut!"* Blunt but true. Gossip hurts the one in which it is stored, as much as the one on whom it is poured. It's deviously detrimental to both. *Have you ever experienced heartache from someone gossiping about you?* It hurts! No doubt about it!

Charlotte, NC, was my home for many years. For about 14 of those years I attended a Church of God in Kannapolis. It was a joy for me to be involved in music, the choir, playing keyboard, leading *Joy-bells,* a Christian girls club, and teaching. The ninth grade Sunday School class was my joy. One very hectic week, out of pure exhaustion, teaching the class was gladly given over to my assistant. But, alas, I missed the kids so much that I decided to sneak in at the end of the hour, just to say hi and give everyone a hug before going to the sanctuary to play for worship.

Walking down the very long hallway where the classrooms were housed on either side, I heard my name. Not someone calling me, but in conversation. It was a little unsettling. At the end of the hallway was a Sunday School office where the attendance and offering was recorded. Usually only one person handled the task; however, on this particular day, there were three women. Their voices were undisguised.

I was, at that time, the wife of the Minister of Youth and Christian Education. These women were serving up Regina on a platter of gossip!

I had purchased a beautiful used red Corvette. Yes. RED. The Lord was blessing my Home Interiors business. So after discussing it, and looking over the budget, it was absolutely a no-brainer, it would work. These ladies were not only making it their business, they were adamantly against such a purchase. The door was slightly ajar, that's how I heard my name in the first place, so I quietly walked up closer, where they could not see me and listened. *"I can't even imagine a preacher's wife thinking it's okay to drive a Corvette! What in the world? And a red one at that! Where's she getting the money to pay for it? Not to mention the insurance. Do you think it's flashy enough? And she sells Home Interiors, how in the world does she get "all that stuff" in that car?"* Needless to say, I'd heard far more than my heart could bear. They weren't taking care of Sunday School business... they were meddling in mine! Wasn't this a spiritual, uplifting thing to be doing in church on a Sunday morning, or any time for that matter?

As bold as I am now, I was not quite as gutsy at age twenty-four, but that was it. These were elder's wives! I pushed the door open and looked directly into their eyes! Their mouths were no longer moving—they were wide open and their faces were as white as a man's dress shirt. Before any one of them could even utter a word, I posed the question. *"If you all were so upset about me driving a red Corvette, why didn't you just come and talk to me about it? Do you honestly feel there are any solutions being made by your gossip? And you, of all the women in the church, are elders' wives. You are what, in your forty's, and supposed to be my example in the faith, yet this morning the things I've heard you say about me have been anything but Godly. Doesn't Jesus tell us that if we've been offended by someone, to go to them and tell them? But that is not at all what you have done. Honestly, in the whole scheme of doing God's work, I don't know why anyone would really even care about what kind of car I drive."*

With that, I closed the door, walked down the hall, and out the door. Obviously I didn't get to greet or hug my Sunday school class. Fortunately that morning, I was to play the electric keyboard, not the grand, and we had an organist as well so it was ok not to be there. I couldn't have been there. I went home and fell on my knees asking the Lord why people are so cruel and if a red Corvette really was a sin? What was I to do?

Peace did come to my heart as well as instruction. The next day the red Corvette was driven to a dealership where it was traded for a beautiful silver 2-door Buick Riviera with a gorgeous soft gray leather Landau top (now you know it's been a while ago!) The following Wednesday night the new vehicle was parked in the Associate Pastor's space. And of course, the ladies saw it, and ran to apologize to me. My response was kind, but brief. Nothing was worth that kind of gossip. No car was going to be a detriment to my testimony.

Now, it wasn't long before reality set in for me. I would never be able to please everyone, about everything, all the time. We can please some of the people some of the time. We can please all of the people some of the time. But we can't please all of the people all of the time. After that incident, it was my intention to the very best of my ability to make sure I pleased the Lord. As long as He was pleased, that's all that mattered. My life would have been utterly miserable had I continued to try to make everyone in the church happy. Gossip is a killer. Gossip hurts. It damages people sometimes for life. It destroys relationships.

I think Dr. Joseph M. Stowell states it best from His book, <u>The Weight of Your Words.</u> *"By making careless communication an acceptable part of our lives, we strive for spiritual maturity while exempting the tongue from the process. Yet the word-sparks that fly from an untamed tongue can leave an entire life (or lives) in ashes. Until we get serious, about bringing our tongues under the control of the Holy Spirit, our churches, schools, homes, friendships, and relationships with God will be victimized. Social sins of the tongue, including gossip and slander, must be checked. Let me provide a recent illustration of how serious we need to be about controlling our speech. A favorite sportswriter of mine once analyzed a fine levied on a local baseball manager for verbally chewing out the commissioner. His column defended the manager by saying, 'After all, they were just words.' At the time I thought,* **Just words? There's no such thing. It's like saying, 'After all, it's just an atom bomb!'"**

In the rest of the account Dr. Stowell went on to say that a number of years later the *Chicago Tribune* ran an article for ten days reporting on the aftermath of this northwestern Illinois high school's state play-off football game. Lots of very alarming facts came to light after the game. The game had been close, going into overtime. When one team was finally defeated, the fans were disappointed and some even went out of their way to place the blame on a particular referee.

One fan followed him 65 miles home and sat outside his house for two hours. The days and weeks that followed, he received hostile letters and cruel phone calls. Do you know what happened next? The 36 year old referee tried to kill himself because he could no longer handle the horrible *words* and *accusations* that were being *thrown in his face*. Fortunately, the suicide attempt failed.

Just words? They were much more. The power of their weight continued to affect their target, *and for what? A high school ball game! How much better would it be to control our words than cause such toxic harm to others with such cruel and totally unnecessary words?*

MORE *BAD* WORDS

DECEIT AND LYING: More *bad* words, but ones I want to touch on as a reminder that they are not acceptable in the passionate Christian's life. I've heard it said that most people lie (and I'm not talking about on the bed to sleep) at least five times a day. *Is it really that surprising?* It's convenient. A friend of mine once made a profoundly silly statement: "If I tell you I'm lying, then it's really not a lie." Not! A quote from Mark Twain that I like is, "When in doubt, tell the truth. It will confound your enemies and astound your friends." It might seem easier to lie at times so you won't feel so guilty about whatever it is that you haven't done, or did. But the truth (no pun intended) of the matter is, *"be sure your sins will find you out."* Lying never pays off. After a while, when a person lies, they have to keep on doing it in order to cover what they've lied about. Eventually, they lose track and it all comes crashing down. Big or little, deceit and lying never pay off, and these are certainly not words to be found in a Christian's vocabulary.

As we delve a little deeper into the detrimental effects of lying, the scripture has much to say. In Proverbs 6:17 Solomon tells us that a lying tongue is among the list of things that God detests. John says in Revelation 21:8 that *all* liars are included in the list of people who will be judged in the lake of fire. That's not a consequence to play around with. It was used by satan, with Eve, and just a few paragraphs down we will discuss his deceitfulness with her as well. But he lied to her about what God had spoken to her. God told her if she ate of the one tree in the Garden, *she would surely die;* satan, on the other hand, boldly lied to her saying, *"You shall surely not die."* Lying was and still is satan's central strategy focus causing people to sin, or doubt God. He continues to present questions in a way that lead us to believe he's offering some really fantastic options to be considered. Lies are still his main method of operation. He infiltrates society with lies such as: There are no consequences for sin. Just live a good life and be sincere and you'll go to heaven. True freedom is found in doing anything you want anytime you want to. It's your body, go ahead and get an abortion. It's not really a baby. Then there's the classic lie he tells people: *"If God is so good, why does He allow so many bad things to happen?"* Lying is the foundation for satan's strategies; in them his system gains strength. His lies are endless. John 8:44 says that *"he is a liar and the father of lies."* Now there's one thing I know for sure. I do not want to have, in any way, shape, form or fashion, the nature of satan. Whenever we tell lies we are putting on the cloak of his nature.

Lying just seems to be so acceptable and normal anymore. Doesn't everyone do it occasionally, or maybe just in *special situations*, so they won't hurt another person with the truth? Hogwash!

EVEN SPECIAL SITUATION LIES

We need to be cognizant of the times that we are tempted to lie to protect ourselves. We cannot excuse even "special situation lies." You know what I'm talking about. Things that might make us look non-Christian if we tell the truth about not doing something we were supposed to do. Then we conveniently lie to the person so as to not make ourselves look bad.

People have taken one of the Old Testament stories and said, "Well, Rahab lied to the soldiers about of the Israelite spies, and look at all the good that came from that. Lying actually protected others from harm." Hello. If that were the case, then where do we draw the line for absolute truth? When is it ok to lie because it may have redeeming value? Rahab was commended in Hebrews 11:31 for her faith, *not her lie*. She actually had a lapse in faith when she lied. Though she was a pagan, Rahab did embrace faith as a response to the miracles she had heard that the Israelites experienced in crossing the Red Sea and other victories.

God probably would have intervened supernaturally had she not lied. He did a miracle for the spies later when they hid for three days in the mountains and the soldiers who were familiar with the terrain tried in vain to find them. Joshua 2:22. God is able, we don't have to assist Him with satan's tactics and then try and justify them. *Could it be that Rahab is yet another example of a forgiving God who through His mercy uses even our disobedience for His glory?*

Truth is what God wants to dwell in us richly, because it aligns us with HIM and with His attributes of holiness and righteousness. If we are going to live passionately for Jesus, truth must find residence in our hearts. Psalms 31:5 says that

"God is a God of truth." "He cannot lie." Titus 1:2 *"Jesus is full of grace and truth."* John 1:14. When we are committed to truth in our lives, we are in agreement - alignment with the very nature of God. Truth also reflects God's character, so we can become more and more like Jesus. Romans 8:29. Walking in truth, speaking and living out truth is, without question, God's perfect will for every believer. Proverbs 13:5 says that *"A righteous man hates falsehood."* Paul exhorted, *"Do not lie to one another."* Colossians 3:9. That wasn't an option, that was a command, and these cannot be ignored for a child of God who desires to become more passionate in their relationship with Him. Neither can our conscience be clear, nor our joy full, when we partake of, or participate in, lying.

THE SHEPHERD BOY AND THE WOLF

"A mischievous shepherd boy used to amuse himself by calling, "Wolf, Wolf!" just to see the villagers run with the clubs and pitchforks to help him. After he had called this more than once for a joke and had laughed at them each time, they grew angry. One day a wolf really did get among the sheep, and the Shepherd Boy called "Wolf, Wolf!" in vain. The villagers went on with their work, the wolf killed what he wanted of the sheep, and the shepherd boy learned that liars are not believed, even when they do tell the truth." Excerpt from The Family Book of Christian Values by Stuart & Jill Briscoe.

DECEIT: This word we will refer to as the *brother* to lying. The greatest deceiver of all is of course satan. He has used his ploys from the beginning in the Garden of Eden to mess things up for mankind. Look a little closer with me about what he said to Eve. We already mentioned his lies, but one deceitful statement he made caused a huge question in the mind of the *first woman,* which became forever the greatest demise of man. Words desperately need a good editor so that truth spoken will not be lost or manipulated. Eve required much more; she needed a Holy Ghost filled translator!

In Genesis 3:1 satan posed this question to Eve, *"Indeed has God said, 'You shall not eat from any tree of the garden?'"* "The facts may have been there, but the presentation was riddled with deceit. All of a sudden Eve felt that obeying God was keeping her from experiencing a full life. God was being restrictive and enslaving. What God actually said was, *"From **any tree** of the garden **you may eat freely**; but from the tree of the knowledge of good and evil you shall not eat."* Genesis 2:16-17. Thinking about what He said, doesn't it seem that God is being completely generous—it was only one tree? They could freely partake of every other tree in the entire garden. Yet the deceptive way satan approached Eve caused in her wrong thinking about God. He manipulated the facts to ultimately gain an advantage over Eve causing her to doubt and then sin. The Bible calls this **deceit.** 2 Corinthians 11:3 and it is a serious tool used continually by satan in his ongoing tactical warfare.

In our world deception is rampant. It's almost a technique used by people to manipulate, to advance or as a means of self-protection. Sadly to say, it also resides in the church, from pulpit to pew. Deceit destroys trust and ruins relationships. It's found in our government, the media, politics, and business, but the Bible is emphatic about the results of allowing such a word to pervade our lives, Proverbs 20:17 *"Bread gained by deceit is sweet to a man, but afterward his mouth will be filled with gravel."* Bottom line, *"Deceit is in the heart of those who devise evil."* Proverbs 12:20. Deceitfulness is the sign of a wicked heart. "Purify our hearts, Oh Lord, and take away every trace of deceit that may hide within us."

WORDS MATTER

Have you ever thought about why the children of Israel spent 40 years wandering in the wilderness, in dry places? After all the miracles God showed them of His power and might. After all the fulfilled promises and the opportunity of living in the beauty of a land flowing with milk and honey, still they wandered. They stayed on their wilderness-road-trip because of their

WORDS! Their grumbling, complaining, whining, moaning, even criticizing God saying they were better off in Egypt. With our own words we often bring about our own demise! We are often more filled with whining and complaining than praising and adoring. What a difference to wake up in the morning and say *"Good Morning, Lord!"* rather than *"Good Lord! It's Morning!"* How He desires for us to focus on the blessings and not the curses. To see all the marvelous daily miracles He's given us... speaking thanks for all He is and all He has done.

Being in sales for a number of years I loved attending life-building conferences, listening to motivational speakers. These pros mastered the technique of animated teaching—showing people how we could succeed and why we weren't. Among the myriad of strategies taught, words were one of the highest priorities for success.

One of the key ways to implement right words of course is to be optimistic about life, rather than pessimistic, by speaking positive words.

I remember a funny story about a family who had two sons. One was the eternal optimist; the other saw only the negative in everything that happened. The parents were quite concerned, not so much about their son who seemed to always see the good, but rather they worried that the pessimistic boy would go through life not seeing any of his blessings.

They were in the process of moving into a new home that had been under construction and had an ingenious idea. In the optimist son's room they would put off finalizing the decorating, even the flooring or mud and tape on the sheet-rock. They would leave it almost bare bones and fill it with horse manure just to see if he would see or even say anything negative.

In their negative boy's room, they got all the particulars from him on paint color and theme for the room and precisely fashioned the room décor—including computer games and toys that he wanted—hoping he would see something positive.

They day came for the boys to go into their rooms and both parents waited, listening in the hall to observe their responses. In the pessimist's room they heard sobbing and sadness. They ran down the hall and looked at their young son and asked what could possibly be wrong, it was everything he'd asked for? His response, "Well, I know, but my friends are going to come over and break my toys and mess up my room, and then I won't have them any more..." and the negative response continued.

The parents threw up their hands in despair feeling the child would never change.

Down the hall, in the son's room that always saw on the bright side of things they heard splat... splat... splat. They opened the door and watched as he threw handfuls of horse manure against the wall. The mother and father, completely baffled by the child's actions asked, "What in the world are you doing?" He responded, "Mom, Dad, I figure underneath all this manure, there's bound to be a pony!" Oh, the pure joy of a positive attitude!

Zig Zigler, one of the greatest motivational/inspirational speakers of all time said, *"An optimist is a person who, when he wears out his shoes just figures he's back on his feet."* A great definition is one he used in his book <u>See You At the Top.</u> *"The best definition of 'positive thinking I know came from my daughter, Suzan, when she was ten years old. I had just returned from Pensacola, Florida, where I conducted a series of seminars for the US Navy. My family had picked me up at the Atlanta Airport and we were driving toward our home in Stone Mountain, Georgia. I was quite excited about the trip and was giving my redhead some of the details. I overheard Suzan's girlfriend ask her what her daddy did for a living. Suzan told her I sold that 'positive thinking stuff.' Naturally the little friend wanted to know what the 'positive thinking stuff' was. Suzan explained. 'Oh, you know, that's what makes you feel real good even when you feel real bad.'"* Out of the mouth of babes! How you think, and what you say, does determine to a great extent who and what you will become.

ATTITUDE DETERMINES ALTITUDE

How about another word that makes a major difference in our lives: **Attitude.**

Our minds are really computers that are dutiful servants, programmed with the data we input. They function only when the on switch is activated. Then they perform according to our instructions. If we feel negative, they will perform in that precise manner convincing us that life could not be any worse.

A good illustration of this is a story of a man and woman seated at a luncheon for the Board of Realtors in Flint, Michigan. The man was asked how his business was going, and for the next fifteen minutes he elaborated on how bad business really was. General Motors was on strike, nobody bought anything. Things were so bad that the people were not buying shoes, clothes, cars, or even food so they certainly were not buying houses. He hadn't sold a house in so long he honestly didn't believe he would know how to fill out the contract. He finally concluded by saying if the strike didn't end soon, he was going to go bankrupt himself. He really belabored the point. His attitude and words were contagious and he was so negative, he could have brightened up the entire room by leaving it.

The woman, on the other hand, responded by saying, "You know, General Motors is on strike," and she broke into a big beautiful smile and finished the sentence by saying, "so business is fantastic!" For the first time in months, these people have plenty of time to go shopping for the home of their dreams. Some of them will spend half a day looking at one house. These people know the strike is going to end and they have faith in the American economy, but the most important thing is this, they know they can buy a home cheaper right now than they will ever be able to by one again. So, business is really booming."

One person was going broke because of the strike and the other was getting rich, but their attitudes, the words they were speaking, were enormously different.

No matter where you live, what your profession is, or where you are in life, there's always going to be someone, like *Pigpen* in the Peanuts comic strip, who has a cloud of dirt following them. Negative! Always seeing rain instead of the rainbow— people who themselves choose to be depressed, and don't want anyone else to be happy if they're not—people who need to notify their face when they are happy. *Did you ever know anyone like that—someone who couldn't see a blessing if it hit them over the head?* The saddest thing about this type of attitude is that it's quite difficult to change. And... it robs them of good things that could be transpiring in their lives.

I am convinced more everyday that life is exactly what we profess with our mouth. The condition of our mind and our attitude is what makes all the difference. It's not that we are supposed to go around like an ostrich, bury our head in the sand, and never seeing reality. Nor is it that we practice some mind over matter ritual. If you're a believer, than you can be a receiver. James 1:17. *"Every good gift and perfect gift is from above, and comes down from the Father of lights, with whom there is no variation or shadow of turning."* Either good or bad is happening in our lives, and a positive attitude will produce positive words which will produce positive results.

ENTHUSIASM

One of my favorite words is **Enthusiasm.** Nothing great is ever accomplished without enthusiasm. The difference between the good preacher and the great preacher, the good mother and the great mother, the good speaker and the great speaker, the good salesperson and the great salesperson is often one word: Enthusiasm! The word actually comes from two Greek words: En- Theos. It simply means, *God within.* My, what a positive, life changing difference God-within makes in our lives!

Look at the last four letters of the word enthusiasm. IASM forms an acrostic which could stand for **I Am Sold Myself**. If you truly believe that you were created in the image of God for a divine purpose, then you have an enthusiasm that comes from the well-spring of the Holy Spirit residing within. Unfortunately we allow circumstances to dictate our level of enthusiasm. If things are good and finances are plentiful, we're filled with excitement. If things are bad, challenging, and financially tight, we're anything but excited. We're usually negative, even depressed. You've probably heard the saying both ways: If life were any better I'd have to be twins to enjoy it twice as much; if life were any worse I'd have to be twins to be twice as miserable. That reminded me of a ridiculous song from Hee-Haw years ago. *"Gloom despair, and agony on me, deep, dark depression, excessive misery. If it weren't for bad luck, I'd have no luck at all, gloom despair and agony on me."* Makes me almost miserable typing the lyrics. Of course by the time they finished singing, you were laughing hysterically.

Attitude Determines Altitude. *How high do you want to climb?* Go the extra mile with a positive, Godly attitude. On the job, go beyond your boss's expectations. Arrive early, rather than one minute before the hour. Give yourself over and above the call of duty to your responsibilities whenever possible without compromise. Keep your word. Meet your deadlines early. Follow through. Show excellence. If you see something that needs to be done, take the initiative without being told. All of these things are connected to attitude toward work. This applies even more so as to how a Christian's attitude should be in every area of their lives.

Words—what a vast subject. There are so many that can make a positive difference for us. I'd like to list just as few as food for thought. We couldn't possible touch on these in this chapter, but here are some that describe Christian Values: Courage, faithfulness, humility, perseverance, resourcefulness, self-discipline, wisdom, work, devotion, faith, holiness, joyfulness, obedience, prayerfulness, repentance, love, honesty, thankfulness, compassion, forgiveness, friendliness, kindness, unselfishness. *Which of these or how many do you feel are evident in your conversation or in your lifestyle?*

Do words really matter all that much? Oh, come on Regina, life is going to give us what it will anyway. We can't change that. You know, Que Sera, Sera — what will be, will be. No, I'm sorry; I don't believe that for a moment. If that's the case, then why ever do anything that would promote a healthy, happy life? Because whether you eat greasy cheeseburgers, or grilled chicken and romaine salads, what's going to happen is going to happen. I promise you that is as far from truth as anything I've ever heard. I believe truth, and truth says there is power in my words. God's word is truth and that's what He says. I choose abundant life. I choose blessings. I choose favor. I choose health. I choose the best that God has to offer me.

Now saying those words, expressing those statements, does that automatically make me immune to everything bad that might happen — such as tragedy, sickness, financial struggles, disappointment? No, it doesn't make anyone immune. This isn't some magically formula. But it sure builds our inner faith so that if and when those times do come, we have a foundation built on a belief that *"All things are working together for good,"* because we are passionate about God and *"called according to His purpose."* Romans 8:28.

People who are achievers that reach their goals are continually sowing positive words into their lives. People don't fail because they fall down or get discouraged. They only fail if they stay down or stay defeated and don't get back up and get back in the fight! We can't tailor make our situations in life, but we can tailor make our attitudes and our words toward them as they arrive.

I sincerely believe at times, we even hinder our own prayers from being answered because we are continually praying the problem. God does not want us to live in perpetual frustration, or constant begging. He deeply desires us to believe when we pray that he will answer. That He is more willing to give than we are to receive. So we pray, but not in the negative.

This is a negative prayer of desperation:
"Oh God, what are we going to do? We're desperate - things are so bad and they're just getting worse. If something doesn't happen soon, we have no idea what we are going to do, or what is going to happen to us. You've just got to do something God, where are You? What is going on? Why aren't You taking care of us? Don't You even hear us or plan to answer our cries for help?"

This is a positive prayer of affirmation:
"Heavenly Father, we know that You are, God. You are our Father. You said in Your word that if we know how to give gifts as earthly parents, how much more will You, provide for us. So we thank You because you keep Your promises. You know that we live in a real world with frustrating situations, but we know that You are greater than any problem we will ever face. You will either give us the strength to endure, and the wherewithal to handle it, or You are going to completely remove this adversity from our lives in a miraculous way. So we praise You for the victory! We praise You for the provision. We praise You for doing what only You can do because you are God, and nothing is impossible for You! Nothing is too hard for You. We praise You for every miracle and blessing."

When our prayers become more about Him, than us, positive change begins to unfold. Praise is key and quoting scripture moves the hand of God, reminding Him of His Word. *Does this in some way communicate the difference?* We can pray positively, still sharing the need, or we can pray with futility and hopelessness. The confession of our words can hinder the very hand of God in a sense, because we're receiving exactly what we're asking for.

Proverbs 18:21 says, *"Death and life are in the power of the tongue, and those who love it will eat its fruit."* Do you want to eat the fruit of life or death? So where can we begin, right now that will help us start using words of life?

1. **Make a decision today, with the help of the Holy Spirit to become more positive**. Decide also to believe God's word and to keep His promises. I John 4:4 says, *"You are of God little children, and have overcome them; because greater is he that is in you than he that is in the world."* Our tongue cannot be controlled easily in our strength or natural ability. We will fall short. But when we accept Christ and allow the Holy Spirit to be mighty in us, He becomes greater. He increases and I decrease. He will give us the power to speak words of life and not death.

2. **Today, I will *"Bless the Lord at all times and forget not all His benefits"*** Psalms 103:2. With my mouth I confess words of life and blessing. I choose to walk in that. I will not allow the devil to attach his lies and deceit in my mind, and will "take every thought captive" by the power of God. I refuse to whine and complain regardless of how bleak my situation may seem or how much adversity may come my way. I will praise Him. I heard this little quote a long time ago: "God could turn water into wine, but he can do nothing with our whining!"

The power of words is not only in the speaking, but in the doing. Taking action. *"But do you want to know, O foolish man, that faith without works is dead."* James 2:20. Words must be lived out. Words become fully active as we walk them out. For example: I can't say I'm going to prosper and never work a day in my life, or follow God's instruction in giving. Nor can I say I'm going to be in good health and abuse my body by eating the wrong foods and never getting any exercise, etc. I could have said one day a book is going to be published with my name as the author, yet had never prepared a manuscript or taken the necessary steps to bring it to fruition. Speaking the words, then following them in action, brings the manifestation.

This has been a very challenging chapter—one not easily written. It has brought great conviction to my own heart, and a fresh awareness of how important words are for the *Rekindling of Our Passion for Jesus* to take place. It is also a topic that will never be finished. It's inexhaustible. So I'm closing with a comical story. Let's lighten up a little as we conclude this chapter.

A little old lady had prayed year after year that a tavern at the bottom of the hill where she lived would burn down. It obviously wasn't going out of business. The noise was excruciating and there was such mischief and drinking.

She entered her church week after week with the same prayer request. Please pray for that horrible, satan filled place to burn to the ground. I don't want anyone to be hurt, but pray. Please speak out those words to God so that this place of the devil will no longer tempt people to sin!

*Not too many weeks later, she entered the church on Sunday and a clan of inquisitive folks stood near with apparent excitement on their faces. "Oh, Mrs. Ruthbee, the tavern, it's gone! God finally answered all our prayers. He heard our words of request." The elderly lady smiled from ear to ear and replied, "Yep it sure is gone, isn't it? But I don't think it was just our prayers or the words of request we spoke. I believe it was also that I finally decided to put **action** to my prayers!"*

GODLY WORDS
PUT INTO ACTION
ARE SPIRIT AND LIFE!

7

PASSION EQUALS POSITION
"Finding the Place of God's Richest Blessings"

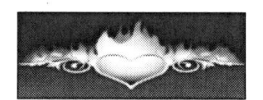

From the beginning of time, *position* has always mattered to God. Placement: the order of things. When He created the universe each planet had a precise home in the heavens to orbit without colliding. Creator God was specific and intentional in His arrangement of the sun. Isn't it pretty miraculous that He didn't position it too close to the earth and cause our bodies to get terribly burned when we went outside? He perfectly placed the moon, and creatively splashed the heavens with millions of stars. He precisely positioned the Milky Way galaxy, the constellation of seven bright stars in the Ursa Major and the constellation of seven bright stars in the Ursa Minor, (also known as the Big and Little Dippers), and spoke the stratosphere, hemisphere and atmosphere into existence exactly where He wanted them to be.

Everything God created had a specified habitation. The mountains—grand and ominous, the seas home for amphibious creatures—the forests, flowers and meadows, all situated with precision for beauty and functionality. The birds of the air were given wings strategically positioned for flight—the field animals were given four legs for standing and running. We see God didn't place their four legs in a row down the middle of their bodies; that would have been just little strange looking, not to mention completely unmanageable. Birds migrate south for the winter for warmer weather (as do some people). Salmon know the exact time to swim the current upstream to spawn. Lions live in the scorching deserts of Africa; polar bears in the bitter cold. They are all strategically placed, on purpose; positioned where they could survive, thrive and multiply. Position matters – Place matters.

God also perfectly placed man, in a perfectly prepared place. But, alas, we messed up so we ended up *out of place and lost from our position of blessing—banned from the beauty of perfection*, out in the cold, heat, weeds, wind and rain. He didn't leave us completely desolate. He placed resourcefulness and skills within us so it wasn't long before man began to grow gardens and create beauty all around to enjoy. Though the Garden of Eden was now a place no longer accessible, God continued to bless mankind in the place that he was—in the position He'd created him to fill in spite of his sin.

History continues to move forward. Now and forever position will matter to God. Heaven is in the perfect place He's designed and prepared; as is the place of torment, called Hell. He cares about where we are right now, both spiritually and physically. I believe position matters so much that we can actually even live in a physical place outside of His perfect will. When we do, we won't experience His richest blessings. He's called us to certain places for certain purposes. If we're not where God wants us to be, then we will be missing what God has for us to do. You've heard the old saying, *"Bloom where you are planted."* Sometimes, let's face it, the soil has not been prepared, nor will it ever be ready for us in certain towns, cities or states, even countries, because we just weren't meant to be there. You may be thinking, *"How in the world would you know?"* Oh, believe me, if you're in Christ, and you're seeking His will, you know. *There's perfect peace in the perfect will of God.* That pertains to place and position. When you are not where He wants you to be, you'll feel and be completely and totally miserable. There have been times, looking at homes within a city, (and I'm not talking about location in the sense of lower income, etc) similar areas where prices of homes are in about the same range, that I would drive into the neighborhood and just feel it. This is not where I am supposed to live. There was nothing wrong with the area—lovely yards, probably nice people—but I just knew it was not where God wanted me. When we are in the right place, not just passionately in our walk with the Lord, but physically in the place where He wants us to be, there will be peace and serenity.

There were a few times our family moved that I would hear Mom and Dad say, *"We just shouldn't have made this move. We knew it, but we did it anyway, and now we are completely out of the will of God. We are not where He wants us to be."* I didn't fully understand this at the time, but as the months went by, I too could feel the tension, the unrest, the "out of the will of God" atmosphere. Life was hard, in a different way. As a family we weren't experiencing the same kind of peace that we'd previously known before we moved. There was unrest and turmoil in our spirits. It wasn't calm. And there also seemed to be financial challenges we hadn't known before moving.

We've probably all heard the saying, "Bloom where you're planted." Yes, and No. One cannot bloom in soil they're not supposed to be planted in. As we desire to grow in our passion for Christ we realize and even come to understand that *position* really does matter. The more our passion grows, the more clearly we hear His voice and the more we understand what this means and how powerfully it can affect our impact for Christ. This may sound a little strange to some of you who may have been born in one town, grew up, married, and are still living in the same town now with your own wife or husband & children. *You know what?* Chances are you are right where you are supposed to be, it's a family thing.

We can bloom beautifully when we are at peace living where we feel God has called us to live. Place matters also in how God's plan will be fulfilled in using us. But we can only know this, IF we hear his voice. His voice becomes clearer with intimacy.

There are others, particularly people called into specific ministries, who have to move "for the sake of the call." There also might be families separated by work, or the military, or vocational placement. There are a myriad of reasons people face choices about relocating. That's when decisions have to be made. These must be *bathed* in prayer. Never move just for money, or convenience, or for just selfish, personal reasons. Move if, and only if, you know without a shadow of a doubt it is God instructing you to do so or guiding you—or that is it is okay with Him. I believe this kind of decision should be made only after *much prayer,* and seeking HIS direction. There should be intercession about any move. *Haste,* in deciding about place or position, *really does make waste!*

Years ago, a personal experience opened my eyes in even a deeper way to this truth. It happened through an Aunt and Uncle of mine who left their home of many years in Missouri to move to Charlotte, NC, to help in ministry.

Bookings had been scheduled in Springfield for both a Women's Conference at their church and a 6 day concert tour in the area. Since their church was hosting the Friday - Saturday Women's Conference, and I was to be there also for the Sunday AM worship service—they invited me to stay with them, making their home my *base* for the tour. I was thrilled. It was such a joy for me to be able to stay with them and get to know them a little better. I had not actually been acquainted with them like Mom's other sisters. They were new in the faith, hungry and already on fire for the Lord! Though most of their adult lives were spent outside the *fold* -when the Lord saved them, He radically saved them. They were glowing and growing new Christians.

We were together about ten days. Of course I was in and out, but we did have some very special times to visit, and shop, play—even time to pray together, and they had the opportunity to become better acquainted with my ministry. During my stay, somehow, the Lord seemed to impress upon them, especially on Uncle Roy's heart, to become more involved and help more in my ministry. By the end of my tour as I was packing my car to leave, they had decided to make a trip to Charlotte in the next month or so. They were seriously considering leaving Springfield to come and work in my ministry. Aunt Laura & Uncle Roy had been retired for a number of years, but had so much to give. He has a great head for business, and she—well, there's little she's not gifted in. I was absolutely stunned, but thrilled, totally ecstatic! Of course we'd discussed the need in my ministry, but never in my wildest dreams had I thought they would move, or even consider leaving their home of however many years they'd lived there. The thought of having family near filled me with more joy that I could express.

It was just a short time and they arrived in Charlotte to visit. They wanted to look over the area and get a feel for things—I thought. They were in my home only a week or so, and my Uncle came in to tell me they had made the decision. They were moving. He had already found an apartment and put a deposit on it. They both loved to golf, and there was a course nearby. *They found an apartment complex named after a golf course in Florida, surely that was a sign.* He'd made arrangements to hook up their telephone, utilities, just everything. It was crazy. I was in a tailspin, questioning them, and saying Uncle Roy, you need to pray about this, don't make this decision so quickly. Are you sure this is what you both want to do? Is this what God is instructing you to do?

He is much older and much wiser, so I didn't push the issue any more. Of course, more than anything I wanted them to be there. But, was the decision made too quickly? Had they given sufficient time to pray about it and make sure it was God's timing and God's place? The decision had been made and they felt the Lord was calling them to position them to work with me in the ministry.

Probably this side of heaven I will never really understand what happened. There's nothing that I can surmise (or conclude) for certain was the reason. They moved to Charlotte, but stayed only six months and went back to Springfield. Their decision to move back was made as quickly as their decision to come. But their living close to me, and their contribution to the ministry, was the most joyous time of my life. It was wonderful having them there. My heart was thrilled to have them work, but when they wanted to golf or have time to rest that was fine too. They chose their hours to work in the office, I was happy if they were happy. They were a tremendous blessing and help to me. But, it seemed as though this place just wasn't right; the traffic, the bigger city, their health. Could it have been their hearts were still in Springfield? And maybe, just maybe, though they thought it was God's will to move, that this was the place they were supposed to be, but it wasn't. And the peace they should have felt and the joy they should have experienced in this position was not the perfect will of God after all?

My heart was broken, of course, when they left, but I also understood that they and we must be in the place, the position God has called us to be, not where we think we might want to be. WE must be led out of a passion for Christ, and obedient to His calling on our lives individually and not for any other reason. Not for the love of someone else—not even out of compassion, but solely because it is God's place, and God's position for us. Otherwise, it will never be successful.

Let me share yet another quite different scenario. If God, in all of His wisdom, had created the majestic Redwood then planted it in Hawaii or Southern Texas, would it have survived? Not. The weather is not conducive to growing Redwood trees. It's just plain too hot all year. Redwoods were not made to grow and thrive in hot, dry temperatures. God created them to grow in a moderate climate, more cool than hot, in lush shady groves with lots of moisture. Neither will a Redwood grow in below freezing temperatures of constant snow, freezing rain or ice. They are planted and placed, exactly where God knew they would flourish. I lived among these beautiful trees most of my life in Northern California. There's nothing more beautiful, but I've never seen them in Southern Texas or Hawaii.

So it is with us. We must be in the place we can thrive because He created us for a particular reason to occupy a special place in His creation. In that place and in that position we will know His peace, experience His hand, and be used by Him for the Kingdom. We can confidently know that we are precisely in the place He desires for us for His greatest purposes to be fulfilled in and through our lives.

THE PLACE OF DIVINE FAVOR

Did you know that we can do nothing to change the vastness of God's love toward us? His love is unconditional, unending. But *favor* is not the same as love. Favor is one of the most incredibly unique gifts from God. It is a marvelous and powerful, yet weighty thing. **Favor** is ***an act of kindness beyond what is due or usual; to esteem, or show approval, goodwill, generous treatment, aid, support. Favor means to experience special advantages; being preferred; affluent, blessed, prosperous, chosen, selected; smiled upon, or promoted.*** So when we add the word divine to the word favor, it is a very powerful, life changing combination.

Divine favor is transforming. It can change one's life forever. Experiencing one day of favor, one person finding favor with another, one situation or moment crowned with favor, one unexpected opportunity or chance meeting of favor — can catapult a lifetime of struggle into promotion and blessing — advantage and prosperity. If you've never experienced it, pray that you will. If you have, pray that it will continue. The blessing of divine favor on our lives is so powerful. It births new meaning to what once seemed an almost futile, meagerly inspired life.

How do we find the place of divine favor?

I believe that divine favor comes in three specific ways.

First, as we align ourselves with God's Word — as we believe, confess, and even claim His promises as our own — as we, by faith lay hold God's Word, asking the Holy Spirit to pour favor into our lives as He would any other blessing. Favor also comes in direct proportion to our love and honor for God.

Second, it is given to certain people specifically, even without their asking by God's design. He imparts divine favor on special people by His own choosing, in His own timing, for His own reasons.

Third, it is a part of our maturing in Christ through adversity, preparing us for the work that He has designed and anointed us to accomplish on earth. We grow in divine favor as we overcome adversity and walk in victory, fulfilling our calling in Christ with joy.

Mary, the mother of Jesus, must surely have already been walking in divine favor with God. I don't believe for a moment God had one of the angels in heaven draw straws or toss a coin to decide who would be *chosen*. We find no biblical record of what brought about the decision. All we know is that God had obviously observed this young handmaiden and knew she was made of the stuff that could handle such an assignment. She was favored for a purpose. It was manifested in her life when her response to the angel of the Lord was, as recorded in Luke 1:38, *"Behold the maidservant of the Lord. Let it be to me according to your word."* She believed and trusted God. As our relationship with Christ deepens, and our passion grows, favor is one of the blessings that God brings into our lives, and is, in itself, a part of maturing in Him.

Those of us who have grown up in the church and believe that God loves everyone the same, may have to rethink this idea. It may be true, but the scripture tells us that even Jesus had to grow *"in favor with God and man."* Luke 2:52. That's quite a unique verse. Understandably He may have found it necessary to grow in favor with man, but growing in favor with God--His own Father? What is that about? He was in fact already perfect, right? Could it be the answer to that is found in the fact that Jesus functioned as a man? He laid aside His divine nature so that He could become the model for us. So, Jesus, as we, had to be tested. Though He was a God-Man, he received His anointing at His Baptism as the Spirit descended on Him and remained. That's when the Father declared Him to be the Son of God. But Jesus didn't go right into ministry at that moment. Rather, He was to begin a journey of testing in the wilderness. The same culprit who continues to test and intimidate, also tested Jesus. He was led into the wilderness to be tempted by the devil. Luke 4:1 confirms that Jesus went in to His testing period *filled with the Holy Spirit* but in verse 14 we are told that He returns *"in the power of the Spirit."* So, He was filled, but the power came after He passed His time of testing. He had received favor, the favor to embrace and walk in His potential in a greater measure than ever before. He did this by meeting the enemy head on with the Word of God.

This favor that Jesus matured in during His time of temptation could be defined as *"the divine grace and empowerment of God being placed upon one qualifying them to accomplish His purposes."*

THE PLACE OF PROMOTION

Then there is King David. So much comes to mind as we think of this mighty man of God. He was just a shepherd boy in the fields tending sheep while his brothers fought battles with the Philistines. The visit, bringing lunch to his brothers, who were not fighting this giant, but David came in the name of the Lord. The five smooth stones and a slingshot with which he dispatched Goliath, one of our favorite Sunday School stories. There are others such as, the bear, the lion and David playing his harp to soothe Saul's savage soul. (say that 10 times fast!) *But what do we remember most about Him, other than the blatant sin he committed with Bathsheba?* He stands high above all other patriarchs in the Old Testament. We remember him not so much for the impact of his actions, but for his *passionate* heart. While he was still in obscurity, God saw Him as a *"man after His own heart."* Acts 13:22. That's what continues to set him apart in our eyes and minds as we read about him and his writings. Even before he was a great warrior with military victories—before he brought about dramatic changes in the nature of worship in Israel and ushered in what is referred to as Israel's *Golden Age* of spiritual and economic prosperity— David's heart was full of passion, tender, contrite and one of love like God's.

What evidence do we have to base this on, what proof? The Bible records two essential aspects of David's life that were evident before he was anointed king.

First: When David was totally alone, not at the temple or in public gatherings, it was then that he poured out his heart to God; he praised, worshipped, sang and prayed while in the fields tending his father's sheep. When no one was watching (which proves genuine relationship), he hungered and thirsted for intimacy with God, and it was manifested by His evident desire to continually spend time in his presence. That alone speaks volumes. David was hungry for God before the idea of such a thing was ever thought about. This is Old Testament, God—was God. Man feared and revered Him, but there wasn't a whole lot of passion or intimacy known or experienced during that time. This was the God who blazed the Ten Commandments on tablets of stone, and parted the Red Sea—intimacy with Him? We know that Abraham also walked and talked with God. This time these people lived was a totally different era. Jesus had not yet come, and the Holy Spirit had not yet been sent as He is today. Yet, David adored God constantly because of His love and passion for Him. This is huge. This is what it's all about. We are strengthened in our inner man and in our walk with Christ as we worship God in private, and spend time in His presence when no one is around. That's when we will receive divine instruction and guidance. This is genuine relationship — not religion.

How many people go to church and serve God just because it keeps their reputation looking good? Often our faithfulness to the Lord comes more from the need to please others and make ourselves look good in the eyes of the community, rather than because our hearts are fervent and hungry for more of Him. We wouldn't want people to miss *seeing* us worship. Not so with David. He heart was so attuned and interconnected with God that His love for Him flowed even while he was caring for sheep or rescuing them from wolves.

One of the reasons for making this point is remind us that during David's lifetime, Israel's worship was focused on animal sacrifice offerings providing temporary atonement for sin. Worshipping with a sacrifice of praise from the heart, as David did, was not taught or even heard of, let alone practiced; this kind of heart is what led David to a relationship with God Himself, way beyond the Jewish teaching or the letter of the law.

Second: David had an unparalleled faith, a trust in God for victory. His faith in God is what gave him the strength and courage to slay the lion and the bear, and even more so when he killed Goliath. He knew it would take far more than a tiny slingshot and a stone. There had to be a supernatural thrust behind the stone when it hit Goliath to do more than knock him out — even if he was a perfect shot. This is evident by his response to the mammoth Philistine. I Samuel 17:42-46 *"And when the Philistine looked about and saw David, he disdained him; for he was but a youth, ruddy and good-looking. So the Philistine said to David, "Am I a dog that you come to me with sticks?' And the Philistine cursed David by his gods. And the Philistine said to David, 'Come to me, and I will give your flesh to the birds of the air and the beasts of the field!' Then David said to the Philistine, 'You come to me with a sword, with a spear, and with a javelin. But I come to you in the name of the* LORD *of hosts, the God of the armies of Israel, whom you have defiled. This day the Lord will deliver you into my hand, and I will strike you and take your head from you...*

that all the earth may know that there is a God in Israel.'" You see, we can never face the giants in our lives, if we have no faith in the Lord, or if we have not spent time in His presence so that our faith grows. That's why David was filled with great faith—and that great faith motivated him—both in saying no to wearing Saul's armor and in his willingness to obey God by picking up the stones and using such an inferior weapon. He completely relied upon and trusted God to defeat this intimidating giant. This trust was indicative that David's heart for God didn't vacillate because of circumstances. His heart was filled with integrity. Neither was he doing it to receive the glory. I Samuel 17:37.

Though David was just a shepherd boy, God saw a King. But even though he was chosen for this place of leadership, David was not taken from the pasture to the palace. He was the last choice when Samuel came to his father's house to find one to anoint among the sons of Jesse. Though seemingly hidden away, **he was not hidden from the eyes of God**, or Samuel. But even after he was anointed to be king, it was 10-13 years before he would assume the throne. In those interim years, the difficulty, persecution, and rejection that David endured (more than most might face in a lifetime) prepared him for leadership. *Do you think he anticipated it taking so long for him to fulfill His calling?* Probably not—kind of like us; once we know that God has called us for a particular work or ministry, we feel it should happen immediately. We should just be able to jump in and get going. Why waste time? Most often that does not happen - there must be a grooming time. A time of preparation to ready us for labor and leadership if we are to successfully accomplish His destiny plans. The process of preparation is as important for the work as the plan. God knows when we are ready for our assign-ment. Saul on the other hand didn't face this kind of difficulty or even waiting period.

We still see and feel this same impatience today. Seemingly some ministries step into their destiny and overnight explode with success and exposure. That can be good and bad. With

Passion Equals Position

Saul, it was obviously bad. And God didn't want another King Saul. At one time, Saul was truly the best man that Israel had to offer. I Samuel 8:6. But the problem came when it was evident that Saul's heart had not been readied or proven through testing before the crown was placed on his head. There was a measure of anointing that was automatically entrusted to Saul as king. This was to enable him to lead the people and guide the Israeli army's to victory. Ultimately the hidden weaknesses of Saul's heart toward God were exposed. This revelation came due to his lack of character which had never been strengthened through winning private battles or crucial circumstances in which he would have had to ultimately trust in God, as David had. The public victories Saul had brought a bright light to the hidden darkness of Saul's heart toward God. Besides that, this king had a huge appetite for the applause of men. He wanted the glory and he disobeyed God as a leader. So what was initially entrusted to make him successful ultimately, because of an untested heart, destroyed him.

DELAYED PROMOTION

Even though David already had the heart of a king, he was led into years of testing. *Why?* So that he would be groomed and equipped to firmly stand in the glory and the responsibility of the throne. We read of scriptural accounts in I Samuel of this season in David's life—filled with character lessons and tests that each of us encounter on the road as we fulfill God's divine destiny. *But what is it that ultimately qualifies us, or David, to receive the promise?* What is it that finally, once and for all qualifies us, causing God to say, "Okay, he or she is ready?" Could it be that in the midst of all this turmoil, David did not whine or complain or question what God was doing? He did not bemoan his circumstances or ask God what in the world He was thinking? After all, he had been anointed King. David never thought in his heart (that we find record of), nor did he say, *"Why should I have to encounter or endure such hardship? After all, I'm special. Years ago Samuel poured oil on my head and told me I was chosen. What is taking you so long, God, for you to place me on the throne?"* David patiently endured, because of his unwavering, trustful heart that he was confident that God knew what He was doing. That was obviously never an issue for David. This attribute must certainly have been one that proved he was ready.

Could it also be found in his or our ability to do the right thing in the face of deepest betrayal and rejection, standing completely alone — to respond in the right way? Not with self pity, but with open eyes that completely trust in God. To believe He knows what He's doing. He knows what we are genuinely made of; that our response would be *"to strengthen ourselves in the Lord"* as David did? I Samuel 30:6 *"Then David was greatly distressed, for the people spoke of stoning him, because the soul of all the people was grieved, every man for his sons and his daughters. But David* **strengthened himself in the LORD his God.**"

Even in this encounter David could have retreated, become defeated and despondent. He could have just given up. That's what we sometimes do by our actions and by our words. We throw in the towel. We take a knee. But David did not. No, he displayed his strong, deep, full root system in God. Once again he trusted and strengthened himself, not in his own abilities or even in the anointing he'd been given, but rather in the Source. David was *dead* to things that affected the flesh, and alive in God so much that he was not moved.

Mother used to mentor me especially in the times of my life I felt distressed and abandoned and she would say, *"Regina, a dead man feels nothing. You know I'm not talking about the human part of us; I'm talking about the spiritual. The Lord is trying to get his bride — you and me — to a place where all the stuff just doesn't matter anymore. It doesn't bother us or discourage us in our walk with Him. We aren't moved or influenced by satanic attacks or the negative things people do or say. If we can reach that place, then God has accomplished what He set out to do in this process of making us more like Jesus — useable for the kingdom."* Sometimes I really struggled with this because it made me feel like the Lord was looking for perfection. Mom was a perfectionist. But now, I truly understand what she was saying. God isn't looking for perfect people, He's looking for people willing to do what David did—not be so easily offended or discouraged when things don't fall into place in the timeframe we'd anticipated, or even in the way we'd planned. The right response is to continue to trust Him, and strengthen ourselves in the Lord, our God.

The last reason I believe that made David ready to reign as king was that in everything he did, it was never about him receiving the glory. Over and over again David reiterated that his strength came from the Lord. The battle was the Lords; God was the one who gave every victory. David never had an ego that advanced or promoted self. Not only was he able to stand up under rejection, and not question the Lord's timing or actions, but he also stayed humble knowing that God was the one who was mighty.

PROMOTION ON THE HORIZON, NOT

Even in David's life, there had been years of apparent success. Because of his intimacy with the Lord, he had great courage and had been set apart as no other man in Israel. His righteous indignation against the enemies that taunted the armies of God showed this courage. He had favor in his victories, moved into the palace, befriended the king's son, and married the king's daughter. Everything looked pretty much like it was moving in the right direction; the fulfillment of Samuel's prophecy was on the horizon.

But something happened. King Saul became jealous. Good ol' King Saul heard some women in the city singing—not his praises—but David's. *"Saul has killed his thousands and David his ten thousands."* Jealousy is a deadly weapon, a devilish trait. Saul immediately became consumed with anger, intent on ending David's life. This began the painful dodging, and then running from Saul's attacks. Once loved and embraced by a king, David's own father-in-law now hunted him like an animal. He left his home in Jerusalem completely unaware that this madman would pursue him for over a decade as far away from the kingship as possible. This rejection by Saul was probably the greatest test in the internship David was serving to become king. Would he believe and walk in the Word over his life, even when the situation looked completely the opposite—even denying his destiny? This entire epilogue was not playing out as planned. The beginning had looked so promising, so perfect.

In the midst of every battle David faced, God gave him the ability to master his own distress, see beyond offense, and stay focused on his purpose and vision. He never collapsed under pressure. He not only kept from death, he led others to victory. These are the strong character traits of an anointed leader. These strengths enabled him to stand at the door that was just about to open. The very darkest hours of his life prepared and lead him to the divine destiny God had ordained for Him to be crowned King of Israel.

ULTIMATE PROMOTION

David wasn't just crowned king; he was a great king. The anointed shepherd boy did indeed walk in his divine destiny. Though he was human, and failed, yet his heart was always toward God. He was repentant and contrite, broken, and healed. He served the nation under God's authority and through His divine guidance.

But this ultimate promotion is not the end of the story. The truest importance of David's promotion from the pasture to the palace is seen primarily in his kingly legacy. It would have been historical enough had David only written the Psalms, brought to fruition an unprecedented style of worship in Jerusalem and created architectural plans for the Temple and ushered in the *Golden Age*. But here's the most incredible part of David's kingship—he was so indispensable to God that he was named *the forerunner* of Jesus, the Messiah. Throughout the eons of time Jesus would be known as the Son of David.

He would sit on David's throne. This is huge. Because of the favor and calling of God, David's promotion altered the course of history forever.

The life of this great man—shepherd boy to king—hasn't been recorded just to inspire us. He wasn't a superhero. That's evident by the accounts of his sins. But it is indeed a call to all of us as believers. It should awaken us from our sleep. It should open our eyes to see that one man—a sinner who lived hundreds of years before the Cross, before the Holy Spirit had been sent to earth—could come into such a place of favor with God. *Why then, would we, being forgiven and cleansed by the blood, having the gift of the Holy Spirit not be able to embrace Him in even a greater measure?* Why would we not be more inspired about our rekindling our passion for Jesus? David had only God. And then, in that passionate pursuit take our position on the earth to fulfill our destiny?

God is not the one responsible for us reaching our potential. We are. He can call us and equip us but we have to take action. David could have been given every chance to take the kingship and ignored it. We must engage ourselves and focus. We must walk in obedience. In some things we take action, in others we wait. If David had killed Saul—justifiably so—rather than allowing God to handle it, chances are he would have never seen a crown placed on his head, and history would not have unfolded as it did. We have been called to take our rightful places, just as David was. But God must know that He can trust us with His secrets, the plans of His heart, and be ready to serve. He has to know that we will not use the anointing or favor He imparts to us for our own purposes, but always for the furthering of the Kingdom and His glory.

THE PLACE OF SPIRITUAL STRENGTH

Where does our spiritual strength come from? Men and women by the millions join health clubs to "work out" and become physically fit. They want to strengthen their bodies and enable themselves to function more successfully at work and play, and to look and feel better. Somehow we have failed to recognize this necessity in the kingdom. It's impossible to live victoriously, let alone endure the onslaught of the enemy, without strength—spiritual strength.

Our passion for Jesus will never increase without daily work-outs that strengthen us in Him. These have to be scheduled—planned— just as physical ones are. David joined Jehovah's gym. He opened the instruction manual daily. He used the equipment provided. He raised his hands and voice to God, joyfully giving Him praise and worship. He ministered or strengthened himself in the Lord. Athletes never reach their goals or ultimate dreams without preparation and the daily sacrifice of strengthening themselves in the regimen necessary to equip them for victory.

The same is true in the realm of spiritual destiny, where this incredible abundant life awaits those who will embrace and experience it. The richest blessings of God flow into our lives as we strengthen ourselves in Him. Our passion increases for Him. There is a deeper peace and joy that accompanies life. We are able to hear His voice more clearly. It becomes second nature to trust Him, rather than our own abilities or choices. David was able to make the right decision, at the right time, with his heart not his head because he was so in tune with God. They must have had almost *synchronized* heart beats.

Trees gain strength from not only the soil in their root system, but also from the sap found in the trunk itself and from the sun and rain. You notice we don't feed the trees, at least not the ones in the forest. We receive our strength also from the SON and the WATER, drawing from His Word developing a strong root system that broadens and deepens with growth. Strong trees stand firm and tall in the midst of most devastating storms. Weak trees bend, and sometimes even break. So it is with us.

We are not just called to stand firm and resolute, we are also called to strengthen ourselves in the Lord so that we can touch our *world* for Christ. Each one of us has a different size and kind of circle of influence, but we are called. I believe every person who kneels at the foot of the cross, accepting Christ as Savior, is called.

This calling requires *initiative*. One of the greatest qualities God looks for in His children is our initiative to seek Him in the *secret place*. Psalm 91:1 *'He who dwells in the secret place of the Most High shall abide under the shadow of the Almighty. I will say of the* LORD, *He is my refuge and my fortress; My God in Him I will trust."* The secret place is anywhere we choose to be alone with God. It can be a room or specific place set aside in your home that you go to be with the Lord. That is the ideal if it's possible because we have a place for everything else: A garage for our cars, a closet for our clothing, a bedroom to sleep in, and a kitchen in which to cook. Whatever the case, we need a place to be undistracted so we can focus. If we are to rekindle our passion for Jesus, it's crucial to have a time and a place given only for Him to praise, worship and adore the Lord and for Him to adore, love, and speak to us. *Does that sound foreign or strange to you?* Then I encourage you, my friend, to take a trip to this strange and foreign place yourself. Experience how wonderful it is. It is the only place to be strengthened in the Lord. So when the winds of adversity blow, and the raging storms of life overtake you, you will be able to stand firm, and tall, and strong. I promise you, once you've journeyed there, you will want to go again and again! Corporate worship is great. We all need it. But in order for us to be fully equipped for God's service, we must possess the *initiative* to seek His face in the secret place. It is then that we will be strengthened in Him in a far deeper measure, preparing, equipping and enabling us to fulfill His calling.

Just as in David's life, being strengthened serves as the foundation for spiritual longevity. We need sustaining faith because victorious Christian living is not easy. We need sustaining faith also because sometimes it is years before we see our potential or destiny come to fruition. We have to be equipped to stay in the race for years and years to come. As we discover the truths that guide us in becoming strong in the Lord, we then appropriate them and continually use them to develop huge spiritual *muscles to* defeat the enemy and remain victorious.

Now, please understand the concept I'm endeavoring to portray. Strengthening ourselves doesn't mean nurturing an independent lifestyle. As Christians our lifestyle is focused on serving, loving, encouraging and depending on the body of Christ. But in order for us to mature in the favor of God, He allows times of testing and adversity in our lives when we may have to stand alone so we can be a blessing to others. This could be an opportune time to become bitter or angry with the Lord, feeling as though no one cares or we have been rejected during these very difficult times. Again, we see how David responded, and that's what God desires for us. Always being cognizant that there are lessons He has designed for us to learn - to teach us to avoid this trap and continue on in rekindling our passion for Him. He's teaching us to lean on His strength, not the arm of flesh, because it will miserably fail.

Briefly I would like to share a few tools that have kept me focused and continue to keep me aware of how important it is to strengthen myself in the Lord so that my *passion* for Him will bring about the *position* He is designing for His destiny plan.

TOOLS FOR THE JOURNEY TO PROMOTION

1. STAY DEFINED AND SECURE IN GOD'S PLAN

Don't let anything or anyone ever cause you to lose sight of God's plan for your life, regardless of how long it seems to take. Keep focused and connected even when you may not be actively pursuing it. This includes watching over your heart; our thinking and hearts are definitely connected. Proverbs 23:7. *"As he thinks in his heart, so is he..."* The heart actually houses our imagination, desires, will, mind, affections, emotions, conscience and memory. We become what we behold. We continue in agreement with what is unseen —

Passion Equals Position

God's agenda, not satan's, not our own. The devil can make problems seem a lot bigger than they really are. Our passion and intimacy with the Lord, which is the most effective way to guard our hearts, is the strategy needed for the release of solutions and blessings.

2. *USE PRAISE TO CAUSE THE DEVIL TO FLEE*

Nothing causes the enemy to retreat like our praise. He hates praise because it is the optimal way of expressing our love and trust in God. Praise opens doors of blessing and strengthens our passion for Jesus. David was especially strong in this area. He praised God continually—sometimes even in the midst of disaster. Psalm 103:1 *"Bless the Lord O my soul; And all that is within me, bless His Holy name."* Praise needs to become our lifestyle. It keeps us aware of God's presence. As long as we know that nothing can ever be greater than Him, we will live in victory. Praise, with rejoicing, cancels the cloud of oppression and wrong assignment or agreement upon our lives. One last very important note: Praise actually creates a place in our circumstances for King Jesus to truly be Lord allowing His kingdom to prevail in our lives, which in fact destroys and disarms the kingdom of darkness. His light eradicates the darkness.

3. *ALLOW THE HOLY SPIRIT TO CONTINUE THE TRANSFORMING PROCESS*

As you know from previous chapters, one of my *loves* is Interior Decorating. It is quite fulfilling to take a house that needs to be gutted and remodeled, then with strategic planning, budget and materials, watch the transformation unfold. It is challenging, but rewarding. It is, in today's youthful verbiage—like, so cool! We are, as a metaphor in scripture, *the house of God*. I Peter 2:5 *"You also, as living stones, are being built up a spiritual house, a holy priesthood, to offer up spiritual sacrifices acceptable to God through Jesus Christ."* The moment we accept Christ, and the Holy Spirit moves in, we have agreed to an ongoing process of spiritual transformation and renovation. God desires that we become a house that can completely express the glorious nature of Him to the world. Our part is to let Him be the architect, let Him finish His handiwork in us.

4. *HOLD TO THE PROMISES - REPRESENT THE FATHER - POSITION TO RECEIVE*

David's declaration—His calling and anointing, came from Samuel. Yours may have been from God Himself, or in some another way. However it's given, never let go of the promise. Hold on tenaciously to the declaration—to what God said He would do. Don't allow anyone, anytime, to try and discourage or steal that calling from you. Don't let doubt or delay or detours cause you to lose sight of it. Proclaim the Word in faith, never questioning, believing it will come to fruition.

Be His representative—represent the Lord. Jesus *re-presented* God perfectly by doing all that the Father did, and by saying all that the Father said. That's one of the most glorious parts of the gospel. Jesus came ONLY because of God. It was His plan, and His purpose. It was God's LOVE for us—God's design to send Jesus. Jesus loved us because God did. *"For God so loved the world that HE gave His only begotten son..."* John 3:16. That's why Jesus said, *"If you've seen me you've seen the Father."* John 14:7. That too is our assignment. A relationship with Him so deep and so strong that we can say what Jesus did, if they know us, they will also know the God we love and serve.

We position ourselves for **God's Richest Blessings** as we continue to be faithful and constant in our time with Him, worshipping Him—listening, obeying and waiting without whining. The perfect positioning also comes as we remain attentive, persevering, and constantly ready to receive from Him all that He has to impart to us!

***Ultimately our PASSION
FOR CHRIST,
Positions us to fulfill
our DESTINY IN HIM!***

8

GO LIGHT YOUR WORLD
"The Power of Giving Jesus to Others"

In Chapter 7, we focused a great deal on David's life. Let's continue with more about his story taking a closer look into a revelation that transformed him, and will change anyone who embraces this truth—The Power of Giving.

Giving to others shows our gratitude for what Jesus has given to us. Can we even begin to grasp the magnitude of the gift we have received from God? Because of the Father's love for us, we have received an inheritance beyond measure. We have obtained victory over sin, hope and the glorious promise of heaven. Not to mention all the other blessings and joy we find in a life of serving the Lord. How do people live without Him? That's the question we want to answer. You see people who have never embraced this marvelous Jesus that we know, aren't really living; they just survive or exist in their world. They live without a *real* hope or a *real* purpose, or a promise of a *real* future. That's why we are compelled as never before to "win the lost—at any cost." Jesus said in Matthew 5:14-16 *"You are the light of the world. A city that is set on a hill cannot be hidden. Nor do they light a lamp and put it under a basket, but on a lampstand, and it gives light to all who are in the house. Let your light so shine before me, that they may see your good works and glo-*

rify your Father in heaven." This glorious Gospel that we have to share is more than enough to *"Light Our World!"*

During the time that David was *on the run* from Saul and waiting for the fulfillment of Samuel's prophecy to unfold, he and his men made Ziklag their home. This was a city located in southern Judea. For one year and four months all the families of David and his men had been living there. Not too much had transpired during this time. This was a period of waiting—an interim place for the "yet to be crowned" king of Israel. But there was still purpose in being where he was. It was all about continued preparation for the kingly throne, yet more training for battle, lessons to be taught and learned. Probably every person reading this book has been in their own personal Ziklag; you may be there even now, waiting patiently somewhere between promise and fulfillment. There were of course times to share about the wondrous victories God had given him; he had great testimonies of God's protection and intervention. These were moments *to light his world*, even though it seemed while he was there it was without incident; it was just the ordinary day in—day out living. Still, the process was necessary for the destiny plan to unfold as God had designed. Then, out of nowhere, *everything* changed.

The men had been away visiting a neighboring city about three day's journey from Ziklag and they were on their way home. As most guys would be, they were anxious to return to the comfort of their own homes, wives, and children. They traveled joyfully, drawing closer to their destination and eagerly anticipating their reunion, but as they approached visual distance they saw something horrifying. A, huge, ominous cloud of black smoke was rising directly above their city. First, they were stricken with anxiety and then total panic enveloped them as they swiftly rushed toward Ziklag, horrified at what calamity had befallen their friends and loved ones.

A CITY IN RUINS

When they arrived what they saw was worse than they even imagined. It was horrific. The city had been brutally attacked and completely destroyed. There wasn't a building or home left standing; it was a smoldering heap of devastation. Much to their amazement, in the midst of this warzone there were still a few sobbing, broken survivors. David was able to gather enough information from them to access what had happened. It was the Amalekites. A looting band of several thousand riding on camels attacked the city. They confiscated everything of value. Their herds and livestock, their possessions and, worst of all, they took their women and children captive. The hoarding bandits departed as swiftly as they had swooped in, taking the fortunes and families with them leaving Ziklag a pile of burning rubble.

Next time we think we've had a bad day; it would be a good thing to remember this story. It's true, so often we think we've had the worst things happen, kind of like the old adage, "I complained about the shoes I wore, until I saw the man who had no feet." So we hear of another's plight, and realize ours is not nearly as horrible as we first thought. But In the midst of total chaos David's proven track record remained true, he did not retreat. He first came to grips with what had happened. He wept, but moved from weeping to believing. He did what he did best. **He turned to God to show him the strategy for recovery.** There was a whole lot of rejection from David's men—they were angry, to say the least. So much so that David again feared for his life.

Through it all David remained focused and intent in his pursuit of the enemy. God gave him a plan of attack so that he and his men could avenge themselves on the Amalekites—so that they would be able to recover their families and possessions. The battle raged as these men seemed to attack with supernatural endurance but, as the sun began to set after twenty-four hours of fighting, they did indeed win the victory.

THE BATTLE OF THE CHRISTIAN FAITH

Could David's victory not serve as an example for us in the battle for our Christian faith – in the battle for our Christian witness? The devil has no intention of backing off from his pursuit to hinder and defeat our walk with Christ, and certainly not in our sharing Him with our world. He will do everything possible to thwart God's plan to war against us. He will, with concentrated effort even try to steal the very light of Christ within us.

Are we not in a state of warfare against the arch enemy of our souls? Are we not fighting against principalities and powers of darkness – wicked spirit beings who intentionally desire to rule the world and destroy our light? Yes, Ephesians 6:12 makes it clear. *"For we do not wrestle against flesh and blood, but against principalities, against powers, against the rulers of the darkness of this age, against spiritual hosts of wickedness in the heavenly places."* This is the real deal – a genuine struggle between good and evil, Holy and unholy. We cannot think for a moment that we can just lie down, pull the covers over our eyes, and pretend that it will all go away. We can't gaze upon a star in the heavens and wish it into oblivion. We can't just nonchalantly dream of a nice, happy, quiet place and *hope* that *fate* will smile on us. This warfare has been waging for eons of time and will continue until Jesus returns. We know that Christ has already defeated our foe, but as we go through our own personal battles, we have to stay in the fight, obey the Lord's instructions and follow His fighting strategies and tactics so we will overcome. The greatest truth about this warfare is that that we are destined to ultimately always win if we continue in faith. It's up to us. Jesus completed His part.

So David positions himself for victory by following through with every minuscule detail of God's instruction. Even when it looks like we're going to lose, don't forget, it looked like Jesus was going to lose. His own disciples heard Him explain on several occasions what would unfold. Somehow they just could not comprehend it. So those doubtful eleven followers thought for sure it was all over. Jesus had been defeated. But His story is *the* testimony of victory: A three-act drama — His death, burial, and resurrection. We cannot afford to leave out act three — the winning scene.

How often do we choose not to follow through with sharing Jesus with others because we think we will fail? We may get crushed and never recover. But don't forget those who follow Christ and hold on to the empowering effects of the Cross cannot help but be more than conquerors. *"Now thanks be to God who always leads us to triumph in Christ, and through us diffuses the fragrance of His knowledge in every place."* 2 Corinthians 2:14. This triumph *in Christ* because of His death and resurrection actually deactivates or defuses the *principalities and powers* that we are at war with. Colossians 2:14b-15 *"...And He has taken it out of the way, having nailed it to the Cross. Having disarmed principalities and powers, He made a public spectacle of them, triumphing over them in it."*

THE VICTORY PARADE

There was a specific imperial practice that was known at the time Paul penned these words. He was comparing Christ's victory on the Cross with what was then called the Roman Parade of Triumph. Whenever there was a long yet victorious battle, the conquering Roman general would return to the capital city to be honored with a great state-sponsored parade. The general would arrive, entering the city along the *Via Triumphalis* and everyone would attend to witness the great event. The general and his captains would ride in splendor down the street in royal chariots pulled by gorgeous white horses. While the vanquished foes were chained and led through the streets of the city so everyone could clearly see they had been defeated. There were musicians, flowers and incense that filled the air with the fragrance of victory.

Are you seeing the comparison, the picture? This is Christ, our great conquering General, and His display of final triumph on the Cross. He triumphed. He entered His Kingdom — the

Kingdom of God with an incredible victory parade. He is crowned King of Kings and Lord of Lords. A few hours earlier, He was wearing a crown of thorns, but not anymore. He has won the ultimate battle of the ages forever and satan with all his demons have been brutally disarmed and publicly identified. We have been invited to join the celebration. We have been summoned by King Jesus to march in victory to the sound of triumphant singing and dancing.

Though we continue to live on earth, fighting these battles against *principalities and powers*, remember that Christ Jesus has already conquered satan. He still temporarily has the right, as the prince and power of the air, to torment and tempt us, but satan has already ultimately lost the war. Jesus won it 2000 years ago. We have powerful weapons: the name of Jesus, the blood of the Lamb, the power of our testimony, the armor of God, and the Word of God, all because of Christ's death and resurrection.

However, it is still our *choice* that determines who we will ultimately march with. Who we will serve, and who we will testify of. *Will we march with Jesus – giving Him to our world and being His light?*

RECOVERING ALL

When the battle against the Amalekites was over and the victory was secured, David and his men once again found rest. They then began to survey the warzone. They realized that everything that the Amalekites had taken from Ziklag was there, and so much more. The inventory that David and his men were now taking included not just what had been stolen from Ziklag, but from all of the places that they had previously attacked. So not only had David recovered their own possessions—the herds and flocks, the silver and gold—but also the wealth of the other cities that the Amalekites had destroyed. And of course, most importantly, they recovered their children and wives. These men who only moments earlier were holding swords and violently destroying the enemy

Go Light Your World

now sheathed those same weapons and heard children's happy voices shouting, "Daddy, Daddy!" With joyful hearts and tear filled eyes families were reunited.

David, only thirty-six hours earlier had been given difficult words with a seemingly impossible outcome. But He was confident because God had never lied to him or tried to sabotage him. *"So David* (once again did the only wise thing to do when in doubt) *inquired of the Lord, saying, 'Shall I pursue this troop? Shall I overtake them?' And He answered him, 'Pursue, for you shall surely overtake them and without fail recover all.'"* I Samuel 30:8. One of the most incredible parts of this story of victory is how God prepared everything in advance so it would fall into place and David would gain the victory.

The same truth applies in our lives as Christians. As we grow in Christ, rekindling our passion for Him, and asking for direction in sharing His love with others, He will prepare the way and even prepare hearts that will be receptive. Scripture tells us that the men came upon an Egyptian in the field, and David's men brought the young man to him; they fed him and gave him water to drink. They fed him some more with cake and figs and two clusters of raisins. He was obviously so famished that he was unable to even communicate. He was a young servant of one the Amalekites, but he'd been left behind by his master because he was sick. He freely told them of everything they'd done, including the attack on Ziklag. Amazing! So David asked him if he could take him to down to the troop. The young servant agreed to do it, but only if David promised not to kill him or deliver him into the hands of his master. And the *rest of the story* is history. I Samuel 30:11-18.

SHARING THE SPOILS

The amount of wealth that was gathered by David and his men after the great victory over the Amalekites was unbelievable. As they packed up to return to Ziklag with their families, David realized that the volume of *spoil* they were taking home was far greater than any wealth he had ever possessed. His character was again revealed through his actions. David gave of all the wealth to his men. There were 200 men out of 600 who were too weary to cross the Brook Besor. I Samuel 30:24 seems to give the impression that these were the men that carried the supplies. But after the battle when they came out to meet David, some of the men who fought (the Bible describes them as *"the wicked and worthless of those who went with David"*) were saying *"these guys didn't go with us to fight so they will get nothing we've recovered, except their families."* However David's response was epic — so like God. *"My brethren, you shall not do so with what the Lord has given us, who has preserved us and delivered into our hand the troop that came against us."* I Samuel 30:23. Even beyond that, David gave offerings to all the places that he and his men had previously camped.

Our circumstances may in some small way parallel with this account of David in Ziklag. We are pretty much living our lives, nothing really spectacular, outlandish, or earth shattering happening. We talk a little about what God's done in our lives, but it's really not *impacting* others in a great way. Then, out of nowhere our world falls apart. We are on the verge of disaster. We may have even faced total devastation and lost everything. We may have come upon our homes and seen everything in spiritual ruin. God has gotten our attention, and without His help we have no idea what we are going to do, but He has the plan that will lead us to total victory. Just as David inquired of the Lord what to do in the face of his dilemma, so it is for us. As we seek Him, then follow Him, we will embrace a greater power and direction than we've ever known before.

So many things in life that we would consider "the worst thing in the world that can happen" — often the last thing we would ever want to happen, God uses as a divine appointment to accomplish manifold blessings. Experiences and opportunities we would not have otherwise been privileged to enjoy or embrace — blessings emerging from what seem like such a catastrophe. A *divine appointment* is being exactly where God wants you, precisely when He wants you there, so that His perfect plan unfolds. One tiny detail out of sync could thwart what God has intended to transpire. This is such an awesome lesson for us to learn. In the midst of life's most difficult adversity we can be assured that there is a purpose beyond what our eyes may see at that moment.

David had been given the *cure* that would ultimately restore everything to Ziklag and heal the city. He just had to share the plan with his men…then obey. Jesus is the cure for a world needing to be saved and restored. The devil has pillaged, stolen, killed, and destroyed people, leaving them in ruin and on the ash heap. But we have Christ Jesus who has called us to be the light of the world to shine into the darkest places to bring healing and wholeness; to restore everything that has been stolen by the enemy.

If you knew you had a cure for cancer, wouldn't you be ready and more than willing to tell everyone you met? You'd dial up the most important people in the world and tell them "I have a cure for cancer. Let's get it on the market so people can be healed." Guess what? We have the ultimate cure for broken, ruined lives. We have the cure for people who have been torn apart by sin and heartache. There are faces everywhere—waitresses in restaurants, cashiers in grocery and convenience stores, attendants at gas stations, business men and women—who may be facing more than they can bear. They are in a war all their own, fighting for their lives every day. They are looking for someone to *rescue* them with even just a smile or you're doing a great job. Are we passionate enough about Jesus to share the cure that we have with people that we come in contact with on a daily basis? Or are we so preoccupied with our own lives, our own problems (that we're not entrusting to Him ourselves) that we forget people are dying every day without Him?

God has granted us, through Christ, the greatest victory of all. It is greater than any battle fought in the past, from Biblical times until now. It is greater than any yet to come; it is victory over the battle for our souls. We have received the victory and now it is up to us to share the spoils! We have a greater gift than material wealth or possessions. He designed us to be His light in our dark world with the truth that pervades our hearts and has changed our lives. Jesus Christ has saved us from destruction and defeat. God wants us to *share Jesus* to the world.

WHY DOES IT MATTER?

It matters first of all because of the incredible joy and privilege we feel when we share Christ with someone else. We are blessed to be a blessing! The common term would be of course "witnessing," and is referred to as the Great Commission. In other words, regardless of whatever else we may do as Christians, this is our ultimate purpose, to "Go Light Our World" with the Good News. Maybe when you even hear the word witness, you feel panic stricken. Could it be that many of us feel that this is something we just **can't** do? Let's leave this one thing for the evangelists and preachers, the missionaries, or people who are really *called* into Christian service. *I would ask you today, have you accepted Jesus as your personal Savior? Have you asked Him to forgive you of your sins, followed Him in baptism, and asked Him to be the Lord of your life?* If so, guess what? You too are called. Every person who kneels at the foot of the cross, inviting the Holy Spirit to live in their heart, has now been called of God; called to witness and to light up their world sharing Jesus.

Maybe you're a shy person, not comfortable or don't even know how to go about sharing what Christ has done in your life. You may be a brand new Christian, timid and uncomfortable about "pushing this new experience" on your friends or those you work with or any one for that matter.

Well, I have some words of encouragement for you today, my friends. Yes, you can. As we already shared, David didn't become a king straight out of the shepherds field. It took time. So it is with learning to share Jesus with others or fulfilling God's divine plan for your life. It is a process and it rarely happens overnight for most people. Others may find it very easy to share their faith, and immediately begin witnessing and winning others. There's no particular mold to fill or way that works for everyone. But think about this as another reason that it matters. Where would you be today had someone not shared Jesus with you, illuminating your world with His love?

WHAT DOES JESUS SAY ABOUT IT?

"Go therefore and make disciples of all the nations, baptizing them in the name of the Father and of the Son and of the Holy Spirit, teaching them to observe all things that I have commanded you; and lo, I am with you always, even to the end of the age." Matthew 28:19-20. We witness first in obedience to what Jesus told us to do.

Talk about lighting your world. Saul, the zealot Pharisee who was literally hunting down Christians and dragging them to prison, got his world turned upside down (or maybe right side up) and immensely illuminated when Jesus himself showed up on the scene. We go into some detail about this in Chapter 9. He really did see the light. Acts 26:16 said that the light was shone into his life to turn others from darkness to the light. *"to open their eyes and to turn them from darkness to light, and from the power of satan to God, that they may receive forgiveness of sins and an inheritance among those who are sanctified by faith in Me."* This verse was not just for Saul, who soon was to become "Paul," the great warrior of the faith-Apostle. This Word was not given to one man only, but rather to show us, everyone who reads the Word, that anyone, anyone can be completely changed when the true light of Christ comes into their lives. Anyone's life can be turned around. Even the vilest sinners (if there is such a category) can be totally transformed once HIS light shines onto their path and into their hearts. After this experience, Paul was never the same again; in a very short span of time he began to witness! If he could do it, once his life was transformed, so can you and so can I. Some may have reservations so let's discuss a few of the reasons people honestly don't feel comfortable, or that they can't witness.

Paul said in Romans 1:16 *"For I am not ashamed of the gospel of Christ for it is the power of God to salvation for everyone who believes..."* We can't afford to be ashamed of the gift of forgiveness that we have received. It is what offers eternal life to all who receive — we will indeed be accountable to God for our obedience in witnessing to others without embarrassment or shame.

WHAT MAKES SHARING JESUS SO DIFFICULT?

First – *I wouldn't know how to approach someone.*
Second – *I wouldn't want to push my beliefs on anyone else.*
Third – *I wouldn't know what to say.*
Fourth – *I don't think people really care or are that interested in God.*
Fifth – *It doesn't really matter anyway, just so I know I'm saved.*
Sixth - *God will reach them, He has His ways.*
Seventh – *When it's time, they'll find their way, I did.*

Okay, we'll call these the seven deadly witnessing lies. All of these are actually excuses to justify our lack of or neglect of sharing Jesus. Let's take these individually and briefly find out why it is a lie and how we can overcome these very real, but actually totally false lies

First – *How do you approach others?* Obviously not head on. You don't have to carry around a huge King James under your arm and preach hellfire and damnation. Rather you begin every day by praying and asking the Lord to "give you opportunities to be a witness for Him." The Lord does open doors; we just have to be listening and watching for those opportunities so we won't miss them. Pray...watch, and then be obedient. Don't let these moments get away without taking a chance for Christ and saying something that will make others know you care. You have been introduced to the

ONE who CARES more for you than anyone else ever has, can or will. So, don't be afraid to just share your story in your own words of what Christ has done in your life—whenever the door opens. God will open doors if you'll ask Him to.

I was sitting in an airport one Saturday afternoon, flying out of Myrtle Beach, SC to Louisville, at the conclusion of a Women's Retreat. This was kind of the "second leg" to my tour with a week of concerts and speaking engagements in Kentucky. Traveling to the airport, my heart was filled with praise for a great week-end, and prayers that God would give me opportunities to be a blessing, not just in Kentucky, but on the way, wherever He might lead me. He answered those prayers just moments later.

My scheduled departure from Myrtle Beach was delayed for over an hour. Guess what? Yes indeed, a chance to talk to a gal about Jesus who was really going through some serious battles in her life—physically and emotionally. She was so open and reaching out for someone to just care enough to pray—so I did, and it was awesome! I was able to share with her some of the pain I had suffered in my own life, physically and emotionally, relating to her situation. A seed was planted, and that's the start in witnessing. God opens doors when we ask. We keep our eyes open for ways to witness, listening, then, relating to them with our story. It's kind of like the "feel, felt and found" method. *I feel what you are feeling, I have felt the same or (similar) pain, here is what I found.* Sometimes we have the joy of leading someone to Christ right on the spot. Other times we sow the seed, praying others too will water and nurture it so one day it will be ready to harvest.

Who me, speak to someone about the Love of God? Oh, Yes! Give me opportunities everyday!

Another way is to just live the life before people. Often that's more of a witness than words will ever be. Offer acts of kindness and show the love of Christ, follow through, keep your word—be available. Do the things that Jesus would do and others will see that witness loud and clear. Act like the devil, and they'll see that too. That will most always cancel out anything you might ever try to say to them about the Lord at a later time.

Our lives, our actions, especially our words are the only "Bible" some people will ever read. Living a Godly life as a witness to others means keeping in mind that others are observing the way we live, where we go, what we say or don't say, our attitude, our tone of voice, our actions and reactions, sometimes even our expressions. To sum it up, just living like Jesus would live, and acting like Jesus would act—is the answer for WIN-WIN witnessing. If we want Jesus to be seen in us, then we have to look like Jesus. Be attentive to how your life is witnessing to others.

**Who me? Share Jesus?
Absolutely, every chance I get!**

Second – *I don't want to push my beliefs on anyone else.* If someone were drowning would you stand on the banks of the river watching, worried they may not like you or your techniques, or what you know about rescuing a drowning person, or would you dive in and bring them to safety? Ok, same answer. Jesus is the only one who can rescue us from certain death. There is no other way to God but through Jesus. That means that people who do not know Him are drowning and will end up eternally lost if we don't dive in, so to speak, and share the truth of the Gospel with them. Eternity awaits every man. Can we really think sharing truth with others is pushing on another person some belief that doesn't really matter, that it is unimportant? We're talking about eternity here, forever lost without Jesus if we don't witness and tell others about Him. This is far more important than sharing with someone about a new product line for laundry or weight loss program. It's not a matter of pushing a belief on another person; it's a matter of realizing that someone once told us. If they hadn't where would we be today? Someone cared enough about you, enough about me, to tell us about Jesus and offer us the opportunity to accept Him as our Savior. Why wouldn't we feel others should have that same chance—in fact who are we not to share it?

Who me? Go light my world with the message of Jesus? Yes, Lord, Yes, to Your will and to Your way!

Many years ago Mother and I were in a conversation about this topic of witnessing. She shared an incredible story with me that happened to her. She never forgot it. The impression it left on her heart compelled her to share her faith in the future, no matter how insecure she might have felt, or even when she thought she might be pushing her beliefs off on someone.

She and Daddy were new in the faith, brand new Christians. Mother was so hungry for God's Word she devoured it day and night. She said she remembered looking out the window one morning and noticed her neighbor preparing for a fishing trip. It was wintertime so it looked as though he was going ice fishing. She felt a strong urgency to talk to the man, ask him about his relationship with the Lord and if he knew Jesus. But she was a brand new Christian—not confident, and not nearly knowledgeable enough in the Word to share it, (or so she thought) at the time. So she said she just kind of shrugged off the urge, not thinking it would matter one way or another. A few days passed and she continued to feel this urgency, but suppressed it. Finally the man pulled out for his trip. A week passed, then two. The man hadn't returned home after several weeks. Mother inquired and found out the man had passed away. There had been a fishing accident on the ice, and he fell through. They were unable to rescue him. She was devastated. She felt such guilt and remorse, but it was too late. Of course, in time she knew the Lord had forgiven her, and she forgave herself. From that moment on, to the best of her ability, she never again disobeyed when she knew she should talk to someone about Jesus; even if she felt inadequate—she knew it was so important to obey. It wasn't long before she gained confidence and found great joy in witnessing.

Who me...witness?
Yes, Lord— lead me to the lost.

Third - *I wouldn't know what to say.* The main thing to remember is not how much scripture you've memorized, although God's Word is powerful, and so important to continue reading every day, and memorize. But initially what is most important is *your personal testimony*—what Jesus has done in your life? That's reality. Has He changed your life? Has He given you a real reason for living? Has He filled the emptiness in your life with His love and presence? Now, if you don't have a testimony that's certainly a must. There must be some kind of transformation in your own life before you can share it with someone else. Has He delivered you from any habits that once tormented you? Have you seen any miracles since you began this journey with Him? I promise you when Paul began witnessing He didn't have a seminary degree. You don't need one either. What He had was an incredible, miraculous, life changing encounter from and with God. Your experience is what you have to share. How Christ has changed your life. Ask the Lord to give you the right words to say at the right time. Be sincere – praying asking the Holy Spirit to empower you. He promised that when we don't have the words, He will give us the words to speak. Our part is to be humble, and obedient, not super-spiritual, not perfect, just forgiven. God does the work, we are just the vessels He uses.

Who me... talk about Jesus?
Yes Lord, give me the words.

Fourth – *I don't think people really care or are that interested in God.* Believe it or not, everyone cares about God in one way or another. Atheists believe there is no God and agnostics don't believe in God. He *might* exist but they think it's all bogus. So why is it that both are still trying to prove what they believe? If there is NO God or they don't believe He is real, why are they still trying to convince people of that fact? Think about it. When something or someone isn't real — its fact, no one needs to prove it.

Here's another thought to ponder concerning sharing God with others. People need heroes. From comics, to giving awards to actors and actresses, or *singing* idols, or policeman, firemen, EMT, the armed forces (and they really are heroes, by the way) but people are always is looking for heroes. God is the greatest of all heroes. Funny how people care about God when they're desperate, or in a life-threatening situation, or some catastrophe comes into their lives. What then? Everyone gets religious. What that really means is that at the core of every single human being is a need for God — Often they may not realize it, but I've found in my own life in opportunities to witness that just about every time the door opens the people in my path are crying out for hope. People really not only care about God, they need HIM! He is the one hero who will never fall from His pedestal, fail, or get old!

**Who me…share the light?
Yes, Lord, even when it seems impossible
to penetrate the darkness.**

Fifth - *It doesn't really matter about other people, just so I know I'm saved.* Now honestly, this is about the lamest excuse — not to mention the epitome of selfishness I've ever heard. Actually — it would be difficult to believe that a real Christian could even feel this way, let alone express it. Bottom line, as we've mentioned already, this is paramount to our salvation — bringing others to Christ is the Great Commission. Not just so we can enjoy our salvation and our inheritance, but rather to bring as many to Him as we can. This sounds is the mindset of society pertaining to most things, "well, I got mine, don't really care about you." "Lord, help us never to have this attitude about sharing the light of Jesus with those who are living in such darkness. May we see through your eyes those who have not embraced your saving grace and take away our selfish attitude."

**Who me? Tell others what you've done in my life?
Yes, Lord, because it is a matter of life
and death that others hear the gospel.**

Sixth - *God will reach them, He has His ways.* Bah Humbug. God's way to reach the world is US—you and me. He told us to go into all the world. We are His way. Jesus came once in the flesh, ascended into heaven and sent us the Holy Spirit to empower, comfort, and convict of sin. Ordinary people like you and me are to be His instrument— even the most unlikely people like Saul. He chose us. Remember, we read it earlier in the chapter *"To open their eyes and to turn them from darkness to light, and from the power of satan to God, that they may receive forgiveness of sins..."* Acts. 26:18. Now God can use other means of course, He's God. He can use miracles, angels, and divine intervention. There are a million ways God can reach the lost, but more often than not, He is looking for us to be His voice to the lost. He called us, He equips us, He provides for us, and He will prepare the way. I have a little card taped to the bottom of my computer that a friend gave me years ago that says, *"Where God Guides, He Provides."* God's way is for His people who are called by His name to reach those who do not know His name. We do our part—He does the rest. That's His way.

**Who me? Send the light?
Yes, Lord, to whom and where and when?**

Seventh - *When it's time, they'll find their way; I did.* Yeah, you and I found our way because someone told us. No one will ever receive Jesus by osmosis. There are times when God reaches people, like He did Saul, supernaturally, but the most significant way people find their way to God is through the witness of others—and the time for all to come to Christ was chosen 2000 years ago.

The day Jesus uttered His last words on the Cross, took His last breath, gave up the ghost and died— that was the time. At that moment, God desired that every lost person would accept the forgiveness of sins by the precious shed-blood that flowed from the body of Christ: When that priceless, precious, perfect blood, poured from His head, His hands, His back, His side and His feet, that was when sin was washed away. But if people don't hear, if people aren't told they're lost and are never given the opportunity to come to Jesus, how can they? How will they know when the time is right? You see, it is up to you and me. It is our responsibility because the people you meet today or see today or talk to today I may never meet, evangelists or pastors or missionaries may never meet, but you will.

> **So if we don't go light our world,**
> **who then will reach them?**
> **And if no one reaches them,**
> **how will they ever know Jesus?**

SO HOW DO WE GO LIGHT OUR WORLD?

These are some steps to help in knowing how to share Jesus. How do we tell others about this gift of eternal - abundant life that we've been given?

1. **DECIDE** - Make a conscience decision that you want to, that you see the importance of witnessing. We understand that what we have is too good to keep to ourselves. If we can begin to see how vital this message of hope and light is to others, as it was shown to us, then we make a conscience decision to begin telling others. But we will never do it if we don't decide—no one else can make the choice for us.

2. **ASK THE LORD FOR OPPORTUNITIES** - Everyday we will be able to see open doors, and know when He's opening it for us to give Jesus to someone who desperately needs to hear. There has to be a door. You can't just walk up to people on the street (well you could but they would probably not be as receptive.) More often than not, it's not a cold call witnessing method, like selling vacuum cleaners. It's a process of preparing the soil and planting the seeds. We witness to people we work with, or maybe meet in a gym, or at school activities, parents or our children's teachers, the hairdresser or nail technician, how about the dry cleaners, or the clerk at the grocery store if you frequent the same one, and how about your pet groomer? Sometimes, there's a preparation process involved, but there are so many places to plant seeds and to continue to water them until there's a time to really share Jesus with people.

3. **BELIEVE THAT YOU CAN SHARE HIS LOVE** – Hold onto the power of belief in whatever way possible. Sharing Jesus doesn't necessarily mean preaching a sermon and giving an altar call. It means reaching out in love to people wherever you may see a need. There are probably numerous things that happen in a day when we could reach out to someone. Don't be shy, speak to them, be courteous, but never underestimate the power of belief. *"And He said to me, My grace is sufficient for you, for My strength is made perfect in weakness."* 2 Corinthians 12:9. There is unbelievable power in belief.

Nick was a big strong tough railroad worker. He was reliable, always on time and an excellent employee. There was only one thing about Nick that could have been considered an obvious character flaw – he was chronically negative.

One day the entire work crew left the yard early for a birthday party that was being planned for the shift foreman. Nick, leaving last as usual, making sure everything was finished to perfection, accidentally locked himself in one of the empty refrigerated boxcars that had been brought into the yard for maintenance. The car was not connected to any other trains, but needed to be worked on.

Nick, realizing what he'd done, suddenly became frantic. He realized there was no one on the grounds, though he beat the doors with his arms and fists until they were bloody. He called out again and again, hoping against hope that someone just might hear him. But to no avail. His voice finally became a raspy whisper. This was really happening, he had locked himself in a refrigerated box car. Nick guessed the temperature in the unit would be well below freezing, maybe 15-20 degrees Fahrenheit. Nick feared the worst. "What am I going to do? If I don't get out of here and end up in here all night, I'm going to freeze to death." The more he believed his circumstances, the colder he became. With the door shut tight and no possible way of escape, he sat down to await the inevitable – death! To pass the time he decided to chronicle his demise. He found a pen in his shirt pocket and an old piece of cardboard in the corner of the car. Shivering uncontrollable he wrote this message, "Getting so cold... body numb. If I don't get out soon, these will probably be my last words." And they were.

The next morning the crews came to work. They opened the box car and found Nick's body crumpled over in the corner. They immediately called the paramedics and rushed him to the hospital, but of course he was already gone. When the autopsy was performed they found that Nick had indeed died from severely cold temperatures. He had frozen to death! But here's the most fascinating part of the story. Investigators found that the box car refrigeration unit was not even on! It was out of order, and had been for some time – that was one of the reasons it was in the service yard. The refrigeration was not even functioning at the time of the man's death The temperature in the car that night – the night that Nick froze to death – 61 degrees. He was frozen in slightly less than normal temperatures because he believed that he was freezing in that box car. He believed. Oh, the power of belief! Never underestimate it.

4. BOLDLY TAKE ACTION – We can believe all day long and quote scriptures like, *"I can do all things through Christ* *who strengthens me."* Philippians 4:13, but after we ask the Holy Spirit to give us strength and boldness, we need to take action. If we don't get up and get going, then it will only be words and good intentions. We have to act upon our beliefs. It's more than just a matter of believing, it's doing. It's taking the first step, then increasing the strides, and speaking the right words as the opportunities arise. If we are to be obedient to the calling of Christ we have to put our words, desires and beliefs into action.

If we don't share Jesus, right where we are, the community we live in, our own neighborhood, who will? It's up to us, you and me to Go Light Our World, sharing the message of the Cross to people who need the Savior so desperately.

Who Me? Share Jesus?
Oh Yes. Every Chance I Get,
With Everyone I Can,
Everywhere I Go.

9

FOCUS ON FORGIVENESS
"Whew... this is a tough one...
Pardoning the Unpardonable!"

Has there ever been a time in your life you really had difficulty forgiving someone? I mean really forgiving — not remembering and bringing it up continually. You've said you forgave but it's constantly on your mind and you know in your heart there's still a nagging, sensitive, painful wound that continues surfacing. Something happened. Wrongs were committed. Someone, deliberately, without concern for your feelings purposely took advantage, lied or betrayed your trust. How can you ever forgive them, and furthermore, why should you ever forgive them? This is a question we've all wrestled with at one time or another; and most of us, within our own realm of thinking and ability would respond in the same way. "We can't forgive, and no we shouldn't forgive, because people that do wrongs to others deserve no forgiveness, they need to be punished themselves." But just for a moment, think about Jesus. If He were us, how would He respond? What would He do? Since we're on this journey of *Rekindling Our Passion for Jesus,* this is a very important part of our mission. We know the answer, if we know anything at all about His nature.

Forgiveness is a word kind of like *patience* for me. Not a day goes by that there isn't a need for it in one way or another. There's something or someone that crosses my path needing forgiveness. According to God's Word, this is an attribute that should be constant, and evident in our lives, if we are living holy before Him. Forgiving others is at the top of God's priority list for us to be like Jesus. He forgave us, He expects us to forgive. When we desire a passionate relationship with Christ, we will look more deeply into what it means to pardon and forgive.

WHAT HAPPENS WHEN WE DON'T FORGIVE?

First of all, unforgiveness often causes serious separation between us and an intimate relationship with Christ. Why? An intimate, passionate relationship requires two very important things: Trust and Communication. If we harbor unforgiveness we are not trusting God with our present circumstances. Consequently we're probably not talking to Him about them either, unless of course we're blaming God for what's happening. That wouldn't be classified as a healthy, thriving relationship. But as we openly confess unforgiveness, laying it all at the foot of the cross, admitting our inability to forgive on our own outside of Christ in us, then that division is repaired and we are restored to fellowship with him.

Secondly, unforgiveness can cause serious separation between us and those that we love. Why? Sometimes we don't even realize it, but we end up taking out our frustrations and pain on the ones we love the most. We're hurting and somehow we need some release; we need to vent. Jesus is the only one who can carry our burden. We need Him the most, to share it with. He told us to *"cast all of our care upon Him for He cares for you."* I Peter 5:7. But in our human selfishness we have a tendency to unload on the ones who are closest to us, when they may have had nothing to do with the circumstances that occurred.

Thirdly, unforgiveness can cause anger in our hearts toward God. Why? Because we still struggle with the control we think God should have when we want Him to have it. Most of the time we want to be in control; but when it comes to being hurt by others, we don't think God should allow such things—after all we're pretty good people—we really don't deserve to be treated wrongly. So we go back to that age old question, *"Isn't God supposed to be good? Why would He allow such bad things to happen to us?"* Well, let's go even further back to the beginning. Our choices have brought us to where we are in this world, not His. His choice brings us life and that more abundantly. His choice is for us to forgive so we will be forgiven. Jesus is "crystal" clear on the matter—we will not be forgiven if we don't forgive. Mark 11:25-26 *"And whenever you stand praying, if you have anything against anyone, forgive him, that your Father in heaven may also forgive you your trespasses. But if you do not forgive, neither will your Father forgive your trespasses."* Sounds pretty straightforward don't you think?

Fourthly, unforgiveness robs us of a victorious, abundant walk with Christ. Why? Victory means winning. People who refuse to forgive are losers. They lose, not the ones they are holding hostage with their spirit of unforgiveness. They lose their joy, peace, contentment and so much more. They eventually lose it all. Abundance comes from giving. People who don't forgive are leaving out one of the most important gifts we can give: for-giving others. It's impossible to experience the victorious, abundant life when we are harboring unforgiveness.

THE NATURE OF MAN

Most of us at one time or another have probably said, "I don't love this person – and I can't love this person, in fact I actually hate this person!" Is it possible for us to say, "But I want to love them, because I want to be like Jesus, so Lord, I need some (a lot of) help. Love them through me with Your love." Miraculously, God has done it in my life and if He hasn't in yours, He will as you seek Him for the Christ-like attribute of forgiving others. This is so about Him—not about us being able to—or even capable of—but about our *willingness* to be *made* able—to be changed—becoming more like Jesus, the forgiver of all sin. When we feel it's impossible in our own strength, this is what Jesus says, 2 Corinthians 12:9a-10b *"And **He** said to me, '**My grace** is sufficient for you, for **My strength** is made perfect in weakness.' Therefore most gladly I will rather boast in my infirmities,* (not referring only to sickness, but also to inabilities or inadequacies) *that the power of Christ may rest upon me…For when I am weak, then **HE is strong**."*

A little boy named Johnny was quite upset with his brother. They had been fighting a good part of the day. Evening had arrived and they were getting ready for bed. Their mother came in and said "Now Johnny before you go to sleep I want you to forgive your brother." But Johnny was in no frame of mind to forgive him. "No I won't forgive him!" he shouted. The mother continued to try to persuade her son with little progress. Finally out of desperation she said "What if your brother was to die tonight, how would you feel if you knew you hadn't forgiven him?" This was too much for Johnny and finally he reluctantly conceded. "All right, I'll forgive him, but if he's alive in the morning, I'll get him for what he did to me."

Matthew 6:14-15 *"For if you forgive men, when they sin against you, your heavenly Father will also forgive you. But if you do not forgive men their sins, your heavenly Father will not forgive you."* Now this is a little confusing when we first read it. So how can God hear a sinner? One who has never come to Christ certainly harbors much unforgiveness, right? Yes. But Jesus is talking to those who are converted, to those following Him. He was saying, *"This is the way to walk."* If we expect God to forgive us, then we too, must forgive. Why is it that so often we expect God to do things for us that we are not willing to do for others? We pray, "Oh God, bless me, bless me, bless me," but are we blessing others? Are we doing the things we are asking God for in our prayers? So if we're asking for His forgiveness and grace, are we showing the same toward others?

How often have we given forgiveness to others? Colossians 3:13 *"Be gentle, and ready to forgive, never hold grudges, remember the Lord forgave you, so you must forgive others."* Easy to read; easy to say; but very difficult to live out in our own strength.

The reality is none of us, in our own strength or ability will ever be able to truly forgive—even when we think we understand the necessity of forgiving and we know there will always be consequences when we don't forgive—even when we come to grips with the fact that God expects us to. The only way we will ever be able to forgive is to understand it's not about our abilities; it's about Him, the Holy Spirit who dwells in us. He is the one who can accomplish the work in us. It is Christ in us the Hope of Glory. He said *"Greater is He that is in you than he that is in the world."* I John 4:4b.

Even in knowing and understanding this truth the road to forgiving is not an easily traveled one. Pardoning the unpardonable is difficult, very difficult. Why? Forgiving goes against our human nature. We feel that we are in the right—we should be treated as such. What gives anyone a license to step on, abuse, speak disrespectfully, or lie to or about us? Forgiving doesn't just happen - it involves much on our part.

FIRST: ACKNOWLEDGE THE WRONG DONE—OVERLOOKING IT OR EXCUSING IT ISN'T FORGIVENESS - Acknowledging wrong doesn't mean we grovel in it or wallow in self pity. Carrying a chip on our shoulder or feeling sorry for ourselves will not promote a spirit of pardon. But what it does mean is that we are able to embrace the reality of our pain by looking it square in the face, calling it exactly what it is—wrong treatment. That's progress. When Christ forgives us, He tells us that we have to confess our sins— I John 1:9 *"If we confess our sins, He is faithful and just to forgive us our sins and to cleanse us from all unrighteousness."* Then—He will faithfully forgive and cleanse us from all unrighteousness. This is confessing sin committed against us saying *"God, you know, but to keep my heart from becoming bitter, here's what happened."* "Honest confession is good for the soul." Overlooking or excusing wrong isn't forgiveness. Actually it's just the opposite. Harboring unforgiveness sets us up for major problems later on in life because overlooked or ignored forgiveness actually breeds contempt and bitterness toward others as time goes on. And bitterness can grow to a lethal stage in our hearts. When we actually come to grips with our hurt, giving it to the Lord, the process for healing begins.

SECOND: ACKNOWLEDGE TO GOD THE PEOPLE WHO HAVE DONE WRONG BUT DON'T CONSTANTLY TRY TO UNDERSTAND WHY - I read the most incredible story recently about a young man who had undergone a tremendous amount of counseling and psychiatric help in his life. The stories he told of his abuse were unbelievable, but one of these was unconscionable. His mother often would make him his favorite sandwich, peanut butter and jelly. She then would throw it on the floor, open face, take a butcher knife and cut it up into little pieces. Then she'd look at her son and tell him to get down on the floor and eat it like the dog he was. *Can you even imagine the depth of pain this boy had to endure?* What hurt the most was that he had been adopted. He kept asking the therapist, *why did she even want me to come and be her son if she was going to treat me like that? WHY did she do it? Why? Why did she do such horrible things to me?*

There are many things in life we will never understand. People are one of them. Obviously, this woman had deep-seated problems, demons of her own, and needed someone upon whom to vent her anger. Why people do the things they do remains in many ways a mystery. We know that as long as there is sin in the world, and one who is the *prince of the power of the air*, we are going to face wrong treatment. Satan is evil. Everything he does is evil. Often people are used by him, sometimes even unknowingly because they are being controlled by a sinful or demonic nature. Trying to figure it all out, continually asking why, in order to have some kind of explanation will never help us forgive. It may give some

Focus On Forgiveness

temporary comfort, but it won't bring true forgiveness. More often than not it will cause us even more pain in the long run.

One of the greatest examples I can think of is Corrie Ten Boom. While she was in the concentration camp she kept a journal of all the wrongs done to the Jews by the Nazi's—all the atrocities. Don't you imagine she must have wondered why such unthinkable crimes could have been committed to human beings? The Journal would serve upon Corrie's release (should she ever be released alive), as documented evidence proving the heinous acts of crime committed by the Germans, especially to the Jews. One day, the Holy Spirit spoke to Corrie and told her to burn the journal. Burn it with all the recorded truths of horror—the sins of the Germans against the innocent. Could you have done that? Could I have done that? If nothing else we would have justified keeping it for the sake of history. Forgive those evil heretics? Could Jesus have done that? Oh, yes He did, again and again and again! That's what He desires for us—to forgive others as He has forgiven us.

"Forgive our sins, as we forgive," you taught us, Lord to pray;
But You alone can grant us grace, to live the words we say,
How can Your pardon reach and bless, the unforgiving heart,
That broods on wrongs and will not let, old bitterness depart?

In blazing light Your cross revealed the truth we dimly knew:
What trivial debts are owed to us, How great our debt to You."
Lord, cleanse the depths within our souls and bid resentment cease;
Then bound to all in bonds of love our lives will spread your peace.
— Rosamond Herklots

We really do have a choice in pardoning the unpardonable. The real question is, *"to forgive or to not forgive?"* And remember, though we have a part in it, God plays the biggest part of all. He will never make us do anything we don't want to do. We are free moral agents, with the right of "choice." The real crisis in this decision is our will, our own self will. Can we relinquish it to Him?

OUR PART - WILLINGNESS

Are we willing to forgive the wrong doer? Even reaching a place of willingness may involve a lengthy process, but there does come a time when we have to make a definite crisis decision, will we or not? We have to begin where we are. Not where we think we ought to be. "I know I ought to forgive. I really want to, but to be honest with you, the hurt is so great that I don't think I am quite willing to forgive now." Then the next question, *are you willing to be made willing?* This will no doubt involve the possibility of even greater pain in your life. Obedience to God's will always cost us, but it's more than worth the price. Jesus will honor our struggle the moment we say, "Lord, I don't know if I'm quite willing to forgive, but I am willing for You to make me willing whatever the cost." Then, the enabling grace of God goes to work in our behalf. And He is faithful. He will work with us to bring us step by step to the place where we can do our part, where we can progressively say, "Lord, I am willing to be made willing, I am willing to forgive, I will forgive, Lord, I do forgive." This means that we will not hold on to old feelings, but be willing to accept all the new ones God has for us. We give God permission to change the spirit of anger, resentment and unforgiveness in us—and even take it away.

GOD'S PART - HE'S THE REBUILDER - THE CHANGER OF HEARTS

We might feel it is completely impossible to ever get rid of anger or ill feelings toward the person who so deeply wounded us. That's God's part. Romans 2:19 *"Vengeance is mine, says the Lord. I will repay."* We are, with the help of the Holy Spirit going to be able to let go of all the ways we've thought of to avenge ourselves or get even. Only God has that prerogative—God alone.

Another applicable illustration about Corrie Ten Boom concerning forgiveness is one that she shared while holding evangelistic services in India in 1961. It reveals the depth of the power of healing through the Holy Spirit even when a heart has been wounded beyond belief.

After World War II ended, Corrie traveled to many different countries sharing the Holocaust experiences. She had repeatedly emphasized that God had long ago given her the grace to forgive her torturers. Then, she returned finally to speak in Germany itself, the place where it all had transpired. This was where her family had been imprisoned because, by God's direction, they had hidden Jews away from the Nazi's. Her father was a clock maker in Holland and she and her family were Christian. Word came that help was needed to keep some Jews alive, so they built a secret wall in the upstairs of their home—"The Hiding Place"—in which a few could be hidden until taken out of the country to safety. Somehow the Nazis found out, raided their home one cold rainy winter's night. Her father, her sister Betsy (who was extremely ill at the time), and their brother were all taken to German concentration camps. The few Jews in "The Hiding Place" were never located. They made it to freedom. Her story is truly compelling, a great one to read. All of her family died in the camps except Corrie, for by a clerical error, she was miraculously released.

One evening while she was in Munich, Germany, sharing her testimony of faith and how the power of God kept her during these horrific experiences, to her amazement and shock she saw the very SS officer in the congregation who had stood guard at the shower room door in the processing center at Ravensbruck Prison. It was the first time she had actually met or even seen any of those horrible, cruel jailers. She mentioned that she was immediately ambushed by painful memories of the piles of dirty clothing, the humiliation of her nakedness, the roomful of jeering men, and her sister Betsy's anemic face. A flood of vengeful feelings surfaced in her again. She could forgive the others, maybe, but not this one. And then, to her horror the man came up to her, his face completely aglow, "O Fraulein, thank you for your message," he said, "I believe what you *told us, that God has forgiven me and washed all my sins completely away."* He reached out his hand to shake hers. But the hate was too strong. She could not even place her hand toward his. She felt nothing, not even the slightest emotion of pity. How could she take his hand? It would be complete hypocrisy. But the Lord kept whispering in her spirit. *"Just put out your hand, Corrie, that's all."* Finally, breathing a desperate prayer for God's strength, Corrie reached out her hand and took his. When she did, the most incredible thing happened. It was as though an electrical current passed through her shoulder and down her arm into her hand. The hatred melted and a deep feeling of forgiving love welled up inside her! She said, *"I had to obey God and put out my hand. He did the rest."*

The only way we are going to walk in this realm of forgiveness even when feelings overwhelm us is to constantly be aware that the feelings are God's part. We just have to make the effort and wait for God to do the rest. When we are overwhelmed with emotional pain that He wants to remind us to:

RECALL - that the source of all of this is satan, the father of lies. He never wants us to forgive. He is the promoter and instigator of every evil that causes pain and heartache. We have the authority to rebuke Him, as Jesus did, "Get behind me." Get out of my life. I John 4:4 *"You are of God, little children, and have overcome them..."*

REITERATE - the conscious decision to forgive. It is an act of will—tenaciously hold on to that every single day. It is not just about a decision, but about trust in the Holy Spirit to do His part as we do ours. Push the replay button, go back to track one on the CD and play it again and again—I choose to forgive, that's my part—God promises to do His part

REFUSE - to allow guilt or condemnation to have any place in your heart. The devil is the accuser. Oh how he loves to regurgitate all over us his shame and condemnation. Hold your ground tenaciously. Call him what he is. Tell him you don't even have to listen to his lies any more. He is no longer going to be allowed to steal your joy, or peace — he cannot cross the blood line — he has no rights in your life. You belong to Christ. You are filled with the Holy Spirit. The devil and none of his imps have zero right to bring reproach of any kind upon you. You are **forgiven.** You have chosen to **forgive.**

REMEMBER - that God is faithful. He will never leave or forsake us. He always finishes what He begins. Wait patiently for His work to be accomplished in your life. You weren't hurt instantly, it happened over time. You might not necessarily be healed instantly, it may take time. But in the process remember that when God begins a work in us, He will complete it. Philippians 1:6. *"Being confident of this very thing, that He who has begun a good work in you, will complete it until the day of Jesus Christ."*

REJOICE - Nothing thrills the Lord more than to hear our praises. What joy He receives with the sound of our adoration reaching His ear. The scripture says that He *"inhabits"* (that means He lives there) *our praises.* Proverbs 22.3 "So even in the extremely difficult process of forgiving take time to just say, *"Lord, I praise you for giving me the victory, for doing your part, and for giving me the strength to do mine. I praise you because you are a good God, a miracle working God."*

PRAYER FUELS FORGIVENESS

Prayer is the one key that can be applied successfully every time (no matter what the area of unforgiveness is) to strengthen us and fuel our ability to forgive. As we call upon the Holy Spirit to do the work in us, He will make us willing and God will be faithful to do His part to rebuild and provide what is needed in each circumstance. Then we will begin to see results. However, forgiving without prayer is like trying to build a house without a foundation and wood. But, we need more than the little bedtime *"Now I lay me down to sleep"* prayers. Unforgiveness is a tool satan finds great pleasure in using, even in the hearts of Christians; therefore, this isn't a battle to be taken lightly. We need to be praying spiritual warfare prayers that break the very backbone of the enemy who relentlessly fights against us. **God responds to prayer every single time**. *"The effective, fervent prayer of a righteous man avails much."* James 5:16. So when we know we are in warfare we need prayers that get right in the face of satan and address him with holy boldness so he can be rebuked and depart. Of course, these prayers are ongoing. We can't say them just once any more than we can sweep our floors or dust furniture once and think it will never need to be done again. He sneaks into our lives, and into our faith, like little particles of dust! Fighting the enemy is an ongoing process. This is a war that we will continue to wage until Jesus returns, but with every victory we become stronger and stronger in Christ, and our passion for Jesus in the midst of these battles and victories deepens to even greater depths. We stand firm in the fight knowing *"For the weapons of our warfare are not carnal but mighty in God for pulling down strongholds, casting down arguments and every high thing that exalts itself against the knowledge of God, bringing every thought into captivity to the obedience of Christ."* 2 Corinthians 10:4-5.

SHATTERING STRONGHOLDS

So why not use nice little sweet, "Oh Jesus, help me" prayers? Because those kinds will not bring about the results needed with issues like unforgiveness. Those prayers give us peace in the midst of it all, but don't bring about the victory or a complete work of healing. We need the victory. We need to be able to move on. We don't just need a band-aid, we need spiritual cellular cleansing to remove all the toxins within that keep us poisoned, harboring unforgiveness. We need freedom and victory in this battle that can eat away at our souls and can even cause physical illness in our bodies if not dealt with. We need prayers that catch the ear of God and cause Him to move in our behalf. That happens when we approach the throne boldly, and appropriate the Word as ammunition.

A number of years ago a woman of God influenced my life in a tremendous way. Her name is Liberty Savard. At the time she had just released a book entitled "<u>Shattering Your Stronghold</u>s." She was in Northern California. I was in the area as well, visiting Mother and Aunt Nita, so we attended her conference. Her ministry is based in Sacramento, California and continues to thrive.

Liberty's teaching has to do with *binding and loosing*. We've all heard at one time or another about binding satan, and loosing ministering angels or the Holy Spirit. We know that the Holy Spirit was sent after Jesus ascended into heaven to comfort, convict, and guide. Angels are ministering, warrior spirits who have been around since the beginning of time to aid in our behalf. But the revelation the Lord gave her was quite different than most people have been taught. The prayer she shared has transformed my way of thinking about spiritual warfare and intercession. When this teaching was revealed to me, it was a matter of hearing something I'd never been taught before, then also listening to the testimonies she shared about the transforming power of this prayer in her life. This kind of praying has proven again and again to move the hand of God bringing about many miracles in my life and those I've interceded for.

Matthew 16:19 *"And I will give you the keys of the kingdom of heaven, and whatever you bind on earth will be bound in heaven, and whatever you loose on earth will be loosed in heaven."* The way the Lord revealed the application of this scripture to Liberty is that the binding and loosing pertains to our ability through the Holy Spirit to pray prayers that avail much. Rather than *binding* satan, we bind or wrap three of the most important things that are — that we want to live by pertaining to God — around the people or the situation we are interceding for:

1. **The Will of God**
2. **The Mind of Christ**
3. **The Truth of God's Word**

Liberty's illustration to make this more applicable or understandable was by using the example of Chinese women who wrap their babies around their backs so everywhere they go, the baby goes, unable to detach themselves from their mother or to ignore being bound to their mother's purpose for that time. The prayer works in much the same way in the spiritual realm—wrapping the person or situation or thing in the will of God or it around them, the mind of Christ and the truth of God's word. So we bind those three around them in the name of Jesus. Why these three? Because everything in life should be immersed in: Desiring the will of God in decisions and goals, wrapping the mind of Christ around our minds, thinking His thoughts, keeping our mind stayed on righteousness, and embracing the truth of God's word—our roadmap and wisdom for life. This may seem like a "strange" way to pray, but I will tell you from experience that it is the most effective warfare prayer I have ever prayed. It works. This is a way of praying in the perfect will of God. Not praying the problem, or even begging for intervention, but rather addressing the issue head on because every need we face pertains to one of these three areas. What an incredible way to give to God our issues of unforgivness.

So the loosing part of this prayer is similar to what Jesus said when He called Lazarus from the tomb, *"And he who had died came out bound hand and foot in grave clothes, and his face was wrapped with a cloth. Jesus said 'Loose him, and let him go.'"* John 11:44b. Even though Lazarus had been brought back from the dead, he was still bound. He was alive, but unable to move. The loosing in this warfare prayer has to do with loosing the strongholds that keep us bound. Though we are alive in Christ, if we belong to Him, there are times that the "grave clothes" keep us bound. So, anything that hinders us from walking in the will of God or receiving the blessings He

Focus On Forgiveness

---

has for us needs to be loosed. Things such as strongholds, curses, wrong words spoken against us, even words we have spoken contrary to the will of God need to be loosed. So, in the name of Jesus we loose the strongholds, we tear them from us, or those we are praying for. Once we do this, spiritually, we don't just leave those *grave clothes* or wrappings or strongholds lying there; we destroy them, we burn them, we render them helpless or gone, no longer having power over us to keep us bound or hindered. Here's an example of this prayer, hopefully to make it a little clearer. Remember too, that this is an intercessory prayer for you to cover your loved ones, or friends, or anyone who you feel needs divine intervention in their lives, including yourself.

> "Heavenly Father, today we boldly come before Your throne because You gave us permission to do so. Hebrews 4:16 *"Let us therefore come boldly before the throne that we may obtain mercy and find grace in the time of need."* So I stand before You today in the authority that You have given me as Your child to bring my praise, worship and requests before Your throne.
>
> First I praise You for all that You are. I enter into Your gates with thanksgiving and into Your courts with praise. Thank You for every blessing of life You have given me. Thank You for Your love and grace and mercy. Thank You for Your forgiveness in my life. Thank You, Lord, that there is nothing too hard for You. Thank You for being a God that hears and answers prayer. So today, Lord, I stand boldly before you to do spiritual warfare in behalf of _____ and this situation.
>
> So, now, in the name of Jesus I bring _____ before you, **and I wrap _____ (name the person or situation) in the will of God. I wrap the will of God around _____**. Oh, Lord, I decree and declare Your perfect will to be done in this situation and in his/her life

because I boldly stand in Your name, which is above every name, and by the power of the blood of Jesus. Lord I wrap Your will so tightly around them they can't get away from it, no matter how hard they try! Let Your will prevail in their lives and in this situation. We're in warfare Lord, we know we are, and we are fighting for the souls of those we love. We will win this battle, in Jesus name!

Today Lord I bind _____ to the mind of Christ. I wrap or bind the mind of Christ around them, and in this situation. May Your mind, Lord, prevail — Your thoughts, Your decisions — in everything pertaining to them and to this situation. May they begin to focus their thinking on things You would think upon, may what they fill their mind with become more like You every day Lord. May their mind begin to desire what Your mind desires, to think on the things that are good, holy, pure, honest, and righteous. Pour into them Lord Your divine nature, so that they will receive creative ability and creative genius that You want to give them, understanding more and more Your mind and Your thoughts each day-so that they will mature having the MIND of CHRIST. Make them sick, Lord, even physically when they want to sin or want to choose things that are against Your mind or your ways.

Oh, God, now **I bind _____ in the truth of God's Word, and I wrap the truth of Your word around _____.** I am binding the truth of Your Word around them right now Lord, so tightly, that they will not ever stray very far from it, Lord. I'm wrapping every promise, all wisdom, your divine direction to prevail in this life, and in these circumstances for You oh, Lord, to bring victory, provision, even clarity of Your Word to them, understanding, and new revelation. Open their eyes to the truth of Your Word Lord, with a deeper hunger for it than they've ever known before. Giving you all the glory, all the praise, and all the honor for what is accomplished. Let the truth of

Focus On Forgiveness

Your Word prevail in their lives Lord, may they Your Word become more and more their focus. Today, Lord, I remind you of Your promises, that you cannot lie. Thank You for miraculous intervention. Thank You for doing what only You can do!

And today Lord, **I tear down, in the name of Jesus, and by the overcoming power of His precious blood, every stronghold** that satan has erected or tried to put into _____ life and or in this situation. Everything the enemy has tried to do to detour, destroy or thwart the blessings of God upon _____. **In the name of Jesus, and by the power of Your precious blood, I tear down every — every stronghold**, everything that has hindered Your will, and I **burn these strongholds** in Your name Jesus, **I destroy them**, render them helpless, freeing _____ to walk in faith and obtain the blessings and miracles you have prepared for them. These strongholds cannot hold _____ bound any longer. Thank you Lord that the *"weapons of our warfare are not carnal, but mighty to the pulling down of strongholds,"* and we not only pull them down - **we destroy them in the name of Jesus**, *"no weapon formed against _____ will prosper."* I call forth your abundant blessings, every good and perfect gift you have for them, and for the joy of the Lord to be their strength!

Lord, we thank You, oh, we thank You for hearing, intervening and answering our prayer of binding and loosing, and tearing down the strongholds of the enemy of our souls, knowing full well, that *"Greater is He that is in us than he that is in the world!"* Thank You Jesus. By faith, we call it done — and satan, we tell you that are a liar, you cannot cross the blood line… we draw it right now in the sand. We belong to Jesus, and if you try to cross it you will contend with the Holy Spirit and all the heavenly hosts who will do battle in our behalf. You have no right in our lives or in the lives of our loved ones. We rebuke you, you evil, foul, accusing slime bag, and send you to the dry places of the earth, until Jesus Himself can cast you into hell forever. And honestly, we cannot wait for that day. Hallelujah. In the lovely, matchless, wonderful name of Jesus we pray, Amen.

This is not a prayer stating our defeat, rather it is about satan's defeat and taking authority over him and the power he thinks he has over us, our friends, our family, or even our foes. Nor is this prayer a pleading with God or a begging for Him to *do something*. It is boldly facing the enemy, taking God's Word into battle against satan, so that what we bind and loose will respond accordingly because Jesus said it would. As surely as a baby cannot free itself from being bound to its mother, so it is with these prayers as we wrap them around people and situations. As we pray they are wrapped in them, and in a sense they can't do a thing about it because we have the authority to pray for others on their behalf (and even for ourselves) in this manner. Then we tear down strongholds, loosing off the grave clothes or whatever keeps them bound. When we loose these strongholds we don't just leave them there, we destroy them, we burn them, render them helpless, no longer able to harm, hinder or hold. All of this is prayed in the name above every name – Jesus.

Two other things may address a couple of questions you might have:

First, I mentioned it earlier but repetition aids remembrance. ***This isn't a one-time-cure-all-prayer.*** This is an ongoing battle with ongoing warfare prayers. I've said this prayer more than once in a day for people on many occasions. So, don't be timid to continue steadfastly in this kind of warfare praying for yourself, your friends and your loved ones, regardless of the need.

Secondly, some may be thinking, we know what the person is struggling with, or their situation, otherwise we wouldn't be praying like this, but don't we need to know what these strongholds are in their lives? No, we don't need to know. They probably don't even know. It's the enemy that causes

Focus On Forgiveness

us to be bound. Our choices give the enemy access. We loose these strongholds from them and ourselves in the name and by blood of Jesus and through the power of God.

This is a **supernatural** working, *a freeing that only the Holy Spirit can do in the spirit realm*. In place of what satan has wrapped people in, we wrap them in THE WILL OF GOD, THE MIND OF CHRIST, THE TRUTH OF GOD'S WORD, **and** LOOSE EVERYTHING THE ENEMY HAS EITHER HELD THEM OR BOUND THEM TO, OR TRIED TO HOLD THEM BOUND TO.

Results that manifest from this kind of intercession are powerfully transforming—more so than any other prayer I have ever personally prayed.

TRUE FORGIVENESS BRINGS RECONCILIATION

God ordained and designed reconciliation. He gave us instruction to make things right with others. Sometimes it may be a one way street, but there is still healing in forgiveness when we reconcile, whether the other person accepts it or not, whenever it is possible to do so. The blessings of God will come into our lives because we have been obedient.

Reconciliation requires humility; we are pardoning the unpardonable. That is not an easy thing to do. It's one thing to say, *"Okay, I forgive,"* but quite another to be willing to go to them and say *"I'm sorry."* Or, *"Please forgive me."* Bottom line, there's never just one person wrong in any broken relationship. People are people—imperfect. Of course we always want to justify our actions. No one is every entirely in the right. Somewhere along the way everyone messes up. We've said harsh words; we've done something stupid, or inconsiderate. *"Brick by brick my citizens"* we've built the wall as much as the other person.

The truth of the matter is until we are willing to reconcile, we haven't genuinely forgiven. That's one of the true tests as to the reality of total forgiveness. When we are willing to humble ourselves and reconcile with another, regardless of what their response is, we will find a new freedom in Christ we had not known before. He promises if we forgive others, we ourselves will be forgiven. I believe what Jesus was telling us was that total forgiveness is really the only kind of genuine forgiveness there is. If Jesus had given His life, and not paid for "all sin" it would have been a futile death. He has a twofold task: First to reveal that He was and is the Son of God and secondly, that He completely and totally forgives ALL sin.

FIVE PRINCIPLES DEMONSTRATING TOTAL FORGIVENESS

One of the greatest examples of forgiveness in the Bible is recorded in the life of Joseph. Though his brothers hated him, and intended to destroy his life, God had other plans. He obviously saw the heart of Joseph—although early on it seemed he wasn't very humble or tactful about God's calling on his life, the plans of man still went awry. Through his years of imprisonment, and even when he thought he was going to get a break with his interpretation of dreams, his freedom was again delayed. Timing is crucial with God. In God's time Joseph was restored to become second only to the Pharaoh. God had strategically orchestrated it all, placing Joseph where he needed to be to save Egypt and even his own family in a time of famine. Even though he served all those years in prison as an innocent person, he still completely forgave his brothers. He still loved them. That has to be a God thing! There are five principles that depict total forgiveness:

1. *Total Forgiveness is Demonstrated When the Offended Has No Desire for Others to Know What or Who Caused the Hurt*

What was the first thing Joseph did after Judah finished his speech? Genesis 45:1. He sent everyone away and made himself known to his brothers in secret. Joseph didn't want the Egyptians to ever find out what his brothers had done to him. He also wanted them to be able to come to Egypt and live. Had the people been made aware of what had happened it could have created a landslide of problems. Hate and unforgiveness wants everybody to know we have been hurt. A sample scenario: "Did you know what so and so did to me?" "Did they really do that?" "Yes." "Man, that is just wrong." "Isn't it, how could they have done that to me?" What good can come from this kind of conversation? Total forgiveness means protecting the one we forgive. Whew! That's the kind of forgiveness Jesus gives us every single day. *"For I will be merciful to their unrighteousness, and their sins and their lawless deeds I will remember no more."* Hebrews 8:12.

2. Total Forgiveness Desires the Guilty to Feel at Ease in the Presence of the Offended

Genesis 45:3-5 tells us that Joseph's brothers were troubled in his presence because they felt so much guilt about what they'd done. Yet because Joseph had completely forgiven them, he wanted them to come near to him, not to be grieved or angry with themselves because God had sent him before them to preserve life. Is it possible for us to look at our situations that way? Regardless of what the enemy intended, or our offender had in mind, or even what our own choices may have created, God means for it to work together for good in our lives. Romans 8:28. Could it have been that Joseph wanted them to get close enough to him that they could look into his eyes and see there was no hatred or vengeance, not even the slightest hint of unforgivness to make them feel uneasy? Hate wants others to feel uneasy, even guilty. When we haven't truly forgiven, we want the person to feel uncomfortable in our presence; but when we have no desire to hold on to hatred or vengeance, or cause people to feel uncomfortable in our presence, that is complete forgiveness.

3. Total Forgiveness Holds No Pride - Doesn't Allow the Offender to Hold On to Guilt

Pride hinders and weakens the Christian life. Did you know that God can hate? Now you may be saying, "Come on Regina, God is a God of love, He can't hate." Proverbs 6:16 *"These six things the Lord hates, yes seven are an abomination to Him... a proud look."* Solomon lists the number one thing that God hates as pride. We can't seem to forgive because we hold on to the feeling of "why should I? I haven't done anything wrong, it's so and so." We are puffed up and arrogant in our feeling of who we think we are and what others owe us. God hates it.

Joseph never carried a spirit or feeling of superiority toward his brothers. Neither did he flaunt in anyway the dreams he'd interpreted, his promotion, the planning and preparation by his leadership for the seven years of famine. There is never a mention in scripture of him boasting; it was all about what God had done. A prideful attitude hinders our ability to forgive. It is not pleasing to the Lord. The scripture says not only does God hate pride, *"God resists the proud."* James 4:6 *"But He gives more grace. Therefore He says: 'God resists the proud, but gives grace to the humble.'"* Now — if there's one person you do not want resistance from, it's God.

Joseph's attitude was exactly the opposite. He said to his brothers in verse five– *"don't be grieved or angry with yourselves."* Would most people say that? No. More than likely we would say, "You should feel terrible, carry this guilt to your grave for what you've done to me; look who I am." Joseph's mind was on them, not wanting them to carry any more guilt about what they'd done. He got into their heads, even into their feelings and addressed the issue face to face because he had completely and totally forgiven what they had done to him. He didn't want them to grieve about it now that they knew he was alive. He knew there had truly been a divine purpose in all that had occurred.

4. Total Forgiveness Means That the Offended Helps the Offender Forgive Themselves

One of the most difficult parts of forgiving is to forgive ourselves. Genesis 45:5-7. Joseph told his brothers that God's hand was in all of it and had he not been there, in Egypt, he wouldn't have interpreted the dreams, been promoted or been in the position to save the people. So, he told them it wasn't about what they did wrong, it was about what God did right. What happens when we have the Spirit of God so big in us that we can say, "Nothing is going to transpire in my life without God saying, 'I've got a plan that you know nothing about?' " Joseph reiterated it again in Genesis 50:20 stating, *"that they may have meant it for evil, but God meant it for good, and a plan to save people's lives."* The only forgiveness that is worth anything is the kind that allows us to forgive ourselves. People can say all day long that God forgives, yet they still live in the past, feeling guilty about what they have been unable to forgive themselves for. Complete forgiveness shows the sovereign plan of God in everything. When we completely forgive, we show others how mighty God is, that even they cannot thwart God's plan, regardless of what they had originally intended. St Francis of Assisi said it best, *"it is in pardoning that we are pardoned."* The Lord comes into our lives even shaping our past so that we can clearly see His hand in even that. Complete forgiveness reveals the sovereignty of God in everything, even the greatest mistakes or sins. When He forgives us His word says, *"As far as the east is from the west, so far has He removed our transgressions from us."* Psalms 103:12. Oh, that we would help others be able to forgive themselves, and forgive ourselves, as Christ has forgiven us.

5. Total Forgiveness is Demonstrated When the Offended Does Not Want to Return Evil for Evil

Might it have been uppermost in the thoughts of the ten brothers, and caused them great fear to think that Joseph could indeed reveal to Jacob, their father, what they had done to him all those years before? They would probably have rather been killed right then and there. But Joseph said nothing whatsoever that made them feel as though he would inflict more pain upon them by telling their father. Rather, Joseph just told his brothers to go home and tell their father that they found him, and that God had made his son, Joseph, to be lord of Egypt.

Complete forgiveness does not want the sin to be revealed to others that it would hurt most of all. People more often tend to say things like, "Just wait until so and so hears about this." The response might be, "Please, don't tell them, I couldn't bear you doing that." Joseph had the greatest opportunity to react in this way when his brothers came for provision, yet it never entered his mind because he had totally and completely forgiven them. Joseph saw that they were sorry, so sorry for what they'd done, and once he saw that, there was no way he had any desire for anyone else to hurt over the situation that had happened so many years before.

Joseph had no intention of returning return evil for evil. It never entered his mind to try and get back at his brothers. I Peter 3:9-11 *"Do not repay evil for evil or insult for insult, but with blessing because of this you are called so that you may inherit a blessing."* 1 Peter 2:23 *"When they hurled their insults at Him, He did not retaliate, When He suffered He made no threats, instead He entrusted Himself to Him who judges justly."*

One of the most detrimental things unforgiveness does in a person's life is to cause a desire to return evil for evil to grow like a cancer. So often, the longer it is harbored in our heart the more we want revenge — to cause the person pain. The blessings that happened to Joseph came to fruition not just by God's design, but because God saw and knew that Joseph's heart harbored forgiveness for his brothers, even before the "good things" began to transpire in his life. What greater reason to forgive knowing that blessings await as we forgive and sincerely do not want any pain to come to others.

So... here's the plan:

A. Make the choice - decide to forgive anyone and everyone who has ever done you wrong. Say in your heart and to the Lord, *"I want to do this Lord, because I do not want to harbor this in my heart any longer. I do this in obedience to Your word and I want to walk in Your will. I know I cannot forgive, that ability is just not in me, but this is my first step in the process of what You are going to do in me."*

B. Make a list - for your and God's eyes only of the people who you feel have hurt you. If you aren't even sure then ask Him to reveal this to you. He will if you are truly contrite and sincere, because He knows our hearts, He sees everything, even the brokenness that others have caused.

C. Find a place to pray - take the list and your Bible and begin to ask God to forgive you first, for harboring all of this against those people, for having resentment, bitterness, and maybe even hate. Ask Jesus to cleanse you and wash you white as snow. Tell Him you don't want anything in your life that He doesn't want. If you really mean it, Jesus will begin cleansing you. His forgiveness is instantaneous, but the process of knowing that you have completely forgiven may take minutes, hours, days, weeks, months, or years—we don't know. It's different for everyone, but be assured that he has cleansed you just like Corrie felt when she burned the journal of all the wrongs. This is the burning of the dross, the asking for forgiveness ourselves for not forgiving others. Tell Him everything you feel and give it all to Jesus.

D. Pray - for everyone on the list. Pray good things for them. Pray the warfare prayer. Pray blessings on them. This may sound absurd, but it's exactly what the scripture tells us. As we are obedient we will begin to feel a change in our spirit, in our hearts and in our attitudes toward others. Ask the Lord to pour into you His love, agape love, that unconditional love. This isn't our love, it's God's love, given to us by the indwelling of the Holy Spirit.

Forgiveness means to pardon, to release, to absolve, to excuse, to exonerate, to give absolution to, to give amnesty.

These are life-changing words. This is how God, through Christ Jesus forgives us. This is the kind of forgiveness He desires for us to know and experience through obedience, and His miracle working power - everyday toward those who have hurt us so deeply. True forgiveness will bring the greatest joy and freedom you have ever known in your life.

> *"It is in pardoning, that we are pardoned,*
> *It is in dying,*
> *That we are born to eternal life."*
> **St Francis of Assisi**

10

CONTAGIOUS GRATITUDE
"Making Every Day... Thanksgiving Day"

G RATITUDE is not just a word set aside in America as a yearly holiday, rather it should become a mindset—an attitude that we embrace every day in living. Everything in life, everything about life, becomes better and brighter when our spirits are filled with thanksgiving—a heart of giving thanks. We should have grateful hearts rather than sour, bitter, murmuring, ungrateful souls. It's been said, *"God can turn water into wine, but He can't do anything with our whining."* Philippians 2:14-15 *"Do all things without murmuring and disputing, that you may become blameless and harmless, children of God without fault in the midst of a crooked and perverse generation..."*

Rekindling our Passion for Jesus means we begin to put on His very nature. We act like He would act. Talk like He would talk. Do the things He would do. Jesus never complained. The only place in scripture He ever showed any question about God's plan was in the Garden of Gethsemane. For a moment in time, as He prayed, realizing the severity of what lay ahead for Him, caused His supplication to be so intense that His sweat became as drops of blood (how intense a burden for mankind)—but even then, He humbled Himself to the will of God. Matthew 26:39 *"He went a little farther and fell on His face, and prayed, saying, 'O My Father, if it is possible, let this cup pass from me; nevertheless, not as I will, but as You will.'"* At no other time do we ever find Jesus questioning the road He would travel from heaven's deity to human flesh. I wonder how you and I would have responded to such an assignment. Knowing what Jesus knew, living where Jesus lived in glorious perfection, then given a blueprint by God to live thirty-three years among people who would ultimately crucify Him. I do believe we would have been anything but grateful for such an outrageous plan.

Kids look like their parents; we're supposed to *look like our* Father. That means His character and attributes are manifested (or supposed to be) through us. We begin taking on His very likeness, mannerisms and lifestyle.

It was a Tuesday, voting day, November 7th. I made my way to the polls but for some reason they couldn't locate my information anywhere on the registered list of voters or in their book. Fortunately, I had my voter card and I gave it to them, but they still were unable to find my name. They proceeded to give me one of the old fashioned punch ballots. For a few minutes—okay maybe a little longer than that—I was rather agitated, hurt and felt very unimportant. How could they lose my information? How could they have sent me a registered voter card yet not included me in the book? I mentioned to the kind, patient lady assisting that I was certainly glad this was just voting day and that I wasn't standing before God without my name written in His book. She laughed, sincerely apologizing and handed me the cards.

I finished my patriotic duty and enjoyed every moment of casting my conservative vote—though it wasn't done like everyone else—and thought to myself, still slightly agitated at the inconvenience, "sure hope they don't lose my vote like they lost my name."

Why did it even matter if my name wasn't in their book, as long as I got to vote? Right? What was the big deal? It was of course the principle, the lack of organization, an error from people who aren't supposed to make mistakes. Was that it? I thought about the scenario for a while; all I could really come up with was this. Most of us are so used to having everything right, almost perfect in our lives. We're spoiled for lack of a more fitting word. We simply cannot tolerate mistakes or inconveniences. Overall, our lives are good, little lack in regard to serious need. Even our wants are often met. So when something unexpected happens or our plans go awry, we get agitated, aggravated. We're *inconvenienced.* We are so used to having our way, so accustomed to this comfortable; almost perfect lifestyle.

WE ARE GREATLY BLESSED

Now please, understand what I'm saying. Yes, we have hardships. Yes we have adversity. At one time or another we all face, even in America, job issues, family situations, physical pain or health complications, and financial challenges. Living in the land of the free is not void of problems. Things aren't literally perfect. But, here's the reality. We don't live in a third-world country where ice cubes are a luxury, hot baths are only taken from 6:00-8:00 PM because there's no hot water after that time, vegetables are grown in soil that has also been used for human waste so therefore must be soaked in bleach to kill the contaminates to make them edible. Tap water is toxic even in restaurants. A grocery stores meat department might have 2-3 whole refrigerated chickens and 4-5 pieces of cut beef or pork for the population of an entire city for the week or more.

It has been my privilege to travel in ministry to Russia, Poland, the Dominican Republic and Honduras. While in these countries it was evident that adversity is as common as breathing. The residents of Moscow are ecstatic over McDonalds. Third-world countries have few luxuries in comparison to those we enjoy. They are so thankful for the simplest things. We are so blessed. American Citizens who have never traveled to third-world countries have no idea how abundantly blessed we are. We are accustomed to so much that more often than not, we take it completely for granted. It's like living near Niagara Falls; people come from far and wide to see the beauty, yet those living nearby might hardly even notice. They are simply accustomed to it. They are oblivious, knowing they are there, and will always be—no big deal. We have convenience and comfort, knowing we will always have it, after all this is America, but will we indeed?

We have everything people in other countries dream of having—electricity, running water, clean bath tubs or showers, indoor toilets, toilet paper, and plenty of food in every variety. We have shopping malls, outlet stores, beautifully furnished homes with real flooring (not dirt), doors and windows, garages; vacation homes and timeshares; expensive luxury cars, big screen TV's. Not to mention our computers, computer games by the hundreds, stereo/CD entertainment systems, closets full of clothes and shoes, cosmetics, jewelry, dishwashers, washing machines and dryers, electric can openers and every kind of kitchen gadget imaginable. Telephones and fax machines, copiers and instant printing, maid and laundry services, spas, beauty, facial, nail and body salons. And we have our toys: motorcycles, boats, RV's, four wheelers, snowmobiles, bikes, skiing equipment. You get my drift. You name it, we have it in America. **But are we thankful?**

It's time for a wake-up call. It's the hour for us to pray *"Oh Father God, please wake us up to the reality of our ungrateful hearts. Open our eyes to the bountiful blessings You have poured into our lives. You have given us so much, yet we show little gratitude. How long will we not express our thanks for all we enjoy?"*

There's a movie starring Jimmy Stewart called <u>Shenandoah</u>. It's a classic. On several occasions there's a scene that's almost comical. He offers a prayer of blessing over the meal, but rather than recognizing what God has done and thanking Him, the gist of the prayer is *"Lord, we've labored and toiled in the fields for weeks to reap this harvest, we planted the seeds, we've watered and fertilized, we cared for it and nurtured it, we gathered it in and prepared it. So we really did all the work Lord, but we thank you for it just the same."* He says the same prayer every time. The part of course that's missing is, *"But Lord if it hadn't been for you allowing us to be born in this wonderful country in the first place, then giving us strength and health, along with an able mind and skill to know how to do the work, oh, and not to mention that you provided the dirt, the seed, the rain and the sun. Guess we couldn't have done it without you, Lord, so we really do thank you."*

We are profoundly blessed. Whatever needs we have, there's a simple fix. We run to Wal-Mart, or the local grocery, convenience, drug, or Dollar Store where the supply is unlimited. Can you even imagine walking into the meat department of one of our supermarkets and find only three whole refrigerated chickens to purchase? We have so much, yet often show little or no gratitude. We're abundantly rewarded, yet often without appreciation. Rather, we groan and complain about such insignificant things. Not only do we get irritated at the slightest inconvenience, we actually take the conveniences that we enjoy everyday almost for granted. Could we stop and take inventory to realize how greatly blessed we are and how rarely we show sincere gratitude?

A HEART FULL OF GRATITUDE

There is a story about a single mom who was getting ready to spend the first Thanksgiving with her three children without their father who had decided to leave his family several months earlier. The two older children were very sick with the flu, in fact the eldest had been given strict orders for one week of bed rest.

It was a cool, almost depressingly cloudy day outside, with rain lightly falling. The mother grew more and more weary as she cared lovingly for her children with thermometers, juice, and diapers. She was running out of liquids for the children and as she checked her purse found only about $2.50, which was supposed to last her until the end of the month. What was she going to do? At that moment the phone rang.

It was a call from her former church; the secretary was checking on her to see how things were going, telling her they had been thinking about them and that the congregation had a gift they wanted to give her. The mother responded with much gratitude telling the church secretary that she was getting ready to go to the grocery store to pick up juice and soup for the children and she would drop by the church on the way.

She arrived and the church secretary met her at the door handing her a special gift envelope. She told the single mother how often she and the children were thought of, that they continued to be in their hearts and prayers, and that they were very much loved. When the mother opened the envelope there were two grocery certificates inside, each worth $20.00. She was so filled with gratitude she began to cry. Thank you, oh, thank you so much and thank you Lord, for providing right now when it was needed so much. She drove to the grocery store with a heart full of gratitude to purchase those much-needed items for her children.

She went through the check-out counter and her bill added up to $14.00. She handed the cashier one of the gift certificates. The cashier took the certificate, then turned and held on to it for what seemed to the mother like a very long time. She thought something was wrong. The cashier then turned around, and with tears in her eyes asked if she had a turkey for Thanksgiving. And the mother responded that she didn't but it was ok, because her children were sick and unable to enjoy one anyway. The cashier then asked if she had anything else for Thanksgiving dinner. Again, the mother responded that she didn't.

The cashier handed her the change from the gift certificate, looked into the mother's face and told her that she really couldn't explain exactly why right then, but she wanted her to go back into the store and buy a turkey, cranberry sauce, pumpkin pie, or anything else she needed for a Thanksgiving dinner. The mother was so shocked she asked the cashier if she was sure, and her response was, absolutely, in fact she told her to get those kids some Gatorade too.

The mom felt a little strange, but was genuinely grateful as she went back into the store and selected a fresh turkey, a few vegetables and yams, and some juices for the children. Then she wheeled the shopping cart up to the same grocery clerk as before. As she placed her groceries on the counter the cashier with tears welling up in her eyes looked at the mother and began to speak. *"Now I can tell you,"* she said. *"This morning I prayed and asked the Lord to give this day real meaning, for it not to be just the same old routine, but send someone to me today that I could help. When you came to my line, I knew it was you."* The clerk reached under the counter for her handbag and pulled out a $20.00 bill. She paid for the groceries then handed her the change.

The sweet cashier then told her she was a Christian, gave the mother her phone number and said to call if she ever needed anything, reached out, gave her a hug and said *"God Bless you, honey."*

As she walked out the door with her children the woman was overwhelmed by the stranger's compassion and the realization that God loved her family this much, to show His love through a person she'd never met before and a church's kind deeds. Her heart was filled with thanks; great thanks to a great God, who heard her prayers and provided her every need through people who loved Him—and showed a heart of Christ to someone who was not even family.

WHAT DOES IT MEAN TO SHOW GRATITUDE?

In <u>Reader's Digest Oxford Complete Word-Finder</u> the definition for gratitude is: *"being thankful; readiness to show appreciation for; to return kindness; acknowledgement; recognition; thanksgiving."* Being grateful simply means having common courtesy for people when a favor or blessing is extended. Just saying thank you means a great deal.

Years ago, while still in management with Home Interiors, I had purchased a new Pendleton gray pin-stripe business suit. It was really sharp, tailored, with some very attractive detail. I wore it to the meeting on the following Monday. One of my rather challenging displayers (she was a difficult gal to work with, not grateful, always expecting special treatment) at any rate, she said to me, *"Regina, I love that suit, if you ever decide to get rid of it; you can give it to me."* My response was, *"Alrighty then, this is the first time I've worn it, but I'll keep you in mind."* Paul said he had a *thorn* in the flesh and this gal was mine. The Lord placed her right smack dab in the center of my team to keep me on my knees.

The following Monday morning, I was up very early, preparing once again for another sales-motivational meeting. While walking to my closet, the Holy Spirit spoke to me, as only He can, and said, *"Regina, take the new suit to _____ today, and give it to her."* Oh, I knew it couldn't be the Lord speaking to me. I wasn't hearing Him, was I? There's a little three question quiz that's great to use when in doubt about an instruction, you know, just to make sure it is *God*. First, *"Did I tell myself to do this?"* Duh! I really liked the suit, and had only worn it once. (Oh by the way, she was the same size, go figure. No pun intended). Secondly, *"Did the devil tell me to do this?"* Now this question was slightly debatable since he was probably thrilled with making me miserable by telling me to give away something I paid a lot of money for and liked, but then he doesn't tell us to bless anyone. So, that was strike two; who was left. *"Did God tell me to do it?"* My resolve—there was no doubt it was the Lord. He was prodding for my obedience. So, after yet another moment of struggle, I said yes. Among the deepest of my core beliefs is that no material possession should be so dear that I would not easily give it away. Do not hold tightly to things. Such great joy can be experienced in giving—it always outweighs the sacrifice. Here's the ironic thing. The suit was presented to her after the sales meeting; no one was there except her and me. The response I got was anything but gratitude. She grabbed the suit and said, *"I knew you would give it to me eventually—yes!"* No thank you. No wow, what a blessing response. I didn't hear *I can't believe it, are you really giving this to me?* She received the gift as though it belonged to her and I had borrowed it.

Oh yes, it troubled me—tremendously—deeply. Did I mention *"expensive-not-at-all-on-sale"100% Pendleton wool?* After she left I had some major questions for the Lord. Why did He instruct me to give such an expensive gift to someone who would not even show a smidgen of appreciation? Hmmm, was I in fact sharing in the sufferings of Christ? There is a *biblical account* of Him giving an extraordinarily costly gift to people who would completely take it for granted, even reject it. So… the peace came; the reassurance that I had obeyed, and that was all that mattered. Of course we don't give gifts to people to receive thanks but it sure is nice when we do. Thanks certainly must bring Jesus great joy as well, not just the thanks, but knowing their decision has changed where they will spend eternity. A genuine heart-felt, *"Jesus, thank you for all you've sacrificed and given to me."*

Here's the greatest attestation pertaining to that incident and other challenges the Lord required of me at different times in my life — **we will never be able out give or out thank God**. His blessings come abundantly and frequently when we obey, they are immeasurable. There has never been a day that a need for clothing has arisen that the Lord has not more than *provided, above and beyond, beautiful expensive clothing for a fraction of the cost.* Example: A girlfriend of mine in Charlotte NC works in retail by hosting Sample Sale events. Brands that range in the hundreds of dollars per item, I have purchased for as little as $25.00, and even less. *The Lord has blessed me exceedingly, abundantly; above all I could ever ask or think.*

As we obediently release what is in our hand, God will also release what is in His hand. One of the wisdom keys from Mike Murdock. Remember, His hand holds the whole world. That's a big hand. There's nothing more rewarding than submitting to His will. We can rest assured the outcome will always be tremendous blessings. Mary Crowley used to wear a lovely unique necklace around her neck. A lovely delicate chain with 2 deli crafted shovels. One was big the other was little. She was asked once what the story was behind them. She said, *"Oh, they are my reminder of God's provision and blessing. The big shovel belongs to Him; the little shovel belongs to me. I shovel in and He shovels back, so the rewards are always huge, because His shovel is bigger."* So it is. We can't beat God giving. My heart never ceases to overflow with thankfulness for His great provision in every area in my life, but especially clothing.

"...To obey is better than sacrifice..." I Samuel 15:22b. I waited, hoping against hope that a thank you note would arrive in the mail. But alas—none came. However, my peace never left, and hopefully, there came a time when God was able to open her eyes to the generous gift that she had been given.

Can you think of a time in your life you were appreciative for gratitude that was shown to you for something you did for someone else? It's grand. These two words, *thank you*, are huge.

WHAT'S THE BIG DEAL ABOUT BEING GRATEFUL?

➢ **1. Gratitude is the Will of God**

➢ **2. Gratitude Transforms the Mundane into Meaning**

➢ **3. Gratitude Expands Our Vision to Serve**

➢ **4. Gratitude Expresses One's True Heart**

➢ **5. Gratitude is Contagious**

➢ **6. Gratitude Brings Blessings**

➢ **7. Gratitude Causes Positive Change**

GRATITUDE IS THE WILL OF GOD

I Thessalonians 5:18 *"In everything give thanks; for this is the will of God in Christ Jesus for you."* That is a perfectly clear directive. Sometimes we may wonder what the will of God is and other times it's boldly black and white. If we desire our passion for the Lord to be rekindled we pursue it in obedience to His will. His will is for us to give thanks.

If we look at the words in this verse in phrases, we get an even greater understanding. Paul, by the Holy Spirit, wasn't instructing us to give thanks sometimes, once in a while, or when it's comfortable or convenient. He said in everything I love the word all and everything in scripture—it leaves nothing out. Everything means—the entirety—the total—the good, the bad and the ugly. It's a stretch of human comprehension to entertain the thought of thanking God for tragedy. What is that about? We can easily be grateful for the good, but please? What could we possibly find to be grateful for in pain and heartache? This is what we do. We thank Him for *being with us in* the tragedy. We thank Him for *carrying us*—for *"making His strength perfect in our weakness"* by His strong arm. We are grateful that He will accomplish something *good* in the midst of or on the other side of the adversity. The word *good* is actually quite spectacular. In Genesis, *good* is the word God used after everything He created. His promises assure us that good will come even out of the worst circumstances. *What could be better than good?* So we aspire for a place in our relationship with the Lord—*believing* what he says—to give thanks in everything. He will reveal what we have to be thankful for in every situation. You know what I had to be thankful for in the crazy situation on voting day? An opportunity to witness—first by not letting them know I was frustrated and second by the mention of God's book. We can give thanks in everything, regardless of what it is, when we realize that ultimately God will use it for good.

The next portion of the verse says, **"for this is"**—another definitive phrase. Not it might be the will of God, or sometimes is the will of God, or probably is. *Is* means always, every time, no questions asked—to positively remain, continue or exist in giving thanks— *is* His will.

As for **"the will of God,"** there are clearly defined specifics woven throughout the Word of God concerning His will for mankind. We call that the Gospel. There are other times when

He speaks precise instruction to individuals specifically pertaining to their personal destiny. In either instance the will of God is His intention unconditionally; He compels, ordains, desires, longs, purposes, wants and chooses that we walk in obedience to His intention, His instruction, or His will.

"In Christ Jesus,"—Jesus fulfilled the law, all that the Father required, and ushered in grace and mercy. He is now in us, that's how we are able to fulfill God's will.

"Concerning you" refers to me, you and everyone who would ever read this verse. Listen up, He's talking to us.

GRATITUDE TRANSFORMS THE MUNDANE INTO MEANING

Remember the grocery cashier and the single mom story I shared earlier in this chapter. The clerk awoke that morning and made a decision on that day not to just go through the motions. She wanted the day to have real meaning. She asked God to change her daily routine from mundane into something meaningful. Why don't we ask the Lord to do the same thing in our daily routine? To cause us to envision ways to transform seemingly unimportant everyday tasks into purposeful opportunities. When we're folding our laundry instead of grumbling about the constancy of it, give thanks to the Lord for a family with clothes to wash, not to mention that we don't have to use wash boards like the pioneer women did. Oh my, that opens up a whole new venue of reasons for women, especially, to be thankful. When washing dishes, (hopefully it's not always paper plates), *thank your Lord for beautiful dishes, and food to cook for my family.* It's true, life can become almost burdensome, the everydayness of it all. But there is still so much to be thankful for in the midst of it all. Honestly, it's just a matter of looking around, then making a conscience effort to move from the mundane meaning.

A perfect example of this was man who worked in a toll booth on the Oakland-San Francisco Bay Bridge. It was shared by Dr. Charles Garfield in <u>Chicken Soup for the Soul</u>. Talk

Contagious Gratitude

about a mundane job. But he chose to make this time count. He chose to find something (a lot actually) even in this job, to be thankful for and enjoy.

"Now if you've ever passed through one of these toll booths, you know the people that work in them for the most part are not ones you would ever know on a first name basis. You just hand over the money, get change if necessary, and drive off. But one morning going to lunch in San Francisco, Mr. Garfield heard music, kind of like a loud party, or some kind of concert. He looked around, there were no other cars with their windows open. No sound trucks. He looked at the toll booth, inside it, the man was *dancing*. He pulled through and asked, "What are you doing?" "I'm having a party." The man said. He asked him about the rest of the people in the other booths: no one was moving in those. The toll man's response was "They're not invited." Mr. Garfield had a dozen other questions, but knew the traffic was beginning to pile up. Horns were honking. Something told him to find this guy again.

Months later, he found him, still with the music, still having a party. Now he knew either this guy had totally "lost his mind" or had incredible optimism. Again, He asked him the same question, "What are you doing?" The guy responded that he remembered him from the last time. "I'm still dancing." Mr. Garfield asked, "And what about the rest of the people in the other booths?" The guy responded. "Stop." "What do those look like to you?" He pointed down the row of toll booths. Mr. Garfield responded, "They look like — toll booths." "no imagination" Mr. Garfield said "Okay, I give up. What do they look like to you?" The booth guy said, "Vertical coffins." Mr. Garfield then asked, "What are you talking about?" The guy in the booth said, "I can prove it. At 8:30 every morning, live people get in. Then they die for eight hours. At 4:30, like Lazarus from the dead, they emerge and go home. For eight hours, brain is on hold, dead on the job- going through the motions." He asked the man in the booth what was so different about him. He looked at Mr. Garfield and said, "I knew you were going to ask me that. You probably think I'm crazy. But one of these days I want to be a professional dancer. See those guys up there in that administration building, they're my bosses. And they're paying for my training."

You could say that 16 people were dead on the job, and the seventeenth, in precisely the same situation, but he decided, in his mind, to figure out a way to live. He was thankful for everyday—and enjoying it. Most of us wouldn't have probably lasted 3 hours. The booth fellow went on to say, "I don't understand why everybody thinks my job is boring. I have a corner office, glass on all sides, I can see the Golden Gate, San Francisco, The Berkley hills; half the western world vacations here, and I just stroll in everyday and practice dancing."

How many days have we gone without even looking up at the sky? Our lives can become so focused on the appointment book, or our, *to do list*, that we miss the beauty all around us. We just don't notice because we are so absorbed with our schedules. We become so lost in all the stuff or what we need to accomplish, that we is the beauty and joy in living. We almost live in a cave or vacuum, oblivious to the birds singing, or the sun shining, or the most incredibly blue sky.

Gratitude changes that. There was a woman named Barbara Ann Kipfer who began keeping a list of her favorite things as a shy teenager. Soon her list became second nature. She found herself making additions while riding the bus, eating breakfast, and even in the middle of the night. Twenty years, and dozens of spiral notebooks later, her list was published as a book entitled <u>14,000 Things to Be Happy About.</u> Maybe we need to start our own list of things we can be grateful for in the midst of the everydayness of life…and dance more.

GRATITUDE EXPANDS OUR VISION TO SERVE

Jesus came to serve. Matthew 20:28 *"Just as the Son of Man did not come to be served, but to serve, and to give His life a ransom for many."* We, too, are here for a purpose; to love and serve God, and to serve and bless others. As our passion for Jesus

Contagious Gratitude

continues to be rekindled, we become more aware that gratitude expands our vision to serve. There's a metamorphosis that transpires in us through gratitude. Our eyes are opened to the needs of others in a greater sense because we are more aware of all that we have been blessed with. Serving others can be shown from the smallest gesture of kindness to mammoth acts of benevolence. It's a matter of seeing then seizing the opportunity.

There was a high school freshman walking home from school one day. He noticed another kid, named Kyle, walking as well, carrying a ton of books. It looked like he'd cleaned out his locker for the weekend. The freshman thought to himself, *"Why would anyone take home all his books on a Friday? He must really be a nerd."*

He thought about his own weekend plans—a party and football game with friends the following afternoon. He shrugged his shoulders and went on. As he continued walking he saw a bunch of kids running toward this other guy. They got to the kid and knocked all of his books out of his arms and tripped him so he landed on the pavement. His glasses went flying and he saw them land in the grass about ten feet away. He looked up and saw this terrible sadness in Kyle's eyes. His heart went out to him. So, he jogged over to him and as the boy with the books was crawling around looking for his glasses, he saw a tear in his eye. He continued the story.

"As I handed him his glassed, I said, 'Those guys are jerks. They really should get lives.' He looked at me and said, 'Hey thanks!' There was a big smile on his face."

It was one of those smiles that showed *real gratitude*. I helped him pick up his books, and asked him where he lived. As it turned out, he lived near me, so I asked him why I had never seen him before. He said he had gone to private school before now. I would have never hung out with a private school kid before.

We talked all the way home, and I carried his books. He turned out to be a pretty cool kid. I asked him if he wanted to play football on Saturday with me and my friends. He said yes.

We hung out all weekend and the more I got to know Kyle, the more I liked him. And my friends thought the same of him. Monday morning came, and there was Kyle with the huge stack of books again. I stopped him and said, 'Good grief boy, you are gonna really build some serious muscles with this pile of books everyday. He just laughed and handed me half the books.

Over the next four years, Kyle and I became best friends. When we were seniors, we began to think about college. Kyle decided on Georgetown, and I was going to Duke. I knew that we would always be friends, that the miles would never be a problem. He was going to be a doctor, and I was going for business on a football scholarship.

Kyle was valedictorian of our class. I teased him all the time about being a nerd. He had to prepare a speech for graduation. I was so glad it wasn't me having to get up there and speak.

Graduation day, I saw Kyle. He looked great; he was one of those guys that really found himself during high school. He filled out and actually looked good in glasses. He had more dates than me and all the girls loved him!

Boy, sometimes I was jealous. Today was one of those days. I could see that he was nervous about his speech. So, I smacked him on the back and said, 'Hey, big guy, you'll be great.' He looked at me with one of those looks *(the really grateful one)* and smiled. *'Thanks,"* he said.

As he started his speech, he cleared his throat, and began. 'Graduation is a time to thank those who helped you make it through those tough years—your parents, your teachers, your siblings, and maybe a coach...but mostly your friends. I am here to tell all of you that being a friend to someone is the best gift you can give them. I am going to tell you a story."

I just looked at my friend with disbelief as he told the story of the first day we met. He had planned to kill himself over the weekend. He talked of how he had cleaned out his locker, so his mom wouldn't have to do it later, and was carrying his stuff home. He looked hard at me and gave me a little smile. 'Thankfully, I was saved. My friend saved me from doing the unspeakable.'

I heard the gasp go through the crowd as this handsome, popular boy told us all about his weakest moment. I saw his mom and dad looking at me and smiling that same *grateful* smile. Not until that moment did I realize its depth.

Never underestimate the power of your actions. With one small gesture of kindness you can change a person's life forever — for better or worse.

"...but whoever desires to become great among you, let him be your servant." Matthew 20:28b.

GRATITUDE EXPRESSES ONE'S TRUE HEART

There are hundreds of references in the Bible pertaining to the condition of our hearts. The heart is the core of our being — the who we are. I've mentioned already in a previous chapter that all of the issues of life come from our hearts. Our hearts are the *"dwelling place of Christ"* Colossians 1:27; *"which is Christ in you, the hope of glory."* Our responses to others, the way we treat people, even our thought processes are a product of what is in our hearts.

Our hearts mature and grow (as our minds do), by what we feed them — not, of course, in the natural sense, but in the spiritual sense. The more junk we allow into our minds and lives the more spiritually weak we will become. i.e. junk = *"Profane language, strife, anger, alcohol, drugs, immoral — gory — bloody or even satanic movies, or entertainment, hellish music, sexual behavior outside of marriage — any activity, or person that tears us away from God toward the devil."* Our spiritual hearts are strengthened as we feed upon God's word, as we position ourselves to receive scriptural teaching and biblical preaching, as we read inspirational books that mature us in Christ, when we participate in praise and worship, and music that lifts the soul, and entertainment that uplifts and inspires.

All of these actions create in us a tender, compassionate, righteous heart. David, mighty David, had a heart after God, but it was His constant relationship with God that created that kind of heart—a strong, healthy, vibrant heart.

A person who is genuinely grateful will have a heart that exhibits thankfulness; as is true with those who are ungrateful. Grateful people have tender hearts toward God and others. It's so easy for them to say thank you or I appreciate it. While getting a thank you from those with scrooge-like-bah-humbug attitudes, is like squeezing blood out of a turnip. They are miserable, unhappy, ungrateful people. Matthew 12:34b *"...for out of the abundance of the heart the mouth speaks."* The condition of a person's heart is obvious by words of appreciation or words of contempt. Negative attitudes like bitterness, anger, hatred, or strife will not continue to reside in the heart of a grateful person. Gratitude purges and makes room for tenderness and forgiveness. As we express gratitude toward others, the genuineness of a caring, compassionate heart will be revealed.

As we express our gratitude toward the Lord for all He has done for us—for all He means to us—our hearts are expanded to love Him in an even greater measure. People without gratitude have become blinded or hardened in their hearts, and the true condition of their hearts also becomes bitter.

GRATITUDE IS CONTAGIOUS

Some things you want to catch—others you don't. A cold or the flu, you can keep, but let's catch gratitude and pass it on. *"It only takes a spark to get a fire going, and soon all those around will warm up in its glowing."* That's how it is with gratitude. Once you've experienced it, you want to share it, and pass it on.

It was my joy to lead a Bible study with the women of our church this past spring. The topic was Gratitude. During that time it was awe-inspiring to see so many soaking in the study and seemingly embracing a genuinely new desire to share this *attitude of gratitude* with friends, neighbors, other church members and family.

It will make a huge difference in the quality of life you experience and others enjoy as you saturate your world with this incredible attribute.

GRATITUDE REAPS BLESSINGS

"Do not be deceived, God is not mocked; for whatever a man sows, that he will also reap." Galatians 6:7. Helen Steiner Rice once wrote a poem entitled A Flower Leaves its Fragrance on the Hand that Bestows It. So it is. We cannot bless without being blessed. A portion of the words of St Francis of Assisi were quoted at the end of Chapter 8— but I love this entire verse.

> *"Lord, make an instrument of thy peace. Where there is hatred, let me sow love, where there is injury, pardon, where there is doubt, faith, where there is despair, hope, where there is darkness light, where there is sadness, joy; oh divine Master, grant that I may not so much seek to be consoled, as to console, to be understood, as to understand, to be loved, as to love. For it is in giving, that we receive, it is in pardoning, that we are pardoned, it is in dying, that we are born to eternal life."*

We cannot give gratitude without receiving it in return. Naturally, our purpose in showing a thankful heart should never be for a pat on the back or compliment, or even in order to receive something back; it happens none the less because it's a kingdom law. It's called reciprocity. God designed it and implemented it. When we plant a seed—there will be a harvest.

GRATITUDE CAUSES POSITIVE CHANGE

We will not remain the same once we embrace a spirit and heart of gratitude. There will be positive changes—from self-pity to praise. From being blind to blessings to becoming more and more aware of even the smallest things we have to be thankful for. I've heard it said that *attitude determines altitude* in life. That is still something I firmly believe. The most successful people in the world are often the most grateful. It's not that one is supposed to ignore reality or act oblivious to all the negative, rather, it's a decision to focus not so intently on the negative but to focus on all the good and cultivate a more thankful heart. We then begin to experience this freedom of less stress and more joy and peace.

HOW DO WE SHOW GRATITUDE?

We show it through simple, sincere, and timely recognition. There are so many ways we can share our gratitude through or with:

Kind Words – even to strangers
Notes or Cards – to people who would least expect them
Time or Talents – wherever and whenever they are most needed
Tokens of Appreciation – little gifts from the heart
Gestures of Kindness – even opening a door, or offering a smile

Look today. Watch tomorrow. Be in constant pursuit of ways to show gratitude toward others. Through the ways I've mentioned, and other ideas that you may creatively think of. One of the greatest ways we can *Rekindle Our Passion for Jesus* is to exude thankfulness and an attitude of gratitude in everything. As we close this Chapter 8, I've shared one of my poems that hopefully will give you yet more reasons for gratitude.

A Time to Remember
Written by Regina Elliott – Revised 2011

Thanksgiving is a time to remember,
The bountiful gifts from above,
The countless blessings God gives us,
To show of His great love.
Thanksgiving is a time to remember,
The freedom enjoyed in our land,
Came from lives and courageous hearts,
Of soldiers who firmly did stand!

Thanksgiving is a time to remember,
There are people in such great need,
That we can share with abundantly,
And pray, "Lord, forgive all our greed."

Thanksgiving is a time to remember,
What Jesus has done in our life,
He loved and cleansed us by His blood,
Redeeming from all sin and strife.

Thanksgiving is a time to remember,
And whenever this day draws near,
Our hearts and hands join in grateful praise,
For His divine blessings each year.

11

MORE THAN CONQUERORS
"Oh Mighty Captain, Prevail in Our Lives!"

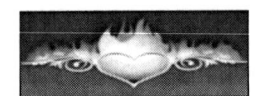

This chapter was originally to be named "FACING THE CHALLENGES." But the Lord yet again has tugged and pulled and broken my spirit with a new message, so, the title was changed. Not a new message in that the "Word" itself is new. Obviously, God's Word is not new, but rather it is the revelation that He imparts *opening our spiritual eyes in a new way* to truths we might not have ever seen before. That's the *wonder* of His Word. How many times have we read scripture, but then one day a passage literally jumps off the page with enlightenment not previously seen? The Holy Spirit also knows when we are *ready* to *see and receive* such truths. He patiently waits until that time when we have our spiritual 20/20 vision glasses on. When He imparts such *Rama* into a prepared heart, it is supernatural—life-changing. The message opens our eyes once again to how mighty He is and what little understanding or comprehension we have of His greatness. Even the way He chooses to show us reflects His very character—it's nothing we could have done within ourselves. God-things don't just happen—God has to orchestrate them.

GOD'S POWERFUL WORD

A number of years ago when I first began radio broadcasting, I remember walking into the recording studio with manuscripts in hand. Five days of 15-minute broadcasts for our session that day. The studio owner (and only staff person, musician, engineer & producer—it was a small place) chatted with me for a few minutes. Those were some very difficult days because this place was not dedicated to anything holy. On weekends, only God Himself knew what kind of devilish music was being recorded. Often I would come in—walking through the place, quietly praying; telling the lingering evil spirits to leave—inviting the Holy Spirit to please come in—to anoint. I also prayed for the hearts of those who had been there to have an encounter with Jesus; to be saturated with His presence, because we were also leaving the presence of the Holy Spirit during our time there.

Al asked me what my plans were for the future. What was I going to use for my materials to gain writing knowledge and information? I was confused and asked him what he meant. He knew this was a Christian format called *Seasons of Hope*. What are you going to use? You've got five days a week, for however many years of 15 minute broadcasts, so how are you ever going to come up with enough stuff to talk about?" Holding up my Bible... kindly responding - " *God's Word, Al. His book is so full of truth, wisdom, answers for life's issues, and amazing promises, it would take a lifetime to even begin to touch on the wisdom that is in these pages. Undoubtedly this will be more than enough material to research for years of radio broadcasts."*

God's Word is rich, and deep, and full. One verse could easily be exhorted for weeks, because it is the infallible, inherit, sharp, and powerful—God-breathed Word. Just about the time we feel we have grown to some extent in Him—and we might have a bit more understanding, or clearer idea of who He is—we find out that we really know nothing. As Isaiah said... *"Woe is me, for I am undone."* We look right into His face to see His glory and we fall on our knees before His feet - as Holy God, and say *"Oh, Lord, forgive me."* *Lord you are everything — I am nothing — be glorified in my life."*

Once again His Spirit draws us to Himself and He reminds us that we are covered in His grace and cleansed by His blood. His work is a finished work. But we are still on the Potter's wheel. We continue to be fashioned, shaped and molded — as long as we're willing — into the image of Christ. Our passion for Him will either increase or diminish, it will not, in our lifetime ever remain unchanged.

SEEING GOD FOR WHO HE REALLY IS

More than anything God wants for us to see Him for who He is — not only as our heavenly Father, who sent Jesus, but as our Mighty God, Conquering Captain, Sovereign, Able and Holy. In one of my favorite choruses the lyrics are *"Turn your eyes upon Jesus, look full in His wonderful face, and the things of earth will grow strangely dim, in the light of His glory and grace."* Helen H. Lemmel. Nothing seems impossible or insurmountable when we are looking into the face of Jesus, rather than in the face of the obstacle or problem.

There are some precarious potholes, at times, on the road to rekindling our passion. We find difficulty differentiating between *our* doing and *God* doing; in serving Him not in our strength, but in His — acknowledging that He is more than able. But He's called us, doesn't He need us? He actually doesn't need us. We on the other hand greatly need Him. He has called us. He has provided the way for us to walk obediently, even be more than conquerors but He never intended for our walk or calling to be accomplished *by our own will*, or *by our own* efforts, or *for our own* glory. Yet, more often than not, even with the most honorable, humble intentions, it is still a snare that can trip us up. When that happens we must fall on our faces before our mighty God and repent - reminding ourselves that *it is all about Him* - **not about His** — that the purpose of our passion is Him - and Him alone. Everything that will ever be accomplished will be through *His* plan, through

His effort, and for *His* glory. We are simply the vessels, the instruments that He chose to use.

Let's examine four accounts in scripture concerning people who actually *caught a glimpse* of God: Isaiah, Saul of Tarsus, the Disciples, and Joshua. These commentaries aren't just in relation to their seeing - they are most about the effect or impact of what the vision of God had upon their lives. Each account reveals the life-changing transformation that takes place in one who has truly seen Him. The sequence in which I have chosen to discuss these people has primarily to do with their particular *revelation*, rather than chronological Biblical accounts.

THE PROPHET ISAIAH - THE VISION OF HOLY ONE - Isaiah 6:1-9

Isaiah. What a prophet. In Chapter 6, Isaiah tells his vision of the Lord. This visualization had a life-changing effect on the man that he was. Nothing about His relationship with God was ever the same after this encounter. His ministry began to impact his generation with powerful anointing and conviction, promise and hope. Isaiah's words are as much alive and relevant today, as in his day, spoken from the very heart of God to our generation.

Here's what's ironic. This man was preaching before this vision was revealed. There are five chapters of messages recorded that he had given before he *"saw the Lord high and lifted up."* Apparently Isaiah had never seen Him until this sixth exhortation. So what was it that he was preaching about all those years before he had this of vision of who he was preaching about? He was obviously working very hard for the Lord, but without *vision*. Sadly, we too, can be very busy in our service for God, but without vision, or at least without a fresh vision, serving in our own strength or stale strength. The word busy makes for a convicting acrostic that represents
   B-Being
   U-Under

S-satan's
Y-Yoke

We get so caught up in working *for* God without God-inspired passion—just for the sake of being busy for Him. When this happens there can be serious repercussions. The work becomes heavy, one sees meager positive results and discouragement sets in. But, knowing little else to do, we trudge on, as Isaiah did, not seeing the root of the problem. But the day came, when God granted Isaiah a new vision of Himself. What a wonderful day in the life of this prophet.

During those early years Isaiah's message was always *Woe* – woe to evil doers, woe to you that do this, and woe to you that do that—six woes. But we notice that there is never a woe to him. Not until Chapter 6. Then when he sees the Lord high and lifted up, he says *"Woe is me, for I am undone... mine eyes have seen the King."* Isaiah 6:5. He had seen the God whom He had for so long preached about. He had been working without passion, without vision, without humility— without a contrite heart. Isaiah spent much of his time pointing fingers at others, pronouncing woes but never looking into his own spiritual mirror to see the reflection of his own lack. Could we be doing the same; living as though we are more than conquerors, mighty in battle, passionate about Jesus, yet still—*undone?* Passion grows deeper in our hearts when we embrace truth; the Lord draws near to a *broken and contrite"* spirit— those who truly see their need for Him, and cry out in repentance and humility.

CRUCIAL TIMING

This happened in Isaiah's life at a very crucial time. King Uzziah died. 2 Chronicles 26 gives the account of Uzziah, at one time a God-fearing king, who had sought the Lord. He prospered but in all of his success he himself became lifted up. Long story short, his pride became his demise. He thought he was qualified to do what only the priests were anointed to

More Than Conquerors

do. Stubbornly, he proceeded with the incense offering into the Holy Place at the temple in spite of the warnings. He was stricken with leprosy because of his sin, never allowed in the kingdom again. All of a sudden Isaiah realized that this God he had been preaching about was not one to contend with. He would indeed judge sin - even the sin of a king who had been at one time extremely blessed by Him. God meant what He said and He said what He meant. Obey Me and My commands, or suffer the consequences. We are looking at an Old Testament account, which lays the foundation for our faith. God is the same God, but because of Christ He no longer deals with mankind the way He did when they were under the Judean law. So, don't panic. His grace is sufficient. All of this is leading up to some incredible things the Lord has revealed for catching a vision of Him, so that we will allow Him to be the *Captain* causing us to be *more than conquerors.*

In order to grow in passion - all of us must have, like Isaiah, an occasion when we truly *see the Lord*. For some it may be a crisis, others a dream or vision, maybe a book or sermon. Sometimes it might even be from someone else's judgment of sin. I read an account about a couple who, together, had a wonderful ministry of sharing Jesus. He had been an elder in a church when their minister was overtaken in a moral fault. It shocked the church and the elders who had to deal with it had asked the minister to resign. He said that it was in the year that the scandal broke out that he himself saw the Lord — how Holy He was, and he saw his own sins in the light of His holiness. *"I might not have done exactly what my pastor had done,"* he said, *"but in God's sight I saw sin, my sin, being just as bad as his. I had things to reconcile with my wife and others. I entered into a new experience with Christ."* When we see others who are broken from sin, it can definitely bring conviction to our own hearts. However, the myriad of things God chooses to show us our own wretchedness, and His awesomeness, is infinite.

What did Isaiah see that made him say these words? The scripture says he saw the Lord, high and lifted up, sitting upon a throne. Around the throne were seraphim - beautiful creatures illuminated with light - whose task was to proclaim to one another the holiness and glory of the One upon the throne. As they did so, the temple was shaken to its foundations. Isaiah shook with them. The temple was filled with God's presence revealed as a cloud of smoke. This was the same cloud that appeared in other times in Israel's history symbolizing the presence of glory of God. It was also referred to as the Shekinah cloud of glory. The glory of God is so powerful, then and now, that it's almost humanly impossible to stand in it. In the newly erected tabernacle in the wilderness, Moses was unable to enter because of God's glory. Centuries later when the temple was built in Jerusalem this same Shekinah filled it to confirm that God was there, and the priests could not even stand to minister—the glory of God was so powerful. And here was Isaiah, held captive by God's spirit, to gaze upon it all.

THE SERAPHIM - "An angelic being, one of the highest order of the nine-fold celestial hierarchy - gifted with love and associated with light, ardor (zeal; burning enthusiasm; passion) and purity."

But what caused this brokenness to come into Isaiah's spirit? Could it have been the action of the awesome seraphim veiling themselves before Holy God? Each of them had six wings; with two of them they hid their faces, with two of them they hid their feet, and with two of them they flew. Why would they do this? Were they using four of their wings to hide themselves before the face of the One upon the throne? Although they were beautiful, the One upon the throne was infinitely more so. Were they not so aware of this so that in no way would they have considered, in any degree, to allow their beauty to distract or divert attention from the greatest Beauty? So, they made it their supreme task to hide themselves with four of their wings that only the Lord on the throne might be seen. Only two of their six wings were used for service. Certainly this sight must have had a profound effect upon

Isaiah. In the light of the action of these glorious creatures, so much more powerful and mighty than he could ever be, whose supreme concern was to hide themselves before God. Yet his foremost interest had been to display himself and his knowledge. It seems as though his attitude up to this point had been "If I am gifted by God, called of God, working for God, then others should take notice—and see it." Isaiah was certainly not trying to hide himself. Oh, yes, he had been doing it all *for* God but there were a lot of perks that came with the j-o-b. Bonuses from the praise and applause of men, and he probably did secretly enjoy them, as most do. Had allowed them to become the main motivation for being in *the work of the Lord?* Now, as he was observing this amazing worship around the throne of God He became completely convicted of his own wretchedness. This awakening caused him to realize that his service was self-inspired—being performed in many ways for his own self gratification. In complete brokenness *"Then he said; Woe is me, for I am undone, because I am a man of unclean lips."* Isaiah 6:5a.

THE WOE OF UNCLEAN LIPS

Let's look at two reasons for the woe of this man who came to see himself as one with unclean lips. What did he mean by this expression? Our lips speak words that are the tools of our hearts, so if they are unclean, then our hearts are also unclean. Even more than that, Isaiah's lips represented his service. He was a preacher. If there was one thing that was supposed to be consecrated to God it was his lips. He had golden lips - a gifted mouth. But that day he saw that even his so called consecrated service was unclean and unacceptable to God because it was all self-inspired. He probably would have never seen this had his eyes not looked upon the King, the Lord of Hosts, and the seraphim, in all their beauty, rightly there to be in His presence, yet hiding themselves before His throne. It was a revelation to Isaiah from the Lord, and we too must experience such an awakening for ourselves if we are ever to embrace who He really is. Holy, Holy, Holy, Lord God Almighty is the resounding song in heaven.

Here we see Isaiah's conviction of sin that God desires for us to see about ourselves as we gaze upon His holiness. If we're not careful, our service also will be done in the flesh without our even realizing it. Self has a way of intruding especially into holy things, and so much of what we do will be done in the power of self—rather than in the power of the Holy Spirit. There are three main forms of self life for us to identify.

1. SELF-WILL: We previously discussed this extensively in Chapter 4 but it also fits in this portion of the book. Making the plans ourselves—I, rather than the Lord, initiate things. As each day dawns, I am the king of that day, and if I want to indulge in something, I will. Not your will, Lord, mine be done.

2. SELF-EFFORT: It's all about me - trying to do God's work by my own efforts, expediencies, and design. What begins with me has to be done by me. This applies not only to service but in living the Christian life itself. The Lord says, *"I thought you understood that the Christian life was My responsibility in you, but you are making your promises and trying to do it all in your own strength."* This is another intrusion of self.

3. SELF-GLORY: This is the desire for people to think well of us; the doing of things ostensibly for God, but really for our own glory, hoping that people will think, "What a victorious Christian." or "What a wonderful preacher." or "What a great writer." or "What a beautiful Christian home." Self-glory is also known as pride. There's nothing wrong with aspiring for greatness, if we do it in a spirit of humility, always remembering who deserves the glory; who gives us what we need, the strength and provision to accomplish each day's tasks.

BLESSED TO BE A BLESSING

This is the most evident of the self-life. God's plan is completely otherwise. Romans 11:36 *"For of Him and through Him and to Him are all things, to whom be glory, forever. Amen."* Acts 17:28a *"For in Him we live, and move and have our being."* Often I will use this scripture in my concerts to remind the people when they applaud that we applaud the Lord! He alone deserves the applause. We gather everything up that we have done in worship into a big bouquet and hold it up to Him and say to You Oh Lord, be all the glory and honor and praise. Thank you for loaning me these gifts of music and speaking, to give back to you, to bless others. That is my prayer but, believe me, as the Lord opens my eyes to this revelation even more clearly—the writing had to cease for a while for some weeping, to pray and repent myself for any of these sins that may have been hidden in my heart. It is my deepest desire and constant prayer to continue to be humble before Him and ever so mindful that this is **all about Him** and to be thankful for every talent He has loaned me to use for His glory. Each day, more than anything, I wish to surrender all - **all** to Him, keeping focused on who He is—to keep balance with a heart pure and humility before Him.

God blesses us to be a blessing. It has nothing to do with what we have done to merit or deserve it. It has nothing whatsoever to do with any work we've accomplished to obtain His blessing. The gift of God for service in our lives is simply about Him making us a blessing. But it's when we try to take over that the problems surface. We obey what God has instructed us to do and leave the rest to Him. Obviously we don't just sit around and do nothing. But neither do we embrace a controlling spirit that makes us our own *Captain*. That's been my greatest sins—trying to do it all myself, rather than releasing it to God and letting Him do what only He can do. So today, if any of these seem familiar, look into His eyes, today, catch a glimpse of Him and say woe is me, I repent before you Lord, forgive me, I am looking full in your wonderful face.

When Isaiah cried out, *"Woe is me, for I am undone; I am a man of unclean lips."* Isaiah 6:5; then and only then flew one of seraphim to him. Here is the glorious gospel for a penitent heart.

Can you even imagine this contrite cry reaching the ears of the seraphim? Might they have said, "Did you hear something? It sounded like a sinner repenting. I heard a 'Woe is me, for I am undone.' There is a man in distress. He has lost hope; he thinks there is no mercy for him." "O Lord, of the throne, could you spare me for a moment?" And the Lord replies, "Go quickly to him; he needs all the comfort heaven can give him, for I will not contend forever, neither will I always be wroth. Go, lose not a moment." Isaiah 6:6 *"Then one of the seraphim flew to me, having in his hand a live coal which he had taken with the tongs from the altar. And he touched my mouth with it and said: 'Behold this has touched your lips; your iniquity is taken away, and your sin purged.'"*

This would be also a prophetic picture of the altar at Calvary's cross—when Jesus, the Lamb of God, by His own precious blood washed away the sins of the world. The Holy Spirit continues to convict us as we realize and confess our carnal nature. He points us back to the cross, where our sins have been expiated by the blood of Jesus. So when we hear Him say, *"Whom shall I send, and who will go for us?"* We will hear the Lord say *"Go."* — our hearing and response will be radically changed.

> *"No more let it be my working,*
> *Nor my wisdom, love, or power,*
> *But the life of Jesus only,*
> *Passing through me hour by hour."*
> — F. H. Allen

When self intrudes again we are cognizant of where to go and what to do. The blood of Jesus causes us to triumph, to become more than conquerors because we have caught a glimpse of the *Captain* of our souls.

SAUL OF TARSUS - THE VISION OF THE CROSS - Acts 9:1-9

This is truly one of the most extraordinary stories written about the grace and mercy of God. If someone were dragging us off to prison because we were preaching the gospel, we'd probably hate him. It's difficult for me right now to stomach some of the things that are happening in our nation, but God calls us to pray, not to despise. He shows again His true nature in this chronicle. God saw the very *heart* of Saul. He knew that if He got his attention, Saul would be a powerhouse for Him – and His church would be established in a greater way on earth. God chooses the most unlikely, but His choice always has purpose behind it. God doesn't see man as man sees Him. We look on the outward appearance and judge by that most of the time. If a person looks like they should be a leader – or carries themselves with dignity – or has enough education required meriting the position, then we assume that they are qualified. I Samuel 16:7 *"But the LORD said to Samuel, 'Do not look at his appearance or at the height of his stature ... For the LORD does not see as man sees; for man looks at the outward appearance, but the LORD looks at the heart."*

Here was a rebel, intent on destroying the very essence of the plan for redemption. But God saw much deeper, something man could not see. Saul didn't just dislike Christians. He hated them. He was a totally self-righteous, staunch charter member of the religious sect called Pharisees. They considered themselves *fair-you-see* because of their fame for perfectly keeping even the tiniest detail of the law. They liked who they were. They piously flaunted their religious refinement and condemned those who didn't keep the law.

Saul was probably the last person anyone every thought would become a believer in the Lord Jesus, let alone an on-fire evangelist. Act. 9:1-2 *"And Saul, still breathing threats and murder against the disciples of the Lord, went to the high priest and asked letters from him to the synagogues of Damascus, so that if he found any who were of the Way, whether men or women, he might bring them bound to Jerusalem."* All of his effort was in the name of God.

Saul was just a tad bit detained on this journey. The light from heaven was blinding, so much that he fell off his horse. The voice from heaven was frightening, asking a question completely absurd to him. He was a Pharisee, why would God think he was persecuting Him or talk to him this way? He was on his way even then to do *His* work. Yet the voice that answered replied something that was more than he could bear. *"I am Jesus, whom you are persecuting."* Acts 9:5a. We know by his answer that He thought it was God, because he answered with a question that finished in *"Lord"*. But when this voice said Jesus; Saul was perplexed and confused. *"Jesus, Jesus, aren't you dead?"* Surely that must have been the thought that ran through his head. Then his next statement revealed his true heart. Acts 9:6a *"So trembling and astonished, said 'Lord what do You want me to do?"*

Saul feared nothing. He was a leader of the Sanhedrin. He was an up and coming Jewish Pharisee. But he was trembling in the presence of the Lord God. He didn't respond with *"leave me alone, I have a mission to accomplish here."* He was broken, and trembling. He responded with a heart that said, *"Here am I, what is it that you're trying to communicate to me?"* This blinding vision literally took away his sight for three days. God intended for Him to be convinced that He was the real deal, and the impact had to be life-changing, unwavering. Jesus was making sure Saul was fully committed to this new assignment and that the transformation would be a permanent one in his life. This wasn't just an accident or a little thing that was happening. This vision couldn't be taken lightly. Then the Lord brought yet another miracle revealing his mighty power through Ananias— to touch the eyes of Saul for healing. These words spoken to Ananias confirm that God already knew the true heart He had placed within Saul. The fire that had once waged war against Christ would became a blazing light of transforming testimony to bring hundreds to salvation. Acts 9:15 *"But the Lord said to him, 'Go for he is a chosen vessel of Mine to bear My name before Gentiles, Kings, and the Children of Israel.'"*

So what effect did this vision have on Saul? Everything about Saul changed, even his name. He cast away his own pathetic righteousness in order to embrace Christ as his own. He not only counted loss the things that were once gain to him, but when he actually suffered the loss of them. He was treated as a criminal himself in the circles of society and influence that he once emanated - even then he had no regrets. He spoke of them as *refuse* compared to the infinitely marvelous relationship he now enjoyed in Christ. He was never the same after this encounter. His fervency remained - all the guts and determination, intestinal fortitude that Saul had - Paul had; but now in the power and anointing of the Holy Spirit. He was a mighty man of God. People that once knew him didn't think it was possible. In the years that followed, he was never hesitant to tell anyone about the transformation that took place in his life because of this encounter from Jesus.

Saul was a man full of pride, though at times even he wasn't aware of it. He had reputation and status with men. He thought even God would have regard for a man of such stature. He was proud of his bloodline. He was of the tribe of Benjamin—a Hebrew through and through. He was arrogant about knowing and keeping the religious doctrine. Saul was proud of his activity, his zealousness to persecute the Christian church and to carry out the demands of the Sanhedrin and he was proud of his moral stand. He kept the law to the letter and wasn't sinful in any way!

But God saw Paul—warrior for the righteous—defender of the faith. Once Saul truly met God, through Jesus Christ, he was never the same. The light of truth was shone into his life so profoundly that scales literally fell from his eyes. They were opened and for the first time he saw and embraced truth.

Saul was on a worldly road trip going up. God from heaven was coming down to meet him. And when the man going up met the Man coming down, it broke him; what things were gain to him, after that he counted as loss, and the Pharisee took his place as a sinner before God in a way he would have never even considered, or even thought about, before. The man going up was now content to be the man going down with Jesus.

This is the effect that the vision of the Cross should have. To change our attitude about our righteousness, our own reputation — to the things that used to be gain to us. We can no longer just sweep our sins under the carpet, with prideful intention of our need to repent. When we see that He gave His all for us, then we should be melted by that love and willing to be broken and contrite; guilty in need of pardon. When we are willing to turn back the carpet and allow Jesus to apply His blood to cleanse us from all sin, that is when we realize that everything we thought mattered — the things that gave us status with God and man — mean nothing, we count them as dung.

May that same illumination fill our hearts and lives every day. May our passion for Jesus increase, be rekindled; that in this walk we become *more than conquerors* adhering to our Captain, responding as Saul did, *"Lord, what would you have me to do?"*

THE DISCIPLES AND THE BLOOD - John 20:19-20; Hebrews 13:20-21; Hebrews 9:11-12

What can take away my sin? Nothing but the blood of Jesus. What can make me whole again? Nothing but the blood of Jesus. Oh, precious is the flow, that makes me white as snow, no other fount I know, nothing but the blood of Jesus." Nothing But the Blood - Robert Lowry

There have been times in my life that it seemed a neat idea to walk and talk with Jesus as the disciples did. Just to be around Him physically. To see His miracles first-hand as HE touched blinded eyes or opened deaf ears. But on the other hand, this is a marvelous relationship we have with Him, because we don't ever have to say good-night, or I'll see you tomorrow. Though we can't see Him with the natural eye, He is always with us. He lives in us. In that sense, we have an even deeper intimacy with Him than they did, because the Holy Spirit lives in us.

The disciples were with Him, but it seems like they didn't listen very well at times—normal human behavior. Because of the frequent communication that Jesus had with the disciples, it seemed they would have been aware of all that was happening when He was crucified and buried, but, no...the boys had golf, or football, or something else on their minds. Or maybe it was fishing, or tax collecting? All they focused on was that Jesus was there, and surely He wasn't going to leave. He was too young. He had too much to accomplish.

When Jesus appeared to them after His resurrection He even had to prove to them it was Him. *Why would He have felt the need to show them his hands and His side had He not seen the doubt in their eyes?* He saw fear, because he spoke *"Peace be unto you."* Jesus also perceived sadness. But when they saw Him, they became glad. What wonderful truth this leads us to.

The scriptures linked together in John 20 and Hebrews 13 has everything to do with the truth that Jesus was brought again from the dead through the blood of the everlasting covenant. This revelation gives us peace when we feel that we are still not living the victorious life - we still fail or fall short - we still feel guilty or condemned. We repent, but somehow that in itself does not give us a clear conscience. So, we still beat ourselves up. Yes, we desperately need this vision—a vision of the mighty power of the precious, cleansing blood of Jesus by which He was resurrected from the dead, that the efficacy of that blood is applied for our sins. He shed His precious blood for us.

> *"He took my sins and my sorrows,*
> *He made them His very own;*
> *He bore the burden to Calvary,*
> *And suffered and died alone."*
> "My Savior's Love" - Charles H. Gabriel

The moment Jesus did this He gave Himself for our offenses and did so by God's decree. Though we deserved punishment for our sin, a just advocate chose to make the payment once and for all through Christ. Jesus was raised for our justification. Just-as-if-we'd never sinned. *If the wages of sin is death, how was it that God raised Jesus, having all the sin of mankind placed upon Him?*

A little boy came out of Sunday School one morning to be met by a kind, elderly gentleman who greeted the lad with some questions, gently teasing him. The young boy seemed to take it very seriously. *"So, what is it that you've been doing in there?"* asked the man. *"I've been learning about Jesus,"* responded the lad. *"And who is Jesus?"* asked the man, *"and what did He do, what happened to Him?"* The boy began to tell him all who knew, finishing the story of how wicked men put Jesus on a cross to die. Then the boy ran to meet his family. As quickly as he'd left, he ran back breathlessly and said, *"Please sir, I didn't tell you everything; He didn't stay dead."*

The Hebrews 13 account answers this question—*"If the wages of sin is death, how was it that God raised Jesus having all the sin of mankind placed upon Him?* In one way alone—Through the blood of the everlasting covenant. The **value of His blood**—the blood of the spotless Lamb of God, not the blood of goats and sheep, but His very own precious, powerful blood in death was enough for all sin for all time. **It was about *whose* blood it was**—the all-encompassing, infinite value of Jesus' perfect blood. The glory of His final cry on the Cross—*"It is Finished."* The grave had no right to hold Him for the awesome price was paid in his judgment-bearing death on the cross. That included cleansing from every sin that He took responsibility for at His crucifixion. Sin could no longer condemn even Him. It might sound daring, but His blood even forgave Him. He became sin. So if, *"the wages of sin is death,* Jesus too had to be forgiven. If His blood was enough to bring Him from the dead, it is certainly enough to bring me again out of all the darkness and death that sin brings into my life. He had more sins upon Him that day than we will ever have. He carried the sins of the world. The most we will ever have is our own. So it is that He lives and that, by His blood, we live also. The glimpse we catch here is:

1. HIS VICTORY OVER ME: It's not even so much about us conquering sin, it's more about Him conquering us — in a sense it's about Him allowing us to be broken and restored. Then He becomes victorious and reigns as Lord of all in our lives.

2. HIS VICTORY FOR ME: This is the setting free we experience from the hangover of our own guilt and self-accusation. We need to remember to embrace the joy that comes with forgiveness; replace shame with praise for righteousness in Christ. He has given us the victory so we can rejoice, not live in constant condemnation.

3. LIVING IN HIS VICTORY: As someone once said, *"There is only one victorious life, and that is the life of the victorious Christ."* Remembering that He is the vine and we are the branches. The only way to live in victory is to abide in Him. We don't just experience it occasionally; we live and share that victory consistently.

There was a church lay leader/playwright directing a Children's Easter performance and overseeing the casting so that each child felt comfortable with his or her part. One young boy insisted that more than anything else He wanted to be the stone in front of the garden tomb. Over and over he pleaded. The director could not understand and continued to ask, *"Wouldn't you like to have a speaking role?"* But the boy would have no other part. The presentation went wonderfully. At the conclusion, once again she asked the lad why he had wanted to play the stone. The glowing smile on his face almost said it before the words... *"Oh, Miss Martha, you have no idea how good it felt to let Jesus out of that tomb!"*

JOSHUA - THE VISION OF THE CAPTAIN -
Joshua 5:13; 6:3

Joshua was a mighty man of God, initially named Hoshea (may Yahweh save) but given a new name by Moses as an acknowledgement that all his victories in the future would depend on God's fighting the battle for him. He and Moses were the only ones permitted to go onto the mountain of God to receive the Ten Commandments. Exodus 24:13.

Joshua's vision came to him before the battle of Jericho. It affected him as well as the entire army that accompanied him. Joshua had been called and anointed by God.

Forty years of wandering by the Children of Israel has come to an end. The old believing generation had died off and the new generation, under Joshua, was ready to be led into the Promised Land. However, there were two obstacles in the way — first, Jordan But that had been conquered in an incredible way by the miraculous power of God. In the crossing of the river, God set His seal on Joshua for leadership. The second obstacle was Jericho. Jericho was a fortified city that stood smack dab in the way of the destination. They could not advance until it was overcome. They couldn't simply pass through it. This was enemy territory. They would most certainly all perish. The problem; Joshua couldn't see any plan or possibility of conquering this safeguarded fortress. He had not an inkling of a strategy that might give them the victory.

One day Joshua decided to take a walk in the field to think – possibly to ponder what options he may have, maybe even to worry a little. He felt very much the *Captain* that day, the leader of Israel, burdened with the weight of responsibility. But beyond that, he also knew that the resources that were at his command were inadequate against the forces of such a city with ominous walls towering down upon them. Probably at that moment had we reminded him of the Lord miraculously bringing him through Jordan, he might have responded, biting his nails... *"I know it, I know it, but this isn't Jordan, this is Jericho."* Once again we see that God chooses but *frail* human beings, who seem to forget the mighty God we serve, yet He still calls us to become mighty Captains.

Then suddenly Joshua lifted up his eyes to see a man in front of him with a strange and glorious appearance. He was obviously a man of war, with a drawn sword in his hand. Joshua immediately jumped to his feet, ready to fight, because he was unsure if this was friend or foe. Joshua walked closer and asked, *"Are you for us or for our adversaries?"* Joshua 5:13. The answer he received was in the original translation, *Nay* - which means neither. In other words, I am not on your side, neither am I on their side; but you are on my side. *"but as Commander (Captain) of the army of the* LORD, *I have now come."* Joshua 5:14. *Not just Captain, but Captain of the army or the host of the Lord.* I just want to say hallelujah right here. Now that is back-up arriving on the scene like no other, and just at the right time! If you've ever felt alone, or totally at a loss as to what to do next to conquer your Jericho—remember God will never fail you. He will always show up with whatever resources you have need of—right when you need them the most. Sometimes He waits until we've reached the impasse— with no options but Him.

The Mighty Warrior continued the conversation by telling Joshua to take his sandals off his feet because he was standing on holy ground. The *Captain* was claiming Deity for Himself.

Who then was this person who stood before Joshua? Could it have been the eternal Son of God? Many believe it was He, appearing, our Immanuel, the One who always desires to reveal Himself to us when we face life's challenges.

Often we feel as though we are standing before a fortified city, unable to enter, to go around, or to conquer it. Who will tackle the situation if we don't? The responsibility lies heavy upon us. But our resources are so limited and inferior. God would say to us today: *"Let me be your Captain, one who will bring you through, more than a conqueror."*

Let's look in a positive way to three glorious negatives concerning the *no* response the Captain gave to Joshua.

1. **NO** in that the taking of Jericho was not going to be Joshua's idea, it was the Lord's. All the pressure was off him and placed on God. Yes, it's God's idea.
2. **NO** in that this city was not going to be defeated in the strength of Joshua's army, nor by Joshua's efforts or ideas. It would be taken by one *infinite* and *invisible*.
3. **NO** in that the only one who would receive the credit for this battle was going to be God. The main reason for the ludicrous method that God planned to be used to overcome Jericho, was so only He would be glorified. Could a strategy have been more impossible- let alone downright crazy. We would have probably been thinking, surely not even God would consider this idea of marching around the walls of a city? What? No weapons? No plan of attack? Has there ever been city conquered without a battle?

God was indeed the *Captain* of this undertaking. The instruction (as lame as it may have seemed) the method of marching was to demonstrate that God could do anything He wanted any way He wanted to, even conquer a city in this fashion. Then when the walls fell and the city became defenseless, all the glory and applause would go to God. That included also, all the loot. Everything in the city was to be devoted to God.

In order to see the application for ourselves in the *Captain* being the one who tears down our Jericho walls, it still works the same as it did for Joshua:

1. **It's not going to be about self-will** — *"Not my will, Yours be done, oh* Captain *of my life"* – it is all about God's will. He has every strategy in place and even the victory assured. He will implement His will not ours, His ideas, not our agenda by His power. His ways are not our ways.

2. **It is not about self-effort** or in our own strength, or our good qualities. It is about the *Captain's*. Our strong points will be of no help, our weakness no hindrance. *"Not by*

might, nor by power, but by my Spirit, says the Lord of Hosts." Zechariah 4:6

3. **It is not going to be about self-glory.** Whatever He does for us is not to be regarded as a prize or for our own gratification. Any other motive we have besides God receiving the glory, must be repented of as prideful.

So what was Joshua's response? What effect did this vision have on his life? He fell on his face before the Lord. Before the walls of Jericho could fall, Joshua had to fall. In doing so he vacated his own place and surrendered completely, giving the *Captain* the leadership position that was necessary for victory. In the process, Joshua repented for trying to be captain himself. The falling on his face was far more than worship, his words showed that of a subordinate to a superior.

When we see Jesus as our *Captain*, with His army infinitely vaster than we could ever fathom, then we too will fall on our faces to worship Him. We also humbly surrender our self-will, our self-effort and any self-glory over to Him, we will know fully His decisions and His orders, and acknowledge Him as the receiver of all the glory because He alone deserves all the glory. As we fall at His feet—the walls that have hindered or threatened or discouraged us will also fall. The Lord will have no difficulty in bringing them down once He has seen our repentant hearts.

After Joshua asked what the Lord was saying to His servant, all the instructions were laid out before him. All that was left to do was to obey. Follow the instructions. Sometimes we even mess that up. Cooperate with the Captain. Obey. Then we are no longer trying to do God's work for Him. No doubt, in our challenges of life, we would choose a different way than He would. But once we know what He's instructed us to do, we must cooperate with Him if we are to see His results transpire.

Joshua was told to have all the men of war walk around the walls once a day for six days and, on the seventh day, walk around the walls seven times, and then all together shout. The shout was the shout of faith. God delights in our obedience, and in our faith.

There are actions, as this one with Joshua, where it is blatantly evident that it's a God-inspired instruction. By all human standards it would be considered ludicrous — outlandish. What? You have got to be kidding?! I believe there are times when the Holy Spirit speaks to us to do something and we feel it's a little *ludicrous* so we don't obey. We rationalize and sermonize it away until ultimately we miss the miracle that He wanted to unfold because we think we know better than God, or we're too afraid to walk by faith. *Oh Mighty Captain, Prevail in Our Lives.*

God's results for the walls of the city with the instructions given to Joshua, were not only humanly impossible, they were scientifically unattainable. It could not happen. City walls — fortified walls in particular — cannot collapse because a few thousand people march around them every day for six days. *Now using a few sticks of dynamite here and there might have helped.* Isn't that what our thought process would be? But this was God's very own strategically planned method being carried out because He wanted Joshua to be convinced that it was completely about the *Captain* and the *Captain* alone.

One of the most enlightening truths about each of these encounters; in none of them was the seeker seeking. Isaiah, Saul, the disciples, not even Joshua had asked to have some miracle or mighty revelation to increase their faith, or even have their eyes opened in a greater measure to see the Holy One. We don't read of any specific request they made to God for some life changing, supernatural experience. The receivers only received. God did everything else. He chose the recipient. He chose the place. He chose the time. He chose the plan. He chose the blessing. He even chose the results. He did it all. Somehow that hasn't been something I've ever really seen or understood until now in my own life. There are times we just have to **trust** God as our *Mighty Captain* to do what only He can do, no strings attached. Not because we deserve it, or because we've done everything right, or haven't done everything right, not even because we've asked Him to. He intervenes just because He can - and because He chooses to do so. He sees our hearts and responds to what He sees because of His great love for us—just because He is God.

O Mighty Captain, I've joined your regiment. I have become a member of your warfare soldiers. I'm signed up, and sold out. Prepare me and send me, fill me and guide me, try me or build me up, strengthen me or test my faith. I've chosen to step across the line and raise the white flag in surrender to your leadership. Today, I relinquish control of my plans and strategies completely over to you. O Captain, I'm your armor bearer. You are the Master and I am the seaman. You are the King. I am the servant. You are the leader. I am the follower. You are the breath of life. I am your creation. I'm willing to stand, sit, run, jump, pray, serve, wait, work, sing, or breathe. I'm completely willing to be totally lead by you.

O Mighty Captain, prevail in my life. Take your rightful place, first place, receive all the glory, take the applause and all the praise Lord. I've joined up to go into combat, to fight every fiery dart of the enemy. I'm willing to finish the fight, count the cost, endure the loss, embrace the consequences, hold up under ridicule, be a faithful, trustworthy servant, and accept the criticism that goes along with the territory. Today, I relinquish all rights, lay down anything that might cause me to be prideful or feel superior to others, shelve all demands, and defer all requests for leave. I commit to serve you as long as I live.

"Oh Mighty Captain, Prevail in Our Lives!"

12

ENJOYING THE JOURNEY
"Embracing the Abundant Life Jesus Provided"

We have begun a journey together *"Rekindling our Passion for Jesus."* To *rekindle* means to kindle again — *to ignite, light, set fire to, burst into flame, shake up, jolt, arouse, awaken, inspire, to enliven or energize.* As a review we recall that *passion* means to have a strong, barely controllable emotion, to be eager, intense, zealous, spirited, enthusiastic — even fanatical. This journey we have traveled together has been about igniting or shaking up a strong, eagerly intense desire to know Jesus more intimately. Maybe even to become a fanatic about Him — for Him. Everyone seems to be looking for heroes in life and who could be a more perfect hero for us than Jesus, Our Redeemer?

So often we get caught up in the whole idea of arriving, the destination rather than the journey itself. People focus on heaven and the afterlife so much it can be easy to neglect or lose site of the pilgrimage, which is the road we're on right now. And why not embrace and enjoy the journey!

Do you remember traveling as a child with your family for a vacation or over the holidays? Almost from the moment you began or maybe an hour into the trip over and over you would ask, *"Are we almost there Daddy?"* or *"Are we there yet?"* *"How much farther?"* Somehow we could not quite grasp the idea of the trip itself being as much fun as arriving. We often missed all the scenery and beauty along the way because we were too excited about just getting there. My brother and I used to take lots of trips with my Aunt Nita and Uncle Keith. David loved to sleep lying down in the back seat, and that was ok with me — I got to sit in the front and see everything even better. I remember Aunt Nita, in her own sweet way yelling at him as he lounged lazily saying, *"David, wake up, you're missing all the beautiful scenery sleeping all the time – you can sleep when we get to the motel."* Sometimes it worked — sometimes it didn't. He enjoyed sleeping during the journey, but especially arriving at our destination, where he could swim in the pool and eat pizza.

Sound familiar? Aren't we like that to a great extent spiritually? *We sleep through life, missing everything except the focus of making it to heaven; waiting to arrive at our destination, without understanding that <u>we are daily living out our destiny</u>. It's the journey that is our destiny. Every single day we are accomplishing Kingdom work. Will there be greater things? Absolutely. But we miss the joy of walking out our destiny always wondering when we are going to arrive. We are exactly where God wants us today. <u>We are already in our destiny</u>. We don't have to keep hoping or wondering when or if we will ever walk in our destiny. This is a profound revelation the Lord recently showed me. It was an incredibly freeing moment in my life. For so long I have cried out to the Lord to allow me to walk in my destiny, the anointing and calling He placed on my life, even as a child. What I just shared was His answer. Quit striving... quit waiting... quit the self-condemnation and the wondering if you will ever be good enough. You are, because of Jesus. God is the one who makes us complete and perfect in Him. If we hunger for Him and are passionate in our relationship with Christ, honoring Him with our lives, we are in our destiny.*

Can you imagine taking a trip, yet never arriving? Years later still asking, *"Daddy, are we there yet?"* Abba God, Daddy says, *"Oh yes, my child you've have been there throughout your lifetime. You have been accomplishing much for my names sake, and I have seen every life you've touched, every song you've sung, every prayer you've prayed. I've seen your worship, your sacrifice, your giving, your love for me, it's all a part of your destiny, and you are walking it out daily by my Spirit."*

Jesus came not just to give His life as a ransom for sin, with the guarantee of *eternal* life, but He also came to give us *abundant* life. Abundant life is the journey. Eternal life is the destination. Are we experiencing abundant life? Do we expect to travel life's journey embracing an abundant life—a contented, fulfilled, even joyful life? Or, have we even thought about it?

More than just encountering a brief journey as we've traveled through the pages of this book learning how to **Rekindle our Passion for Jesus**—is to grasp the most important truth of all. We are a life-long pilgrimage from birth until when we permanently change addresses to our eternal home. This journey must not just *include* Jesus; it must be about putting Him first. Making Him the very center of everything.

God yearns for us to *enjoy* every single moment of our life on earth. Though we have no idea how long that may be, no promise of tomorrow—next week—or even next month—what we do know is that He desires that we live each day as though it were our last, with joy and expectancy. We should cherish every moment, passionately loving and serving Him as well as, loving and serving others.

After being diagnosed with cancer, Erma Bombeck wrote a list of things she would do if she had her life to live over. Here's what she said:

> *I would have gone to bed when I was sick instead of pretending the earth would go into a holding pattern if I weren't there for the day.*
>
> *I would have burned the pink candle sculpted like a rose before it melted in storage.*

I would have talked less and listened more.

I would have invited friends over to dinner even if the carpet was stained, or the sofa faded.

I would have eaten the popcorn in the 'good' living room and worried much less about the dirt when someone wanted to light a fire in the fireplace.

I would have taken the time to listen to my grandfather ramble about his youth.

I would have never insisted that the car windows be rolled up on a summer day because my hair had just been teased and sprayed.

I would have sat on the lawn with my children and not worried about grass stains.

I would have cried and laughed less while watching television and more while watching life.

I would never have bought anything just because it was practical, wouldn't show soil, or was guaranteed to last a lifetime.

Instead of wishing away nine months of pregnancy, I'd have cherished every moment and realized that the wonderment growing inside me was the only chance in life to assist God in a miracle.

When my kids kissed me impetuously, I would never had said, "Later, now, go get washed up for dinner."

But mostly, given another shot at life, I would seize every minute, look at it and really see it...live it...and never give it back.

What would your list say? What would you change if you had this journey to live over or start again? The truth of the matter is we simply take each day for granted. While we're traveling it seems as though this journey will never end. We have all the time in the world. Then we awaken one morning and we're old—our lives are reaching the sunset hour. For many that will be true, for others their lives may be cut short by an early departure for some unexpected reason. Either way, life is often taken so lightly.

My Mother went to be with the Lord in May 2011. By the way, her name is Ina. I didn't say her name was Ina, because she still is—oh yes. Many times during these past few years, I would encourage her to quit working so hard, just to stop and enjoy the time she had left with Pops (her second husband. My Father, Robert (Bob), went to be with Jesus in July 1986). I would tell her to watch a movie, or put a puzzle together, go for an afternoon drive, or simply relax with a good book. But Mother enjoyed staying busy doing all kinds of stuff around the house, remodeling—reorganizing—things that made her in some way feel useful or fulfilled. That's okay too, but in the long run, I wonder if she really enjoyed the journey—or if she ever took time to savor the abundant life? Oh, she loved the Lord, but in her later years it seemed she was caught up with so many other things. It becomes more evident as time goes by on how very precious life is—how very brief. Whatever today is, tomorrow will not be. We have to make some decisions, take inventory if you will, as to what this journey is really all about for us. Are we mindlessly traveling to reach our destination of heaven? Or, are we enjoying the journey along the way—experiencing the *abundant life and living out our destiny?*

STEPS TO TAKE TO ENJOY THE JOURNEY

FIRST: LOOK FOR THE SIMPLE JOYS

Keep your eyes open. How often have we missed even seeing the sky for days on end because we rarely even glance up? Watch for the smallest blessings, the birds, the flowers, and the spring rain. How about mixing a cake and letting your children eat the batter left over in the bowl and on the beaters. Or, making popcorn and watching a movie together as a family; gathering around the piano or guitar and singing "old hymns." Lying on the grass and identifying shapes from the clouds in the sky. Why not time to work on school projects with your kids, or shopping together for nothing in-particular. Why not enjoy a few minutes at Starbucks, with a favorite hot drink with a friend or relative?

One of my fondest childhood memories was when my sister, Revonda, was a freshman in high school. She had a homework science assignment in the spring of the year. The students were to gather different kinds of flowers and put together a notebook identifying each one by attaching a typed, brief explanation and description. It became a family project. We traveled everywhere looking for foliage she could use, picking flowers and weeds or so it seemed. It was great!. Simple joys.

Often we're focused on arriving at our destination. That's when we miss so much, and before we know it, life has indeed passed us by. We look in the mirror, we know time is passing and we see our loved ones growing older too, wondering where time has gone. How could it have passed so quickly? With a feeling like Erma Bombeck's, if we could just live it over again there are many things we might do differently. So, we let's begin today. It's never too late to make up for lost time. Neither you nor I will ever be any younger than we are right now. So, let's decide not to miss the simple joys, asking the Lord to nudge us, to remind us of how very special even the smallest little blessings can be.

"Simple Joys"
Written by Regina Elliott 3.02.06

It's the simple joys God gives us every day,
Which so often pass us by upon life's way;
All the special little blessings
Can diminish daily testings,
Changing sadness to a smile upon our face.

It's the simple joys that causes hearts to sing,
Children's laughter, flowers blooming in the spring,
Sunshine, rainbows, special days,
Snow capped mountains, foggy haze,
Ocean's treasured jewels and flowing meadows green.

It's the wondrous joys Creator God has made,
Within the timeframe of a simple seven days,
For He knows that when we see,
What He's designed our lives to be,
All the simple joys will vanish fear away.

Yes, the simple joys remind us of God's love,
Redeeming, reaching down from heaven above,
So that as we learn to trust,
Decide to live for Christ, a must;
Our hearts will soar with simple joys
On wings like doves.

SECOND: SIMPLIFY LIFE

We live in a culture—a world, if you will, identified and symbolized by super-highways—both asphalt and information. How many people don't long, at least occasionally, for the more simple life? If you really don't think so, the next time you're trapped in bumper to bumper traffic, or making your way through the crowded store in a mall, ask yourself these questions, "Wouldn't it be nice to have a lazy afternoon sitting on *a patio beside a swimming pool sipping lemonade, or in the mountains drinking hot chocolate and laughing with friends? Wouldn't it be nice to have a quieter more peaceful daily schedule so we wouldn't feel so frazzled and spent at the end of the day?"*

Apparently, many people feel the same way, and I'm not just talking about anticipating retirement. There seems to be a national hunger for simplicity again. Maybe that's why the country décor look has been popular for so many years. The desire to move toward an old fashioned way of living again, when life was less complex and seemed much simpler, not necessarily easier, maybe just a little slower, a little quieter, a little less complicated, demanding or stressful. Maybe we long for a time when life moved at an easier pace when there seemed to be time and emotional energy to appreciate each day.

REMOVE THE CLUTTER

The best way to begin to simplify our lives pertaining to our surroundings is to remove the clutter—all the clutter. Don't hoard. Simplify your way of living by disposing of anything that is unnecessary—this will automatically make your residence more pleasant. Our homes are our haven, our place of refuge, peace, beauty and harmony. When we walk into total chaos it is not a pleasure for anyone. Whatever you have that you don't need or doesn't have a function or use, don't keep it. Purge. Throw away. Get rid of all the unnecessary stuff. Pack up what could be used by someone else and make a trip to the Salvation Army or Goodwill. That means everything from toys and gadgets to clothes and shoes—to just plain old junk. The only way to bring simplicity into your life is to get rid of the clutter, the mess. Living in chaos is not peaceful. It certainly doesn't promote the feeling that Jesus wants for us—which is joy.

Not long ago I staged a home for a family to put on the market. When I arrived, after being hired, the woman's kitchen was a total disaster. Yes, my job was to decorate, but it hadn't been cleaned and was a little difficult to stage. So, I organized and uncluttered the kitchen first. When the family walked into the room there was a look of amazement and joy on their faces. They loved it. The children's response was *"Wow Mommy, our kitchen is beautiful."* All of sudden what seemed like turmoil was now filled with peace and beauty. There's turmoil in clutter, not abundant living, but when there's order in a home, it automatically reflects a more peaceful atmosphere.

CLEAN THE CLOSETS

Clean out the closets. I've reached the conclusion that we can have a ton of clothes but there will always be just 365 days in the year. How much can we really enjoy? It's a proven fact that people wear 10% of their clothing 90% of the time. Decide to purge your closets making three piles of clothing. I stand convicted.

- ➤ **The first for** *everything you wear* **or have worn in the past year**
- ➤ **The second for** *everything that needs mended* **or repaired**
- ➤ **The third for** *everything you have not worn* **in the past year**

Bottom line, if we haven't worn a garment for one year, we probably won't wear it the next year so it's taking up space. Maybe you lost weight, or gained weight, and you keep thinking, *"Oh, I'll be able to wear that again, I really like it."* Not. Just let go. Find someone who really needs them.

Release yourself from things that you think you cannot live without and begin to simplify your life from all the unneeded clutter — in every room — whether it's a closet, or in the middle of your living room or dining room, or kitchen. Pray. Ask the Lord to deliver you from whatever causes you to want to hold on. There is no one on earth that is probably not affected in some way with this vice. We just have to let go if we want our lives to become simplified, pleasant, and peaceful. Don't forget, we came into the world naked and we're leaving that way. Nothing we own is going with us. *Have you ever seen a hearse, pulling a U-Haul?*

ORDER BRINGS PEACE

There's no peace more wonderful than walking into a home that's clean, warm and inviting. It doesn't have to be expensive or filled with elaborate accessories but it should be clean, uncluttered, and warm. (Or cool if it's summer time). These three important elements, that most people can afford, affect the mood or attitude of the family and determine how guests feel when walking into their home. Music and lighting also adds an inviting touch.

Kitchen sinks piled with dishes day in and day out don't feel inviting, let alone peaceful. Simplifying life means implementing order. Can you imagine the chaos there would be in the universe if God wasn't a God of order? As we grow in our passion for Christ and an intimate relationship with Him, we begin to understand how natural it becomes to release things into His hands, to seek His strength and help. It is amazing how genuinely interested He is aware of the things that trouble or weigh us down. He's just waiting for us to seek, ask, and know. He will open the door. *Does He really care?* Always. There's nothing that concerns us that He is not knowledgeable of and also is concerned about. It's a matter of first acknowledging that we have a problem in a certain area that we can't seem to overcome on our own and then just saying *"Lord, I'm weak but you are strong. Please, strengthen and help me."*

Something else that's life-changing about removing clutter; we will gain or save more time. Some seem to have convinced themselves that even in total chaos they know where everything is, so don't touch it. Sorry — it's not true; the time we save with things in order is mind boggling. There's less stress and everything goes far more smoothly when we're not pressured because we are unable to locate something that has to be somewhere under the mountain of clutter. Stuff most people have even forgotten they *have* because it's been so long since they've seen it.

Ask yourself how you would feel if Jesus came into your home for a visit, or if He needed a ride in your car? I've been in vehicles that looked like they had two weeks of meals from McDonalds, and they smelled like it. How difficult is it to just throw the trash away and give the car a good vacuuming once in a while? Simplify by getting rid of the unnecessary trash and clutter in your lives. It will be amazing how much better and more peaceful everyone feels. It just takes initiative — and making a choice to see change happen. If we can just get a little uncomfortable in our current state, grasp the idea that we could improve it, with little or no cost except, time, soap and water, the outcome will be totally transforming.

Recently, I transformed an upstairs landing area that was basically being used for nothing (or sometimes a catch-all if I didn't make it to my walk-in closet) ☺ into a secret place — A cozy, quiet, organized, inviting, area for prayer, study and reading. You know, we have a place for our cars, a place to cook, a place to watch television, a place for our clothes — I like a place to meet with the Lord, in prayer and quiet time. So, with a little effort, and creative genius, what was once an empty, useless area is now inviting and purposeful. I love it. Wicker chairs, a fun, colorful area rug, tables and lamps — and of course music playing — not to mention some lovely wall accessories. Almost all stuff I already had, we just hadn't envisioned it in this room. Everyone needs a place specifically for spending time with the Lord on a daily basis; it makes a huge difference as we give Him that priority time. And, you know what? He waits for us there — everyday, to meet with Him.

MAKING THE CHOICE

Simplifying life has to be more than just a grand idea; it has to be a choice. Jesus Himself lived a totally simplistic life. He owned nothing. Had no home or place to lay His head except for the borrowed bed of friends and the table of those that invited Him to eat or on the seashore. He accumulated no riches or wealth. He rode a borrowed donkey into town only days before His crucifixion. His kingdom that he spoke of was not visual or material, rather spiritual and eternal; one not seen with the mortal eye. Even in His death, His burial tomb was a borrowed tomb, owned by Joseph of Aramethea. Jesus was a man of simplicity.

Now, don't misunderstand this example. The lifestyle of Jesus doesn't mean we're not supposed to own anything or have any possessions. That is by no means what I'm portraying. Simplifying life does not mean living in poverty. The mission Christ had was for a limited time on earth, for a specific purpose. God doesn't intend for us to be *poor* and humble. He loves His children just as much *rich* and humble. God's view on wealth is that He doesn't hate it when people have riches, *He actually wants us to be financially prosperous;* but He hates when riches have people; *when people love riches more than Him.* He blesses us so we can bless others, especially the Kingdom work. If you doubt what I'm saying, check out the people God *called* in the Old Testament. See what they owned and how extravagantly God poured blessings upon them.

At the end of Job's life, that was 140 years after he went through all the stuff; God restored to him 14,000 sheep, 6,000 camels, 1,000 oxen, and 1,000 donkeys. That sounds like wealth to me. In the present market the value of these livestock would be worth between 30 and 50 million dollars if sold for top value. The Bible tells us that Job was a man who feared God and hated evil. He obviously wanted to please God in how he lived and with what he had. This is the most important key to God's blessings: Giving.

LIFE-CHANGING CHOICES

Simplifying life really does mean, in its truest sense, keeping control of life in order to enjoy it to the fullest as God intended. We should not allow things, people or situations to pull at us or control us so much that we do not live a fulfilling and purposeful life.

Choose to rid life of clutter, to slow down, or to step back from the frustrating, hurried rush of daily living and enjoy a simpler lifestyle. We need to make wise choices concerning our schedules or calendars so that our lives will become less hectic and stressful. Choosing more or bigger is not necessarily the better life, and debt can be lethal.

Jesus too, had to make choices often. He couldn't possibly do everything people expected of him, or be everywhere people wanted. Sometimes choices require changes. We really do have the ability, with God's help and direction, to slow down our lives and enjoy more by making the right choices and even sacrifices when necessary. We can regulate the amount of things we do, the activities in which we're involved that seem to drain our energy, peace and joy.

When Jesus became weary He chose to rest. How much simpler would life be if we just did that? But simplifying doesn't just happen because we say we want life to be that way. If we're going to have a less complicated life, we're going to have to learn to make simplifying choices—choices that require us using words like no, or not this time. It's just not possible for me right now. We have to realize when enough is enough. Here's the "neat" surprise about simplicity. When we learn to say no to things that aren't imperative for us to do, and no to the things that aren't a necessity for us to have or own; it opens the door to saying yes to what we already have. Simplifying life is learning to enjoy the marvelous abundance of what is already ours.

Could the process mean making room, clearing out the spaces of our cluttered minds and closets and letting some brilliant light come in? Could it be the process of giving ourselves freedom, freeing up our schedules from the overload of work and commitment that most certainly weighs us down?

People, in general, have the basic urge to acquire, to get more, to conquer, or even to keep up with what society dictates is important. It's even more evident now with computers and technology. Every day there's a new phone, or notebook, or laptop — something we must have. We can't live without it.

We have to quit listening to or believing myths such as *more and bigger really is better*. Enjoying this journey has so little to do with material possessions. Going in debt to buy more stuff we really don't need is not the abundant life Jesus planned for this journey. Owing money is an albatross that eats away every ounce of joy. *Why is it that people spend money they don't have, on things they don't need, to impress people they don't even like?* Crazy, isn't it?

We are reminded in scripture to *"Be still, and know that I am God."* Psalms 46:10a. Sometimes we need to do this as we are embarking upon simplifying life. Start by being still and focusing on where to begin — how to simplify certain situations, or have less responsibility committed to things that are not really important — so we can better know God and His divine purpose for our lives. Choosing to simplify our lives and use whatever God has blessed us with to promote Kingdom work and serve others, will effectuate fulfillment and contentment in life.

SOME QUESTIONS TO ASK

Ask yourself these questions that may help in regard to simplifying life:

Is this something I feel God really wants me to do? Is this His will or my will? Is this a job that can be delegated? Is this something that I can pay someone else to do for me to free up more time? Is this a job that could be eliminated completely or do I really need to do this? Is my attitude right, or does it need to be changed, so that I can focus on the role this is playing in my life?

"The steps of a good man are ordered by the Lord, and he delights in his way." Psalms 37:23. These steps are always the right steps; they are ordered, simple, perfect, prioritized, and fulfilling. Oh, for the simpler life—abiding in Christ and being still—allowing Him to order every step, and giving us the ability to make the right choices to enjoy the abundant life He provided for us.

THIRD: FILTER LIFE

Have you ever needed to use a filter for anything? Especially when I was first learning to cook, every time I'd make gravy, particularly roast gravy. I'd bring out this little tiny woven wire strainer and use it to get all the lumps out. Somehow, the concoction of flour and water never seemed to become smooth enough, or maybe my beef broth was just too hot when I stirred it in. At any rate, none was the wiser when that yummy thick brown sauce completed its passage through the strainer. It was completely non-lumpy and delicious.

A great analogy for life, don't you think? I personally don't like lumpy gravy, nor do I enjoy a life that has lumps in it. And by that I don't mean trials and tests but, instead, things that cause undue stress and anxiety. Now this may sound a little radical to you, but we really don't have to look at everything, hear everything, and read everything, anymore than we have to eat the whole loaf of bread when we take it out of the package. Not that we could anyway, but don't you think we live in a society that somehow glorifies the concept of complete-up-to-the-minute information?

If we want our lives to run more smoothly, and if we have a desire to enjoy the journey, experience abundant living, then maybe there are some *filters or strainers* we need to appropriate that would prove to be helpful along the way in smoothing out the lumps or is that bumps on this road of abundant living?

In Philippians 2:5 Paul said, *"Let this mind be in you, which was also in Christ Jesus"* — filter out — have the thoughts of Christ. Be selective. Make a decision as to what kind of stuff will have positive influence on your life and develop ways to keep other information out of your life, mind, thoughts, and hearing. He went on to say in chapter 4 verse 8 to think on things that are true, noble, just, pure, lovely, whatever things are of good report, virtuous things—whatever is praiseworthy—meditate on that. This is going to take some filtering on a daily basis—to allow good stuff in and to keep more of the cruddy stuff out.

FILTER THE AMOUNT AND KIND OF INPUT

Too much information is sometimes overwhelming—especially if it's coming at you with the momentum of a high-speed chase. It's stressful. We have so much stuff to process each day it can eat away at our joy—our peace, and the abundant life. Somehow we have to filter out, turn down the volume, or even completely turn it off so as to limit the data intake we are sorting through daily.

There's no way we can completely avoid violent or upsetting material, though sometimes we intentionally clutter our lives with that. But what about the incredible amount of trivial, shallow, negative or distorted stuff? Things that don't contribute in any way and actually can distract our mind and spirit with thoughts and images—even memories—contribute nothing to achieving the kind of joyful life the Lord wants us to experience on this journey. Paul also said, *"All things are lawful for me, but not all things are beneficial."* That can be true of what we allow ourselves to see, hear and experience. Is what we're permitting in our lives contributing to peace, joy and purpose?

Let me give you an example. Is there literature you read that makes you cynical, or skeptical concerning moral principles or Godly virtues? Are there things you hear or watch, such as violent or bloody movies or television programs that cause your adrenaline to begin pumping at unhealthy levels, causing stress or anxiety? Some programs we call entertainment are almost despicable. If what we view on television or in movies actually happened to someone we know or love, would we even consider it fun or entertaining? Yet that's what we call it. Do you allow close friendships with dominant, shallow people who feed your weaknesses or push you toward pride or sin, or others who are complainers that drain you of energy and joy—or even scoff at the things of God? Who needs any of that? Shouldn't we prefer to surround ourselves with the kind of input that uplifts, expands our minds, and settles our spirits? That's what filtering does. Remember the gravy—smooth, non-lumpy and good.

Life isn't supposed to be filled with stress. If we can learn to filter out much of what we really do not need, there's no doubt it will be much more enjoyable and far less irritating. We need to take inventory of what we're watching. How about the books we're reading? What are our ears listening to? Only you can decide what works for you. For me personally, I don't like sensationalism, or hyped up details of gruesome murder trials and political scandals. I want to know the facts, yes, but not so that newspapers will sell more copies or particular TV stations will have the best ratings at the expense of making people depressed and cynical—not to mention being almost nauseated at the sight of blood and gore.

Jesus taught and brought truth. He is truth. He did not come to get us all torn up in the process. He said the truth would set us free, and far too often today in what we read, hear, and see there is little or no truth.

When we begin to filter out things that create fear, distrust, suspicion, and discouragement, we will begin to live the abundant life promised and provided by God. We won't be so lumpy—weighted down with all the junk. Paul said in Hebrews 12:3b *"to lay aside every weight that so easily besets us, and run the race..."*

As always, the decision is ours to make. Sometimes I wish God would just drill a hole in the top of my head and pour into me all the things I lack; the strength to always make the right choices—to filter what isn't necessary out of my life. It's a daily process, but we can experience true joy and abundant

Enjoying The Journey

living on this journey as we allow the Holy Spirit to guide us and teach us to live and move and have our being in Him.

This is an incredible, eye-opening article that I included in my Legacy series for a week of radio broadcasts.

"12 Steps on How to Train Your Child to Be a Delinquent."

#1 *When your kid is still an infant, give him everything he wants. This way he'll think the world owes him a living when he grows up.*

#2 *When he picks up swearing and off-color jokes, laugh at him, encourage him. As he grows up, he'll pick up even "cuter" phrases that will floor you.*

#3 *Never give him any spiritual training. Wait until he is twenty-one and let him decide for himself.*

#4 *Avoid using the word* **wrong.** *It will give your child a guilt complex. You can condition him to believe later, when he is arrested for stealing a car, that society is against him and he is being persecuted.*

#5 *Pick up after him – his books, shoes and clothes. Do everything for him, so he will be experienced in throwing all responsibility on others.*

#6 *Let him read any printed material he can get his hands on, never think of monitoring his TV programs or computer games. Sterilize the silverware, but let him feast his mind on garbage.*

#7 *Quarrel frequently in his presence. Then he won't be too surprised when his home is broken up later.*

#8 *Satisfy his every craving for food, drink, and comfort. Every sensual desire must be gratified; Denial may lead to harmful frustrations.*

#9 *Give your child all the spending money he wants. Don't make him earn his own. Why should he have things as tough as you did?*

#10 *Take his side against neighbors, teachers, and policeman. They're all against him.*

#11 *When he gets into real trouble, make up excuses for yourself by saying, "I never could do anything with him, he's just a bad seed."*

#12 *Prepare for a life of grief.*

FOURTH: LIVING A BALANCED LIFE

This might be the most challenging factor of all to implement on our journey: Balance. This encompasses so much; finding balance in our eating and sleeping habits; finding balance in our schedules and activities; finding and living balance in the time we give to the Lord and accomplishing His purposes.

Is there anyone reading this that recalls ever having a problem with balance? Maybe you're not actually a workaholic, maybe you're just driven. Or, it's simply a matter of more to accomplish than there's time available to complete the projects. How is it feasible to finish all that we have to do, yet live a balanced life? How is it possible to focus on one project without getting so far behind on another that one will never catch up? Honestly, I'm not sure there are any pat answers to these questions. This is something few people don't struggle with. I certainly wrestle with finding balance. But the more the Lord speaks to me and opens my eyes to truth—God reveals once again that He always has the best plan. He has all the right answers. He will show us how to find, focus, and follow His plan as we invite Him to do so.

FINDING THE PLAN

1. Seek God's Kingdom and Righteousness First – Matthew 6:33 *"But seek first the kingdom of God and His righteousness, and all these things shall be added to you."* This seems to be one of the most difficult tasks for us—putting God first. Oh, we intend to. We want to. But somehow it rarely happens. We begin early, and say as we drink the first cup of coffee, "Now as soon as I get out of the shower and get my clothes on before I do another thing, I'll get my Bible and spend a few minutes in prayer and reading before I go to work." Before we know it, something has come up. The office called and we have to be in earlier than we had expected. We get there, everything is nuts. We're overwhelmed with calls, and responsibilities, deadlines and stuff. We breathe a quick prayer, and dive in. It's now 10:30 a.m. Oh, my we still haven't given the Lord a moment of our undivided attention. But we will—we will, just as soon as… We'll have time at lunch. The day progresses on and we end up having a lunch appointment, or maybe just work during that hour eating a peanut butter cracker and pushing on through the piles of work. We look up at the clock—no way—not possible—5:00 already! *Where has the day gone?* Why I just got here and it's already time to go home. And so it is. The days fly by one after another. Somehow our intentions have been left in the haze of dust we leave behind in the activity of work. We really wanted to, we really meant to—our heart was in the right place. Somehow it wasn't given priority, other responsibilities and demands were more important.

Balance can only manifest itself in a meaningful way as we properly prioritize: seeking God first. Not because we'll feel guilty if we don't. Not because it's our duty. We seek Him first, in obedience and because we love Him. We want to have balance in our lives that will reap the abundant life and eternal dividends.

2. Seek Him First to Direct Our Paths – *"Trust in the Lord with all your heart, and lean not on your own understanding; In all your ways acknowledge Him and He shall direct your paths."* Proverbs 3:5-6. We seek Him first because we trust Him with our lives. We love Him and we acknowledge who He is. We cannot lean on our own abilities or even our own understanding because we know that His ways are best. We focus on who He is and His compass. We desire for Him to make our paths straight, to lead us, and even to prepare the way. We're right back full circle to our love relationship with Him. We spend time in His presence so we will have clear instruction, and then we will experience abundant living – yes, even a joyful journey as He directs our paths.

GODLY FOCUS

As we focus on placing Christ first, we realize that it is far more than a goal or a priority – it's even broader and more compelling. It is the commitment or involvement that will provide the *deepest meaning* to our lives. He gives us purpose. He gives us meaning. Giving Him priority commands our most sincere loyalty. It is the core value that dictates our goals and future success. *"It is in Him we live and move and have our being."* Acts 17:28a. When we've reached the end of our own abilities, He's hasn't tapped the surface of His resources. Our focus to honor Christ first will change our lives dramatically in every sense of the word. When Christ is first, we focus on the importance of life and the overall reason for being born. There is eternal significance and eternal purpose for every person's life. God has equipped us with abilities to achieve our purpose in life, not only for making a living, but to excel and to serve and bless others. Once we have a clear understanding of that, keeping a Godly focus, it will be pivotal to making decisions that keeps life in balance.

God designed us for balance in every aspect of life. We have to find balance in the foods we eat, the time we sleep, the amount of work we can do, physically, mentally and emotionally, finding balance in delegating time to play and relax with our family and friends. We need to apply balance in nurturing our health and getting the proper amount of exercise. There's a balance to be given in our time for worship—for prayer, study and Christian growth.

As we focus on this list our eyes are open to what makes balance so very challenging—almost too difficult for us. There's just a lot to take into consideration. That's why seeking God first makes all the difference in how our time can be expanded. It's kind of like tithing our finances. God can do more with 90% of our income than we can with 100%. So it is with balance as we give to Him the first-fruits.

Focus and balance is a life-long process of choosing, adjusting and changing. So, we do what we know to do to maintain healthy balance in our lives. We focus on God's word and God's promises; we seek Him first and we obey His instructions. We are cognizant of keeping balance to the best of our abilities, through His strength. We say *Lord, direct my paths, I'm trusting in you with all of my heart on this journey of abundant life.*

FIFTH: LIVING TRUE REALITY

There is a concept that's not too new or incredible anymore, but when it was first introduced to our society through technology it was totally mind-boggling. It is called Virtual Reality. What seemed to be believably real wasn't real at all. It was fake, counterfeit, an illusion—it was simulated. Virtual reality was made to *look like* or *seem like* the real deal. You're in a desert waging war against aliens—you're there, but are you really? We can't stay or live in virtual reality. These are games, entertaining videos, or rides at amusement parks. We live in the real world. We live in true reality.

Is true reality cold-hard facts? You know facts: Everyone is going to die and pay taxes. Everyone suffers. Life is made up of disappointment, betrayal, fear, failure, and tragedy. Bad things happen to good people. Is reality by definition, negative and ugly?

I don't believe that for a moment! Reality is far bigger than any set of cold hard facts or depressing statistics. The greatest reality of all has to do with hope, faith, and a future—about the abundant life that God has given us.

True reality is the absoluteness of God. *"In the beginning was the Word, and the Word was with God, and the Word was God. He was in the beginning with God. All things were made by Him and without Him nothing was made that was made." John 1:1-3* He was, He is, He always will be. That's reality.

True reality is that God sees and knows all things. *"The eyes of the Lord are in every place, keeping watch on the evil and the good."* **Proverbs 15:3** So if you're ever in doubt as to whether God knows what's happening—rest assured He does, and more importantly, He cares. Wonderful true reality!

True reality is that God paid the full and final price for sin. We no longer have to worry about our sins being forgiven. God promises that if we *"Confess our sins He is faithful and just to forgive us and to cleanse us from all unrighteousness."* All sin, for all time, paid in full. That is marvelous reality.

> "Jesus paid it all, all to Him I owe;
> Sin had left a crimson stain-
> He washed it white as snow."
> Written by - Elvina M Hall

A young man was getting ready to graduate from college. For many months he had admired a beautiful sports car in a dealer's showroom, and knowing his father could well afford it, he told him that was all he wanted for his gift.

As graduation day approached, the young man awaited signs that his father had purchased the car. Finally, on the morning of his graduation, his father called him into his private study. His father told him how proud he was to have such a fine son and how much he loved him. He handed his son a beautifully wrapped gift box. Curious, but somewhat disappointed, the young man opened the box and found a lovely, leather-bound Bible, with his name embossed in gold. Angry, he raised his voice to his father and said "with all your money you give me a Bible?" and stormed out of the house, leaving the Bible.

Many years passed and the young man became very successful in business. He had a beautiful home and wonderful family, but realized his father was getting older and thought perhaps he should go to him. He had not seen him since that graduation day. Before he could make arrangements, he received a telegram telling that his father had passed away, and willed all of his possessions to his son. He needed to come home immediately and take care of things.

When he arrived at his father's house, sudden sadness and regret filled his heart. He began to search through his father's important papers and saw the still new Bible, just as he had left it years before. With tears, he opened the Bible and began to turn the pages, His father had carefully underlined a verse Matt. 7:11..."And if ye then, being evil, know how to give good gifts unto your children, how much more shall your Father which is in heaven, give good things to them that ask Him?"

As he read those words, a car key dropped from the back of the Bible. It had a tag with the dealer's name, the same dealer who had the sports car he had desired. On the tag was the date of his graduation, and the words written, Paid in Full."

That's exactly what Jesus did for us—He wrote *paid in full* across our lives when we came to Him asking for His forgiveness, receiving the gift of salvation. That's true reality.

True reality is that there are some things God cannot do. We always say there's *nothing* God can't do, but in all reality, there are a lot of things He cannot do:

God cannot lie - Hebrews 6:18
God cannot be given a problem He can't solve
Matthew 19:26
God cannot leave or forsake us – Hebrews 13:5

God cannot allow His people to be ashamed
Joel 2:26
God cannot despise a contrite heart – Psalm 51:17
God cannot change – Hebrews 13:8
God cannot stop loving you – Jeremiah 31:3
God cannot be unfaithful – Lamentations 3:23
God cannot break a promise – Psalm 89:34
God cannot commit sin – Isaiah 59:2
God cannot allow anyone to earn their salvation
Ephesians 2:8-9
God cannot be selfish – Romans 8:32
God cannot be fooled – Hebrews 4:12
God cannot lose anything – John 6:39
God cannot go unnoticed – Psalm 19:1
God cannot be put on a time schedule – Acts 1:7
God cannot leave the work in us unfinished
Philippians 1:6
God cannot sleep – Psalm 121:4
God cannot give us a spirit of fear – II Timothy 1:7
God cannot fail – Deuteronomy 31:6

True reality is that God still performs miracles and answers prayer today. Everyday there are miracles of answered prayer and the salvation of a lost soul. Babies are born and healing occurs. Believe it when you feel nothing good is happening; God is still a God that answers prayer and performs miracles.

True reality is that when we are in Christ all things become new. We no longer have to be a prisoner to yesterday's failures – *"I can do all things through Christ who strengthens me."* Philippians 4:13. I no longer have to live in self-pity or negativism hold grudges, hostility, judgments, will not keep me bound or be a part of my life anymore. I am cleansed and a new creation in Christ Jesus.

A LIST OF REALITY CHECKS

1. God created us for His purposes, His pleasure and His glory. Revelation 4:11

2. God has designed for us to live an abundant life, not one filled with worry, stress and strife. John 10:10

3. God has clothed us in the garments of salvation and covered us with a robe of righteousness. Isaiah 61:10

4. God has called us, commissioned us to share this message of forgiveness and redemption and hope to the lost so none will perish. 2 Corinthians 5:19-20

5. God has placed His spirit within us to equip us and keep us for every good work. 2 Timothy 2:21

6. God has promised us hope and a future. Jeremiah 29:11

7. God has prepared a marvelous life after this one, with Him. Isaiah 64:4 & I Corinthians 2:9

8. God desires that we love him with all of our heart, soul, mind and strength. Mark 12:30

REMOVING THE LAYERS WITH LPT

We're at the end of our *Rekindling Journey*. As I close this final chapter there's one last thought I'd like to leave you with in this process of living and enjoying the *abundant life* Jesus provided.

Ask the Holy Spirit to Remove all the Layers of Anything that Would Encumber or Hinder the Beauty of Christ or the Joy of the Lord from Shining Through Your Life — the passion that's been rekindled on this journey for deeper intimacy with Jesus. "Holy Spirit, remove from us today the layers that weigh us down; replace them with *Laughter*, *Praise* and *Trust*. Cause our lives to embrace you're abundance— to be overflowing with joy, as we laugh, as we praise, and as we place our trust completely in your divine power. " In Jesus name, Amen.

People will see Christ in us and glorify the Father. And you know what else? Others will crave this abundant, passionate, intimate relationship with Jesus that you have, that I have, because they have seen Him, His glory in us ... because we have been with Jesus.

REMOVING THE LAYERS WITH PLT
Written by Regina Elliott - 9.17.09

Looking in the mirror, I see a face that's mine,
In every way so human,
not in any way divine!
Gazing in the mirror the reflection that I see,
Is a person on the outside —
Not at all the truest me!

Oh yes, I want to honor and take pride in how I look,
I'm the daughter of the King,
representing His great Book,
So yes, it is important the image one perceives,
People often judge me,
by what their eyes can see.

But underneath are layers of a woman, oh so rare,
Deep beneath the surface lies
her truest self so fair,
Scarred by pain, and tragedy, unbearable at times,
Yet thru the fire, pure as gold —
priceless and refined!

Layers of discouragement, at times I could not bear,
"Tears, and prayers. . . heaviness,
Even mountains of despair,

Enjoying The Journey

Words others had spoken, treatment undeserved,
Yet, deep within my spirit,
God's nature stayed preserved!

For in those trying moments,
when it seemed that I would die,
Jesus spoke these words to me;
He said "My Child, don't cry!"
Take upon you all My love, feel My warm embrace,
Know that I Am always there, to lift you by My grace!

Hear Me speaking words of peace and joy in who you are,
It's in my presence you will find,
the strength to go so far!
Your countenance will change & glow,
with beauty from on high;
As everyday you laugh, you praise,
you trust the King divine!

The layers of your brokenness will freely fall away,
And be replaced with joy and peace,
as laughter then pervades,
And as you praise and trust Me,
with every part of you,
You'll see true beauty deep within surface into view!

It's in the praise, it's in the laughter, it's in the trust in Me,
Not looking at your life, the way that it should be;
But rather fully leaning on,
My strong, secure, safe arms,
Knowing that My strength & peace,
will shield you from all harm!

And then, my Child, you'll really see,
the layers that you'd known,
Melt away like driven snow, pure beauty to be behold,

*And all who look upon your face, will see the presence of
My Spirit and My healing grace,
flowing from My love!*

God bless you my friends. Thank you for taking this journey with me. I pray your hearts have been challenged and your *passion for Jesus* has been *rekindled* into a deeper more intimate relationship than you have ever known before.

**Walk with Him. Love Him.
He Loves You Unconditionally
You are Loved!**

Copyright Permission was granted for book quotes and lyric quotes by letter or email from ministries represented below.
Reference page numbers are for placement location in this book.

The Wisdom Center
Lyrics by Mike Murdock - I Love Sitting at Your Feet - page 26
Bill Gaither Music
Lyrics by Rusty Goodman - I Am - page 44
Lyrics by Lanny Wolfe - Jesus Be the Lord of All - page 51-52
Ken Davis, Quote taken from Jumper Fables - page 56-57
Dr. Joseph M Stowell
The Weight of Your Words - page 132-133
Phillips, Craig & Dean
Lyrics - I Wanna Be Just Like You - pages 79-80
Chariot Family Publishing
Quote from The Family Book of Christian Values
by Stuart & Jill Briscoe page 136
Zig Zigler Corporation
Quote taken from See You At the Top
page 139
Rosemond Herklots - Lyrics - Forgive Us Our
Sins page 197
Health Communications
Chicken Soup for the Soul Compiled by Jack Canfield Story by Dr.
Charles Garfield - page 228-230
Public Domain
Jesus Paid It All - Levina M Hall - page 28
Eternal Life St Francis of Assisi - page 235
My Savior's Love - Charles H. Gabriel - page
253

MINISTRY RESOURCES

*R*egina Elliott is a sought-after Inspirational/Motivational Speaker and Concert Soloist for worship services, conferences, retreats, revivals, and special occasion events. Her message of passion and hope ignites in audiences a clearer understanding of what it means to genuinely walk with Christ and in His destiny plan for your life. Her full-time ministry is devoted to radio broadcasting, speaking engagements, concerts and writing. The next book she will submit for publication in 2013 is *"Rekindling Our Passion for Prayer!"*

CONTACT INFORMATION to
schedule Regina or to purchase ministry products:
Booking Agent: Michael Booher 260.336.2727
Email: sohwithregina@gmail.com or visit her website
www.seasonsofhopeministries.org

Seasons of Hope Ministries, with Radio Broadcaster, Regina Elliott has anointed programming that encourages listeners to Rekindle Passion for Christ and communicates biblical guidance for victorious Christian living. We are waiting on the Lord for direction in opening up stations across the nation. Her teaching is also available on CD or in transcript form, from the broadcast as well as from recordings at conferences. Her messages include individual topics as well as a variety of series: Here are a few of her topic series:

Ministry Resources

JESUS, OUR MASTER COUNSELOR
HEAVEN, WHAT'S IN IT FOR ME?
UNITY AMONG CHRISTIANS
EXPERIENCING JOY
EXPERIENCING PEACE
RENEWED IN MIND & SPIRIT
OUT OF ADVERSITY...INTO VICTORY!
FORGIVENESS
GOD & GOALS
THE LEGACY
AMERICA WHAT WENT WRONG?
OBEYING GOD'S VOICE
WHAT'S ALL THE CELEBRATION ABOUT?
(5 MESSAGES ON CHRISTMAS)
LESSONS FOR LIFE'S JOURNEY
THE ROAD TO SUCCESS
REALIZING & UTILIZING OUR TALENTS

Also available through **Seasons of Hope Ministries** are 6 - Solo Music CD's recorded by Regina. Prayerfully, with the Lord's financial provision, she is projecting the recording of an Inspirational Christmas CD in 2013. Four of her CD song titles are listed below.

Regina
Original songs and arrangements of adoration, praise & passion for Christ

1. I Say Rejoice
2. Families & Friends (Written by Regina)

Rekindling Our Passion For Jesus!

---

3. Heaven Waits
4. All for the Good
5. Awesome God
6. Can God? God Can!
7. Kindle the Flame
8. Jesus Reigns
9. More Than Conquerors
10. Jesus Your Name (Written by Regina"

REMEMBERING...
Original arrangements of some of the most beloved hymns of the church

1. Glory to His Name
2. My Savior's Love
3. A Shelter in the Time of Storm
4. In the Garden
5. Grace Medley
6. How Great Thou Art
7. The Old Rugged Cross
8. It is Well with My Soul
9. Great is Thy Faithfulness
10. His Eye is On the Sparrow 11. Suppertime

HONORING GOD & COUNTRY
Patriotic songs and narrations honoring our Nation & our Godly heritage

1. Star Spangled Banner
2. America I Still Can Hear
3. America the Beautiful Medley
4. The Price for Freedom
5. Land of the Free
6. Battle Hymn Medley
7. God Bless America Again
8. Statue of Liberty
9. God Bless the USA

Ministry Resources

10. *Military Salute*
11. *God Bless America*

SEASONS OF HOPE
Songs of God's love, care, providence & protection

1. *Just A Closer Walk*
2. *Lead Me To The Rock*
3. *In His Hand*
4. *I Am In His Care*
5. *Quietly In Love*
6. *In A Little While*
7. *I Am*
8. *Wrapped Up*
9. *Led by the Master's Great Hand*
10. *Come Alive*

CPSIA information can be obtained at www.ICGtesting.com
Printed in the USA
LVOW122136281112

309076LV00002B/8/P

9 781619 966611